D1346410

Waiving the Rules: the Constitution under Thatcherism

Waiving the Rules: the Constitution under Thatcherism

EDITED BY

Cosmo Graham and Tony Prosser

Open University Press
Milton Keynes · Philadelphia

Open University Press
Open University Educational Enterprises Limited
12 Cofferidge Close
Stony Stratford
Milton Keynes MK11 1BY

and

242 Cherry Street
Philadelphia, PA 19106, USA

First Published 1988

Copyright © The Editors and Contributors 1988

British Library Cataloguing in Publication Data

Waiving the rules: the constitution under Thatcherism.
   1. Great Britain. Constitution. Political aspects
   I. Graham, Cosmo   II. Prosser, Tony
   344.102'2

ISBN 0-335-15580-4
ISBN 0-335-15579-0 Pbk

Library of Congress Cataloging-in Publication Data

The State, law, and Thatcherism/edited by Cosmo Graham and Tony
   Prosser.
      p.   cm.
   Bibliography: p.
   Includes index.
   ISBN 0-335-15580-4 ISBN 0-335-15579-0 (pbk.)
   1. Great Britain—Constitutional law. 2. Great Britain—Politics
and government—1979-   I. Graham, Cosmo.   II. Prosser, Tony.
KD3989.S73 1988
342.41—dc19
[344.102]   86-19637
                                                                  CIP

Typeset by GCS, Leighton Buzzard, Beds.
Printed in Great Britain by Biddles Ltd., Guildford and Kings Lynn

For Albie Sachs

Contents

Contributors

Keith Ewing is a Fellow of Trinity Hall, Cambridge, and lecturer in law at the University of Cambridge. He has written widely in the fields of constitutional law and labour law. His publications include *The Funding of Political Parties in Britain* (1987) and *Trade Union Democracy, Members' Rights and the Law* (1987, with P. Elias).

Andrew Gamble is Professor of Politics at the University of Sheffield. His current research interests lie in political economy, state theory and British politics. His books include *Britain in Decline* (1981) and *The Free Economy and the Strong State* (1988).

Cosmo Graham is a lecturer in law at the Centre for Criminological and Socio-Legal Studies, University of Sheffield. His research interests are company law and privatisation and regulation.

Ian Harden lectures in law at the Centre for Criminological and Socio-Legal Studies, University of Sheffield. He has undertaken public law research on quasi-government and corporatism and is co-author, with Norman Lewis, of a critical view of the British constitution, *The Noble Lie* (1986). He is currently undertaking research on budgetary processes.

Steve Leach is a lecturer at the Institute of Local Government, University of Birmingham. He was one of the key researchers with the Widdicombe Committee and has published several books, the most recent with Chris Game and John Gyford, *The Changing Politics of Local Government* (1988). His current research interests are the operation of local government in metropolitan areas after abolition and the politics of hung councils.

Michael Moran is a senior lecturer in government at the Victoria University Manchester. His publications include *The Union of Post Office Workers: A Study in Political Sociology* (1974), *The Politics of Industrial Relations* (1977), *The Politics of Banking* (1984) and *Politics and Society in Britain* (1985). He is now completing a comparative study of the politics of financial regulation.

Tony Prosser is a lecturer in law at the Centre for Criminological and Socio-Legal Studies, University of Sheffield. His publications include *Test Cases for the Poor* (1983) and *Nationalised Industries and Public Control* (1986). He was a Jean Monnet Fellow at the European University Institute, Florence in 1987–8. His current research is on comparative aspects of privatisation and regulation.

Gerry Stoker is a lecturer at the Institute of Local Government, University of Birmingham. His previous publications include *The Politics of Local Government* (1988). His current research interests are local government politics, decentralisation and urban renewal.

Paul Wiles is a senior lecturer in criminology and Director of the Centre for Criminological and Socio-Legal Studies, University of Sheffield. He has written on criminological theory and the sociology of law and carried out research on policing and industrial disputes and on reparation in the criminal justice system. He is currently engaged in research into the relationship between crime, residential communities and the housing market.

Bruce Wood is a senior lecturer in government at the Victoria University Manchester. In the field of local government he has published *The Process of Reform 1966–74* (1976) and in public policy *Public Policy in Britain* (1983, with M. Burch). He is currently completing a training manual for Family Practitioner Committees, commissioned by the NHS Training Authority.

Abbreviations

AC: Appeal Cases
ALL ER: All England Reports
CMND: Command Paper
HC: House of Commons Papers
HC DEBS: House of Commons Debates
HL DEBS: House of Lords Debates
ICR: Industrial Cases Reports
IRLR: Industrial Relations Law Reports
QB: Queen's Bench Division Reports
WLR: Weekly Law Reports

1

Introduction: The Constitution and the New Conservatives

Cosmo Graham and Tony Prosser

It is now unarguable that the ascent to power of Margaret Thatcher as Prime Minister in 1979 represented a major change of direction in British political life. Radically different claims have been made as to the legitimate role of the state by her Conservative Governments and their supporters, different not only from those of their political opponents but also from those of earlier Conservative political thought. In practice, there have also been major changes in the political order, and many of these have occurred in areas constitutional. Most notably, the privatisation programme has cut back state ownership of public enterprises to an extent which could never have been anticipated even in the years of the first Thatcher Government of 1979–83; just as importantly, it has radically changed expectations as to the legitimate role of the state in a developed economy. Local authorities have lost a considerable degree of their autonomy, particularly in the financial and political fields; housing provides a particularly striking example, and in 1987 it has been proposed that the authorities will also lose numerous powers in education. Furthermore, the trade union movement has not only been, by and large, excluded from the governing institutions, but a new body of legislation has limited its (already weakened) ability to act as an effective mass movement in the economic and political spheres. Many aspects of civil liberties have seen radical change, most notably the law of immigration and nationality and police powers. The social security system, whilst still of enormous importance in public expenditure terms, has had important changes made in its structure and in conditions of eligibility. Many of these changes will be largely irreversible.

This book does not purport to form a comprehensive guide to the particular changes of a constitutional nature introduced under the Thatcher Governments. For example, there will be only limited coverage of the areas of civil liberties and social security. Rather, it will aim to assess the extent to which these changes represent the symptoms of a deeper constitutional rethinking. It will ask if 'Thatcherism' carries with it a coherent view of the legitimate scope of governmental action, from which a developed concept of desirable constitutional arrangements can be drawn. The later essays will examine the degree to which there have been fundamental changes in the constitutional structure in practice. Before tackling these questions, however, more needs to be said about the circumstances leading to the election of the Thatcher Governments, and about the traditions of constitutional thought characteristic of this country.

Legitimation and constitutions

Discussion of legitimation and legitimacy are now commonplace in sociological literature (see e.g. Habermas 1976). What is striking, however, is that the coming of the Thatcher Governments can be seen as a response to particular, and fundamental, problems of legitimacy in British government. Full discussion of this is outside the scope of this book and is covered elsewhere (e.g. in Gamble 1985; Hall and Jacques 1983; Lewis and Wiles 1984). Suffice it to say that the fundamental problem facing those seeking to govern the United Kingdom, at least since the Second World War, has been the need to arrest the country's relative economic decline. That governments could have a major beneficial influence on the economy was one of the ideas underpinning the so-called 'Keynesian' consensus on macro-economic management. This was central to the images presented by successive governments:

> since governments were so eager to take responsibility for the economy and to proclaim its successes as their successes and regularly to promise in their manifestos that they had the secret for turning the country round, they could not escape censure when their policies came apart in their hands and the economy deteriorated, inflation accelerated and unemployment climbed.
>
> (Gamble 1985: 22–3)

The goal of successful economic management was not something peculiar to the United Kingdom, for it has been identified as an endemic problem for Western liberal democracies. There has, however, been great scepticism among theorists of the state about the ability of modern states to solve problems of economic management, and this has been expressed in a number of concepts within different interpretative frameworks; for example, the 'fiscal crisis of the state' (O'Connor 1973) and 'legitimation crisis' (Habermas 1976). In Britain the problems of crisis-management reached a peculiarly dramatic climax in the problems of the 1974–9 Labour Government, most spectacularly in the 'Winter of Discontent' of 1978–9 and in the adoption of a modified economic strategy under Denis Healey's Chancellorship from 1976. This anticipated (in a more minor key) central elements of the Conservative economic strategy, notably the application of cash limits to public expenditure and the announcement of targets for the growth of the money supply. In these circumstances, it is no exaggeration to write that:

> The present, somewhat confused, state form emerged out of a need for economic restructuring in the context of continuing decline which crystalised into a crisis of legitimacy around the constituent elements of the old state form. It was a failure of the state itself and in such a context the radical re-constitution of the state in an authoritarian manner became a possibility.
>
> (Lewis and Wiles 1984: 86)

In its rhetoric at least, the 1979 Conservative administration promised a sharp break with the policies suggested by the post-war consensus. It took office with a self-consciously radical strategy involving a 'rolling back of the state', the dismantling of corporatist forms and the implementation of liberal free-market policies aiming to reverse economic decline. This could have been dismissed as mere rhetoric, but it now seems clear that fundamental changes have occurred to the map of political power in Britain since 1979.

It is controversial how far these changes have been part of a coherent new vision of the state and society which the Conservative Party has tried to implement (cf. Hall and Jacques 1983; Jessop *et al.* 1984; Riddell 1983; Bulpitt 1986; and see the discussion in Chapter 2 of the present work). However, the policies of the Thatcher Governments do represent an attempt to resolve legitimation problems of the modern state through reversing economic decline, via, at least in its rhetoric, a radically different role for the state. These elements have been fully discussed in the works cited above. What has been less remarked, however, is the role of Thatcherism in relation to the constitutional aspects of legitimation. We do not intend here to develop a detailed definition of a constitution, but (sharing the concern of Harden and Lewis 1986) see constitutions as sets of understandings regarding the boundaries of the public and private realms and establishing principles to which public action must adhere to if it is to be legitimate. We shall examine the assumptions implicit in the institutional changes carried out under the Thatcher Governments and the ideas produced by the 'New Right' of what a new set of constitutional arrangements would look like. To understand these themes, we need to understand the peculiarities of English constitutional thought. (For detailed discussion, see Harden and Lewis 1986, esp. Chs. 2–3.)

The stateless constitution

The uniqueness of the British constitution is a commonplace of legal and political thought. It is less frequently observed that the British polity has followed a substantially different course of development from its European neighbours (though cf. Dyson 1980). It has been described as a 'stateless society' with the concomitant characteristics of a lack of constitutional awareness and of any developed system of public law (Johnson 1977). This has meant that the central legitimating concepts of a formal constitutional document and of a coherent concept of the state as an entity defined and legitimated by law, have been absent. It is also less frequently noticed that the British notion of law is a peculiar one. Any reading of British law journals or texts will show that, especially in comparison with the United States or France, there is a very narrow notion of what counts as a fit subject for legal study (see e.g. Murphy and Roberts 1987: 677–80). Moreover, the dominance of legal positivism in British jurisprudence is a reflection of a broader denial; that critical concepts, such as justice and fairness, play a necessary part in a lawyer's way of thinking. The interplay of these notions has had the result that constitutional claims, at least in the twentieth century, have been founded on the concept of Parliamentary sovereignty and on the rhetoric of the rule of law. However, as we shall explain, the cement of the constitution is a dependence on conventions and mutual expectations rather than any explicit constitutional principles.

We begin with two commonplace observations – that there is no written constitutional document, such as exists in the United States and France, and that there are no distinct public law principles enforced by a specialist court, as in France. Any legal principles we do have are developed from the background of a common-law system, which is predominantly concerned with *private* rights and duties. Only recently has any specialisation in public law developed in the High Court, but this is most emphatically *not* the equivalent of the French public law courts; it is essentially a procedural device.

Although these differences are well known, their implications for constitutional debate are not. A constitution, written or unwritten, outlines a basic structure of the state, the relative powers of the organs and lays down particular principles for the action of public bodies, for example the due-process clause in the US constitution. Whether changes in the mode of governance are in accord with the constitution or not, even whether they are constitutional issues at all, are inherently controversial matters. The existence of a written constitution is not a panacea which provides the answers in debates about constitutionality. A written constitution requires constant reinterpretation and reassessment. Nor does it tell you everything about the workings of the constitution; informal understandings, practices and conventions will grow up around it. An example of both points is that the US Supreme Court's power to strike down legislation as unconstitutional is nowhere explicitly stated in the constitution; it was developed in the case-law (*Marbury* v. *Madison* 1 Cranch 137 (1803)). Nevertheless, a written constitution provides a focal point for constitutional debate. The subject-matter of constitutional debate comprises changes in any or all of these areas.

This is so in two senses. First, certain issues must be seen as raising constitutional problems. For example, the US constitution is a federal one, with certain powers reserved for the states and others for the Federal Government. If the Federal Government were to attempt to encroach on states' rights, for example by attempting to interfere with the amount they could raise through state taxation, this would clearly be a constitutional issue. Secondly, in controversial cases, where it is unclear whether something is a constitutional question or not, the debate must always be pitched at a constitutional level. If, in the United States, a constitutional right to welfare benefits is claimed, this must be justified by an interpretation of the constitution. Conversely, if such a right is denied, it must also, logically, be done on the basis of an interpretation of the constitution (for this debate, see Krislov 1973; Sparer 1970). However, in Britain there are no clear cases, no categories unambiguously delineated as constitutional. There may be certain expectations and understandings, for example that local government has its own powers of revenue raising, but it is always open to those who do not share these understandings to deny that any constitutional issue is involved. So in a fundamental way the British constitution depends on there being shared expectations and understandings of its basic presuppositions.

A further consequence is that changes in the structure of the state, such as the creation of new public agencies, may occur without much, if any, debate on their constitutional implications. Contrast the debate in the 1930s, for example, in the United States over the constitutional status of the new administrative agencies and in France during the 1980s over the constitutional upheavals of nationalisation and privatisation, with the relative silence in Britain (Breyer and Stewart 1985, Ch. 2; *Conseil Constitutionnel*, 16 January 1982 and 25–6 June 1986; Prosser 1986). Elsewhere constitutions serve as focal points for debate about whether new developments in the state structure are in accord with constitutional protections. Without such debate, in Britain at least, we have tended to assume that the old forms will be effective guarantors.

This fundamental uncertainty about what is or is not constitutional also extends to the question of general principles and limits on action by public bodies. Where there is a written constitution, these limits are often policed by the courts and so, through such case-law as that on the due-process clause in the United States and the general principles of law (*principes généraux du droit*) in France, a general morality of public action can be developed. In Britain there are no clearly established constitutional principles which can be derived from an authoritative source. In so far as the courts are concerned, whether an issue is constitutional or not depends on the judges' understanding of the issues and previous case-law. As a result it is again easy to deny that certain issues are constitutional at all (e.g. *Home*

Office v. *Harman* [1982] 3 WLR 338 per Lord Diplock at 341, *Secretary of State for Defence* v. *Guardian Newspapers* [1984] 3 WLR 986 per Lord Roskill at 1011). This fundamental lack of clarity about the nature and limits of constitutional issues has meant that the English courts have never developed any coherent principles about the nature and limits of public action (see Harden and Lewis 1986: Ch. 7).

These problems are exacerbated by certain peculiarities regarding English thought about law. There is a strong tendency, certainly within English legal education, to see the ambit of law as confined to the decisions of the courts and the interpretation of legislation (Murphy and Roberts 1987; see also G. Wilson 1987). This is often combined with the view that issues involving value judgements (moral/political) are irrelevant to lawyers, their sole job is textual exegesis of the relevant rules. This blunts the critical faculties of lawyers and often serves to disguise their ideological presuppositions. Lawyers, then, tend to see themselves as only concerned with a narrow range of actions in public life and are not very concerned with generating a principled approach to problems, especially constitutional ones.

This view of law, which we shall call the traditional view, although it is worth noting that it emerged only after fierce controversies over legal education in the nineteenth century (Cocks 1983), has faced heavy attacks in the last twenty years or so in Britain. The literature on this theme is rich and varied, tackling the traditional view at a variety of levels and through a variety of methods. The broad thrust of this criticism can be crudely summarised as saying two things. First, that law is not simply a matter of what the courts and legislatures do, it is a social practice which must be carried out in any organised society. In other words, to understand the legal practices of a society we must look not only at the way courts deal with disputes but also at tribunals, consumer councils, the way local authority officers and civil servants deal with disputes, and so on. We must look not only at how Parliament makes law but also at discretionary decision-making, for example how public agencies create their own rules and policies. (See e.g. Arthurs 1985; Harden and Lewis 1986, esp. Ch. 3; Harlow and Rawlings 1984; Prosser 1982.) Secondly, and this is *not* a necessary consequence of the first set of arguments, value judgements and moral/political principles are inextricably bound up in legal discourse. This formulation conceals a whole host of controversial questions, particularly methodological ones. (For a general overview of this issue, see Beyleveld and Brownsword 1986.) We want to stress the argument that the lawyer is not simply a technician. Lawyers are essentially concerned with principles of justice and fairness. Their job is critically to evaluate institutions and practices to see if they live up to such principles and to design institutions which will ensure a better match between the principles and practice. (See further, Prosser 1982; Prosser 1986, Ch. 1; Harden and Lewis 1986, esp. Ch. 10.)

In Britain, whether or not there are legal devices to structure or monitor public agencies' actions depends not on any attempt at a principled constitutional approach but on the particular historical contingencies surrounding the agency. For example, contrast the relatively open procedures used by the Civil Aviation Authority in allocating airline routes with the very secretive processes used by the IBA for allocating television franchises (Baldwin 1985: 143–58; Lewis 1975). The differences cannot be explained by claiming the agencies are carrying out different functions, that the information is more sensitive in one case than the other or that secretiveness aids efficiency. In other words, a principled *constitutional* justification cannot be found; as with so much else in the pattern of decision-making in Britain, explanations derive from historical accident and political pragmatism (Ganz 1972).

This is characteristic of the British constitution. Although much energy is expended on the rhetoric of Parliamentary sovereignty and the rule of law, the patterning of behaviour of public bodies is dependent on other influences. In particular, it depends on a shared set of mutual expectations, often unarticulated, on what counts as 'good' and 'responsible' government. This is a fragile structure liable to be upset by the onset of war or panics over immigration, amongst other things. It is particularly vulnerable to takeover by groups who do not share these mutual expectations. As shall be argued throughout this book, since the 1979 Conservative Government there have been fundamental constitutional changes. There has been little recognition of this and little debate. In part, this is due to the inadequacies of our only constitutional guarantors, Parliament and the courts. To understand the inadequacies properly, we need to set them in the context of twentieth-century changes in the mode of governance.

The twentieth-century British state

The twentieth century has witnessed a tremendous growth in the scale of state intervention in economic and social spheres. The version of the rule of law which dominated English constitutional thought assumed that the state carried out few functions and that those it did undertake were done so on the basis of general rules, promulgated in legislation. The limits to legitimate state action were policed by the ordinary courts which ensured a separate, 'private', sphere for citizens. The quantitative extension of the role of the state would in itself cause problems for this model. It has been less remarked that there has also occurred a qualitative change in the nature of state intervention. The rhetoric of the rule of law assumed that it was possible to discern a separation between the state and civil society. It is logically impossible to reconcile this with a notion of Parliamentary sovereignty which insists that, in principle, no area of private activity is immune from Parliamentary intervention. In any event, as a considerable amount of work within the social sciences has documented, it is no longer

conceptualise these spheres as separate; what has occurred is a
ssive 'compenetration' of the state and civil society (Poggi 1978,
.1. 6; Harden and Lewis 1986: 56–62).

This has occurred for a variety of reasons, notably crisis avoidance
through political and administrative interventions in economic processes. In
turn, these influences have shaped the types of policy intervention engaged
in by government; rather than conventionally legal forms of intervention
through statute or statutory instrument, a diverse collection of less formal
devices has been utilised, for example circulars, tax concessions, company
law forms and contractual devices (Daintith 1985). Instead of being
exercised through institutions of central and local government conventionally subject to democratic forms of accountability, an imposing edifice of
quasi-government has been erected posing new problems of accountability
and control. A recent highly publicised example has been the replacement of
the Metropolitan County Councils with appointed Joint Boards to
administer certain services together with the creation of Urban Development Corporations taking over certain functions of local government.
However, at a less well-publicised level an enormous range of bodies span
the public–private divide so effectively as to make the concept of such a
separation meaningless (Middlemas 1979; Barker 1982; Birkinshaw *et al.*
1987). Of course, extended government is by no means a new phenomenon,
but nevertheless it does not fit into the traditional structures of
constitutional accountability. This development has been documented
elsewhere, notably in the extensive literature on corporatism, and we do not
need to replicate it here.

It is important to stress, however, that the twentieth-century changes in
the political and economic spheres were not accompanied by any
reassessment of constitutional forms and institutional arrangements; as
Poggi has put it:

> the state still functions in our time within and through *forms* derived from the
> liberal-democratic nineteenth-century constitution; it does so to an extent
> sufficient partly to disguise and partly to limit the changes in the *substance* of
> the political process, but at the same time it modifies and distorts the forms
> themselves.
>
> (Poggi 1978: 121, original emphasis)

Instead of there being any attempt to design new forms of legitimating
principle or new institutions of accountability, legitimation claims were
increasingly based on the ability of government to ensure continuing
economic growth, to intervene effectively to ward off economic crises and to
guarantee well-being through the establishment of the welfare state. An
example is nationalisation. The motives for this were various and included
improving working conditions, but the central stress was on economic
modernisation and efficiency. Little thought was given to resolving the
central constitutional problem of regularising relations between industries

and government and creating accountability to the workforce and consumers (Prosser 1986). However, with the problems of economic decline and with the growing cynicism about the ability of the welfare state to deliver on its promise of full employment, these claims provided uncertain guarantees of continued legitimation (see Habermas 1976). As we mentioned earlier, it is from this that the advocacy from the 'New Right' of limited state intervention gained much of its appeal. Before analysing the extent to which such claims have been turned into practice, however, we should say more about the limitations of the existing institutions for accountability in dealing with the growth of the modern state.

Parliament and the courts: effective accountability?

In the traditional scheme the twin institutions of accountability are Parliament and the ordinary common-law courts – the former supervising policy, the latter legality. Indeed, even in the 1980s the majority of constitutional reform proposals have concentrated on the promotion of the effectiveness of these institutions by relatively minor procedural changes. However, it is clear that the great bulk of governing activity is outside their effective scrutiny.

First, the role of Parliament has been transformed by the development of political parties reflecting collective and class groupings outside Parliament. Thus the ability of MPs to act independently through debate (in so far as it ever existed), rather than as representatives of interests and of party programmes, has been largely lost. To quote Poggi once more:

> The open-endedness and creativity of the parliamentary process is thus diminished. Increasingly, parliament is reduced to a highly visible stage on which are enacted vocal, ritualised confrontations between preformed, hierarchically controlled, ideologically characterised alignments.... Under such conditions, parliament no longer performs a critical, autonomous role as a mediator between societal interests; instead, its composition and operations simply register the distribution of preferences within the electorate and determine in turn which party will lead the executive.
>
> (Poggi 1978: 141)

Recent events have vividly illustrated the limitations of Parliament as a means of accountability. Thus the Westland affair showed both the irrelevance of traditional conventions of individual and collective responsibility (for the extraordinary process of government decision-making in relation to Westland see HC 519 1985–6 and HC 176 1986–7), but also the problems facing the much-heralded system of select committees created in 1979 in gaining information to provide the basis for an effective critique of governmental decisions (for the difficulties in obtaining information from a minister see HC 100 1986–7, para 18 and HC 169 1985–6: 89–130; in relation to civil servants see Cmnd 9916, HC 100 1986–7, and Cmnd 78).

The weaknesses are particularly manifest in areas central to Thatcherism. The control of public expenditure has (at least until 1986) formed a prominent part of Thatcherite rhetoric. However, the procedures available to Parliamentary bodies for the scrutiny of governmental spending are now generally accepted to be antiquated and ineffective. (See HC 24 1982–3 and the Government's reply at 50 HC Debs cols 260–8. For a particularly critical account of the ineffectiveness of Parliamentary control of expenditure see now HC 98 1986–7.) In the area of 'extended government' the weakness of financial control has been most acute and governmental support for reform lacking. This can be illustrated by the responses to the attempts by the Public Accounts Committee to extend the powers of the Comptroller and Auditor-General to include the nationalised industries and a number of quasi-governmental bodies. In the end it was left to a private member to move legislation to this effect, and the result was a compromise excluding many of the most important institutions of quasi-government, in particular the nationalised industries (National Audit Act 1983; for accounts of this background, see Drewry 1983; Prosser 1986: 204–10). The arrangements have been subjected to continuing criticism by the Public Accounts Committee of the House of Commons (see now HC 26 1986–7) and have also created problems in the process of privatisation and where privatisation will not end the flow of public money (see e.g. on the privatisation of parts of BL, HC 407 1982–3 and in relation to the Royal Dockyards HC 286 1985–6).

If the role of Parliament in the scrutiny of such crucial areas of government would seem to be marginal, it might be argued that this is to some extent corrected by the ability of the courts to engage in more effective scrutiny of the legality of administrative decisions, and there has been no shortage of judicial claims as to the developed nature of administrative law (see e.g. Lord Diplock in *O'Reilly* v. *Mackman* [1982] 3 All ER 1124, at 1130; for detailed discussion of this claim, see Harden and Lewis 1986, Ch. 7). There have indeed been reforms of the procedure for public law litigation and a concentration of cases on a more specialist court, perhaps leading to a greater degree of expertise amongst the judiciary dealing with such cases (Blom-Cooper 1982). In addition, in the *Datafin* case, the Court of Appeal has at last taken the first steps towards coming to terms with the development of quasi-government as a central base of public power (*R* v. *Panel on Takeovers and Mergers ex parte Datafin plc* [1987] 1 All ER 564: cf. *R* v. *Independent Broadcasting Authority ex parte Rank Organisation, The Times*, 14 March 1986). Nevertheless, the principles applied by the courts in dealing with public law cases remain undeveloped and unclear; either they are stated at such a high level of generality as to prevent any prediction of future decisions (see e.g. *Council of Civil Service Unions* v. *Minister for the Civil Service* [1984] 3 All ER 935, especially per Lord Diplock at 950–1), or are contradictory in implication (this is particularly so in the revival of the *Wednesbury* test of unreasonableness as ground for judicial review; cf. e.g. *Wheeler* v. *Leicester City Council* [1985] 2 All ER 1106, *Nottinghamshire County*

Council v. *Secretary of State for the Environment* [1986] 1 All ER 199, and *West Glamorgan County Council* v. *Rafferty* [1987] 1 All ER 1005). There have also been recent signs that the much-applauded willingness of the courts to develop the scope of administrative law is at an end (*Puhlhofer* v. *Hillingdon London Borough Council* [1986] 1 All ER 467, *R* v. *Secretary of State for the Home Department ex parte Swati* [1986] 1 All ER 717). Furthermore, recent empirical research indicates not only that very few cases are taken to the High Court but also that they are unevenly distributed between governmental agencies (Sunkin 1987).

A further problem is that it has become increasingly clear that judicial decisions unfavourable to government will face swift statutory reversal, sometimes with retrospective effect. This has always been a feature of political life (Prosser 1983, Ch. 5), but has assumed new prominence since 1979 (McAuslan and McEldowney 1985: 28–31). This has often occurred in the fields of social security and local government, in which the few local authority victories in the courts have proved extremely shortlived. A special mention should be made of the use of novel forms of clauses designed to exclude any possibility of judicial review. A striking use of such clauses is in the Local Government Finance Act 1987. Section 4(1) provides in relation to rate support grant:

> Anything done by the Secretary of State before the passing of this Act for the purposes of the relevant provisions in relation to any of the initial years or intermediate years shall be deemed to have been done in compliance with those provisions.

Section 4(6) provides:

> Subsection (1) above shall have effect notwithstanding any decision of a court (whether before or after the passing of this Act) purporting to have a contrary effect.

Sections 6(1) and 6(6) have similar effect in relation to the validation of the Secretary of State's past acts in relation to rate-capping. So much for limited government under the law!

Thatcherism and the constitution

The ascent of Thatcherism in British politics coincides with both economic decline and a decline in the effectiveness of the conventional mechanisms of accountability of British government. Indeed, some of the appeal of the new politics can be explained by disillusion with the previous consensus on the role of the British state in economic management. It might be expected, then, that an integral part of Thatcherite ideas would be a reassessment of the constitutional machinery so as to express a new conception of the minimalist state. 'Rolling back the frontiers of the state', if it were to be more than rhetoric, would seem to suggest that new constraints on legitimate governmental action were required.

In practice, there has been virtually no such rethinking. As mentioned above, particular political changes have both dramatically altered the map of political power and contained implicit claims as to the legitimate role of the state and as to who might be acceptable participants in the organised political process. However, at a larger level, there have been virtually no proposals reflecting a conscious and thought-out plan to redraw the constitutional map in Thatcherism's own image.

To a large degree this reflects the *ad hoc* elements in Thatcherism itself. Even the term 'Thatcherism' is misleading in that it suggests a coherent political philosophy, whereas examination of what has actually occurred suggests a much more pragmatic process responding to particular political opportunities. The exception to this was the set of economic policies centred around the Medium-Term Financial Strategy. However, even this was largely influenced in its basic structure by the policies of the previous Labour Government ('If there has been a Thatcher experiment, it was launched by Denis Healey' [Riddell 1983: 59]), and this strategy has now been largely abandoned, as has been acknowledged by the Treasury and Civil Service Select Committee (HC 27 1986–7. For the abusive and patronising reply of the Chancellor, see 107 HC Debs cols 1236–44, 17 December 1986).

The rhetorical claims of Thatcherism have been high, for example:

> We offered a complete change in direction – from one in which the state became totally dominant in people's lives and penetrated almost every aspect to a life where the state did do certain things, but without displacing personal responsibility. I think we have altered the balance between the person and the state in a favourable way.
>
> (Mrs Thatcher interviewed in *The Times*, 5 May 1983, quoted at Riddell 1983: 1; cf. ibid: 19)

However, this does not represent any developed system of ideas as to the legitimate boundaries between the state and personal responsibility. Thatcherism may show a greater consistency of approach than previous ideas espoused by political leaders in Britain, but it is not a consistency of thought-out ideas but of an unarticulated world-view:

> Mrs Thatcher's views, prejudices and style have determined the Government's actions more than any other single factor.... Thatcherism is essentially an instinct, a series of moral values and an approach to leadership rather than an ideology.
>
> (Riddell 1983: 6–7)

Even privatisation has been a much more *ad hoc* process than it appears; in its early days the key influence was the perceived need to influence the figures on public borrowing rather than a principled decision to cut back the state; indeed, the programme did not form a prominent part of the Conservative manifestos of 1979 or 1983. Proposals to force local authorities to engage in far-reaching privatisation were dropped in 1987 when the Government discovered the difficulties involved in drafting an adequate Bill and the problems posed for the legislative programme before the general election. To quote Riddell once more:

> despite all the ideas for detailed cuts worked out in Opposition, the Thatcher administration has never had a coherent strategy for shifting the frontiers of the public sector. Indeed, when Ministers were presented by the Think Tank with alternative ways of significantly reducing expenditure in September 1982, they recoiled in horror and had the paper withdrawn.
>
> (Riddell 1983: 132)

Far-reaching changes are being introduced in the third term, including the Local Government Bill which had previously been dropped. However, there is no real likelihood that this will represent an increasingly coherent political approach, as opposed to the continuation of particular reforms which have appeared politically popular, for example, in housing.

Even the controversial Thatcher approach to the civil service and its alleged politicisation can be seen more as a personal implementation of conventional ideas rather than as a new departure: 'she has taken seriously the constitutional principle that the bureaucratic machine must be the servant of elected politicians ... Mrs Thatcher didn't see the civil service as a machine, but as a collection of individuals, most of them less than adequate' (Young and Sloman 1986: 47–8). Similarly, it will be argued in Chapter 3 below that corporatism is by no means dead, despite the exclusion of the trades unions from the inner sanctums of Downing Street and Whitehall.

The *ad hoc* nature of Thatcherism in practice makes it less surprising that it has not carried with it any new system of constitutional thought. Indeed, conscious attention to constitutional reform has been non-existent. As one writer has put it:

> It is somewhat surprising that Sir Keith Joseph and others who share his commitment to the redefinition of the economic and social aspects of Conservative philosophy appear to show little interest in the constitutional implications of their arguments: the impression is often conveyed that political institutions are rather secondary bits of organisation which a management consultant can re-jig according to need. In contrast the political and constitutional dimension was always central to the arguments of the German neo-liberal advocates of the *soziale Marktwirtschaft*.
>
> (Johnson 1980: n. 24)

This has been confirmed by the Lord Chancellor:

> When I accepted office, first under Mr Heath and later under Mrs Thatcher, I was given no remit to carry through constitutional changes of any kind, and no proposals for constitutional change formed any part of the election manifesto. My sole duty was to be as good a Lord Chancellor in a Conservative Cabinet, as God helping, I was able to be.
>
> (Lord Hailsham, letter printed in *The Observer*, 12 April 1987)

Nor have attempts to effect constitutional change by others been more effective. They have encountered at best lukewarm support from some members of the Government (e.g. the Human Rights Bill, which would have had the effect of incorporating the European Convention on Human Rights into British law) or have ended in rejection or unsatisfactory compromise after Governmental opposition (e.g. the proposals for reforming the scrutiny of public expenditure by Parliament, the Access to Personal Information Act). Even the new select committees were very much the personal brainchild of the distinctly un-Thatcherite (and soon replaced) Leader of the House, and have been prevented from undertaking effective work on controversial topics by Governmental restrictions on the availability of information for them, as the references to the Westland affair and its aftermath confirm.

As the reference to Mr Heath in the Lord Chancellor's letter above suggests, this represents a large degree of continuity with previous Conservative constitutional thought, which has in general been hostile to generalised constitutional reform and has stressed the need to maximise the freedom of action of governments. Ironically, the point was well made by Hayek when he refers to:

> the characteristic complacency of the conservative toward the action of established authority and his prime concern that this authority be not weakened rather than that its power be kept within bounds . . . he believes that if government is in the hands of decent men, it ought not be too restricted by rigid rules.
>
> (Hayek 1960: 401)

This could perhaps be seen as an inevitable reflection of the cynicism of politicians; once in office, whatever their previous beliefs, they will not implement reforms which will limit their effective freedom of political action. However, this would be to dismiss the problem too hastily. Much of the appeal of Thatcherism has been based on the limitation of the legitimate role of the state, and as we have seen, this has addressed a real problem of legitimacy. Moreover, certain constitutional reforms could actually serve to perpetuate Thatcherism (e.g. through a Bill of Rights drafted in particular ways), an idea which must have great appeal for a Prime Minister aiming to end the role of socialism in the British political scene forever (Thatcher 1986).

In fact, matters go deeper than this, for attitudes to constitutional reform reflect deep divisions within English conservative thought. As the quotation from Hayek above suggests, 'It has been a persistent theme in British conservative thought that political institutions should not be constructed on abstract principles' (Johnson 1980: 127). As a result:

> Precisely because so much emphasis is placed on the importance of trust as the cement which binds the polity together, there is a prejudice in favour of allowing to public authorities a discretion in the discharge of their

functions.... In other words, the conservative theory of limited government does not advocate the institutionalisation of suspicions and mistrust, but instead proposes that those in power are restrained by their own sense of the limits to their authority, as well as by the pressures, moral and material, in society which they have to respect.

(Johnson 1980: 132, note omitted)

This paternalism also has its dark side in the authoritarianism of the 'strong state' and the neo-Conservatism associated with the *Salisbury Review*; these elements in the new Conservatism are also highly unlikely to favour limitations on the state's powers of rule (for neo-Conservatism and the state, see Belsey 1986: 174–6; Gamble 1979).

However, there have also been tendencies within recent conservative thought towards the institutionalisation of restraints on governmental power. The source of this has been the fear of a left-wing government, perhaps supported by only a minority of the electorate, introducing fundamental economic and political change. This view has been stated most comprehensively by Lord Hailsham, who came to regard the answer as a written constitution with a Bill of Rights, and if possible clauses entrenched against repeal through the Parliamentary process in order to institution-alised limited government. This was to be combined with devolution, regional assemblies and a reformed House of Lords elected by proportional representation and holding a veto on legislation (Hailsham 1978, esp. 21–2, 129–40, 170–4, 219–21, 226). The fear lying behind such proposals has been nicely expressed by Johnson:

> a relative majority in the House of Commons may rest on a minority position in the country. Government on these terms is tolerable if the party in power recognises that there are limits to what it is entitled to do.
> (Johnson 1980: 139; for more detailed constitutional analysis see Johnson
> 1977)

Conservative claims such as these may now produce ironic smiles in view of the fundamental change introduced by 1979 by governments without support from the majority of electors; nevertheless, such views on limited government have come to form one central strand of the new conservative thought. Indeed, in the United States and France constitutional reform has emerged as a central theme in proposals from the New Right (see Bosanquet 1983, Ch. 4; Lepage 1980: 466–7). It is now time to examine one major example.

Hayek's theory of law and the constitution

There are a number of neo-liberal theorists who have advocated a limited role for the state (see e.g. Nozick 1974). However, the most detailed set of constitutional proposals for achieving this comes from F. A. Hayek, whose recipe for changing society also includes politico-economic prescriptions which have clearly had an influence on conservative policies, for example, trade union reform (see Ch. 8 of the present work). It would be a mistake to characterise Hayek as simply a theorist of the minimalist state or of *laissez-faire*; rather, his concern is with *how* the state should act (Hayek 1979a: 41; Barry 1979: 105). It is this which makes his work so interesting for the lawyer; nevertheless, the *forms* of legitimate state action would impose in practice severe limitations on the *content* of state intervention. The degree of influence of Hayek's ideas on Thatcherism is also debatable; certainly his influence was strongly felt in the early days of change in the Conservative Party (see e.g. Bosanquet 1981), and according to one political opponent, Mrs Thatcher:

> really will enthusiastically tell you about the books she's read and the great panjandrums of the intellectual right, the economic right–Friedman, Hayek. These are people to whom she pays earnest and indeed almost passionate respect in conversation. She has deeply imbibed from them and she does believe that she is carrying out a policy according to the best wisdom of what she thinks are men of the utmost intellectual distinction.
>
> (Peter Shore quoted in Young and Sloman 1986: 58)

Whatever the role of Hayek in giving a veneer of intellectual respectability to Thatcherism, his interest for us here is as the major example of a writer from the New Right to give us a coherent picture of what a reformed constitution would look like. It is useful to consider what his approach entails, as it will serve as a benchmark against which to assess the changes wrought by the Conservatives.

As already stated, the concept of Parliamentary sovereignty is central to the British constitution, and Thatcherism has shown no signs of changing this. It is anathema to Hayek. This is part of his wider opposition to 'constructivism', that is 'a conception which assumes that all social institutions are, and ought to be, the product of deliberate design' (Hayek 1973: 5). This implies that deliberate planning of a society by a public agency is inherently inferior to unplanned development. There is an epistemological base for this; it derives from Hayek's belief that knowledge is to a large extent tacit and impossible to concentrate in a single planning agency (for the epistemological bases of Hayek's theory, see Gray 1986: 25, 36, 40). Thus, 'Society advances by making use of dispersed knowledge: but it does so through the price system and the market. Collectivist central planning is bound to fail: it will be the "road to serfdom"' (Bosanquet 1983: 31).

Hayek makes direct links between constructivism and legal positivism; thus legal positivism denies the existence of law which is not the deliberate creation of a law-giver; indeed, in its most developed form it 'signaled the definite eclipse of all traditions of limited government.' (Hayek 1960: 238; see generally Hayek 1973, Ch. 4; cf. Hailsham 1978: 11, 219–21. The general theory of law in Hayek's work is too complex for adequate discussion here: see especially Hayek 1960, Part II, and Hayek 1973; for discussion see Gray 1986, Ch. 3, and Barry 1979: Ch. 5):

...when the British Parliament claimed sovereign, that is unlimited, power...it proved in the long run the great calamity of modern development that soon after representative government was achieved all those restraints upon the supreme power that had been painfully built up during the evolution of constitutional monarchy were successfully dismantled as no longer necessary.... this in effect meant the abandonment of constitutionalism which consists in a limitation of all power by permanent principles of government.

(Hayek 1979a: 2–3)

Law, rather than forming commands which emanate from a sovereign body attempting to manipulate the affairs of private actors, consists of 'rules regulating the conduct of persons towards others, applicable to an unknown number of future instances and containing prohibitions delimiting the boundary of each person'. It merely provides additional information for social actors; it does not coerce them into the performance of particular actions (Hayek 1973: 122; see also Hayek 1960, Chs. 10 and 14). Moreover, 'because the rule of law means that government must never coerce an individual except in the enforcement of a known rule, it constitutes a limitation on the powers of all government, including the powers of the legislature' (Hayek 1960: 205). Such ideal law is explicitly identified with the English common law (Hayek 1973: 84–5).

Despite the major differences on sovereignty, this would appear to ally Hayek with Dicey in stress on the common law as a protection against interventionist government. Indeed, Hayek shares Dicey's antipathy towards coercive discretionary powers on the part of government (Hayek 1960, Ch. 15, esp. 225–6) and his antipathy to any distinct body of public law based on legislation; Dicey 'restated the traditional conception of the rule of law in a manner that governed all later discussion' (Hayek 1960: 203). However, according to Hayek he made the mistake of assuming that only review by ordinary courts was compatible with the rule of law and misunderstood the role of specialist administrative law courts on the Continent:

The very idea of separate administrative courts...came to be regarded in England...as the denial of the rule of law. Thus, by his attempt to vindicate the rule of law as he saw it, Dicey in effect blocked the development which would have offered the best chance of preserving it. He could not stop the growth in the Anglo-Saxon world of an administrative apparatus similar to that which existed on the Continent. But he did contribute much to prevent or delay the growth of institutions which could subject the new bureaucratic machinery to effective control.

(Hayek 1960: 204)

Thus, despite his respect for the common law, Hayek does not share Dicey's view of its effectiveness as a means of rendering legitimate the actions of a developed state.

In his constitutional prescriptions Hayek departs from the conventional British model far more dramatically. There is no space here to describe in detail the ideal constitutional arrangements suggested by Hayek, but it should be stressed that they represent an extreme rejection of any notion of unlimited Parliamentary sovereignty (see generally Hayek 1979a, Chs. 13, 16 and 17). This does not involve a Bill of Rights in the usual sense, because of the difficulty of singling out the particular rights to be protected (Hayek 1979a: 110); rather he proposes the division of democratic institutions so that general rules would be set by a Legislative Assembly elected on the basis of a once-in-a-lifetime vote by people who had reached the age of 45, who would elect their peers for a period of fifteen years. A Governmental Assembly elected on more conventional lines would be concerned with organising the apparatus of government and deciding about the use of governmental resources. Crucially:

> The one important difference between the position of such a representative Governmental Assembly and the existing parliamentary bodies would of course be that in all that it decided it would be bound by the rules of just conduct laid down by the Legislative Assembly, and that, in particular, it could not issue any orders to private citizens which did not follow directly and necessarily from the rules laid down by the latter.
>
> (Hayek 1979a: 119)

The apparent eccentricity of some of Hayek's constitutional proposals might tempt one to ignore his ideas as too far removed from the realm of practical politics to be of interest. This would be a mistake, for his importance lies in his realisation that any fundamental rethinking of the role of the state is essentially a legal or constitutional matter, and that radical political change needs radical legal change for its effectiveness to stick. This is part of the justification for Hayek's denial of his own conservatism (Hayek 1960, Postscript). However, the recent changes in the Conservative Party might have been expected to have brought it closer to his general thought; yet the constitutional rethinking this might be thought to imply has been totally absent.

The following chapters look at the changes wrought by the Thatcher Governments on the structure and institutions of the British state. If one theme predominates it is that the approach of these governments has been instrumental and tactical rather than strategic and principled. The rhetorical claims of Thatcherism are broad and sweeping, the reality is more complex. What does become clear is the ease with which fundamental changes in our constitutional structure can be made once the implicit understandings and conventions which previously served to ensure 'responsible' government are swept aside and ignored. Furthermore, this highlights the lack of institutions to facilitate debate on the desirability, means and consequences of embarking on fundamental structural change. Such a gap enables the rhetorical claims of Thatcherism to capture the moral high-ground; they are rarely tested against the everyday reality of their implementation. This would matter less if there was a coherent approach to constitutional restructuring, but this is not the case. As will be seen, the claim to have created new forms of accountability, for example, in the privatised industries and local government, is threadbare. Instead, the old constitutional nostrums are wheeled out, despite their decreasing power to legitimate government action. This then is the pass at which our constitution has arrived.

Chapter 2 discusses the response of the Conservatives to a critical difficulty: the relative economic decline of Britain. It traces how and why the Conservatives broke with the previous consensus on economic management and investigates what they perceived as being the key levers of economic management. As the theorists of the New Right see the ills of the economy as being caused by the political system, this raises constitutional problems. How do you design a political system which will not suffer from such defects and move towards this goal when the political system is itself part of the problem? The chapter ends by examining the record of the Thatcher Governments and concludes that they have neither fulfilled the expectations of their supporters nor come to terms with this central paradox.

Chapter 3 is concerned with corporatism and suggests that, although industrial tri-partism may be dead, corporatism as a means of policy intervention is flourishing. It examines the reasons why it may be advantageous for government to utilise corporatist mechanisms, the strategies it may employ and the instruments available for use. This enables a typology of 'government' and 'private sector' relations to be constructed which serves as a foundation for a brief survey of empirical instances of existing corporatist arrangements. It closes by discussing corporatism and accountability and the inability of our existing constitutional arrangements to come to terms with corporatist institutions and practices.

Chapter 4 picks up some of the themes of Chapter 3 in the context of an area which has only recently entered the agenda of 'high' politics: the regulation of financial services. In the course of the 1980s this industry has been affected by revolutionary economic changes which have forced an equally profound change in regulation. The outcome was not to abolish corporatism but to make it stronger. This chapter explains why that option was adopted and concludes by examining the problems in maintaining the new corporatist arrangements.

Chapter 5, by contrast, looks at an area which has had a high political profile: the privatisation of nationalised industries. It critically assesses the claims that privatisation frees the industries from political intervention and creates new mechanisms of accountability, especially shareholder accountability. It concludes that these claims are unjustified and that although the *ad hoc*, inconsistent and secretive arrangements surrounding nationalised industries have been swept away, they have simply been replaced by another set of *ad hoc*, inconsistent and secretive arrangements.

Chapter 6 examines the Conservative approach to local government, through discussing local government finance, inner-city policy, the abolition of the GLC and the Metropolitan County Councils and the

Widdicombe Report. It argues that, although there has been a radical change in local government, this has been masked by the piecemeal and initially uneven fashion in which the reforms were brought about. It is only after these changes that the beginnings of a coherent Conservative approach to local government can be discerned, which may influence future government actions.

The same theme surfaces in Chapter 7, which discusses privatisation in local government and the health service. It examines the attempts to encourage privatisation and the differing mechanisms used for this, which depend, in part, on the differing legal status of the authorities over which influence is sought. The effects of such privatisation are analysed and the Chapter ends by examining the different scenarios which might be envisaged for local government in the future.

Chapter 8 investigates the approach of Conservative Governments to trade unions. By way of background, it discusses general themes in the relations between government and the trade unions throughout the twentieth century, in order to provide a contrast with the Conservatives. A critical look is taken at the arguments in favour of the restrictions on trade union power propounded by Hayek. Particular changes affecting trade unions are then examined, which leads to the conclusion that, as well as formal legal changes, institutional changes, such as the downgrading of the role unions play in the process of government, have had a crucial effect on trade union power.

Chapter 9, 'Law, Order and the State', begins by picking up some of the themes of Chapter 8. It briefly discusses the case for reducing trade union power and points out the lack of debate over the proper place for trade unions in the state. The reforms enacted, particularly as regards picketing, and the problems they created for the police's attempt to portray themselves as neutral guarantors of the rule of law, are examined. The focus then shifts to 'law and order' issues and the failure of the Thatcher Governments to find a coherent approach. Instead, the emphasis has been on a 'technological fix', which has had detrimental effects for the police. The chapter concludes that recent Conservative Governments have too often seen policing and law simply as a means to enforce order. What has been lacking is a philosophy of justice relevant to non-market situations or market failure.

The final chapter begins with the Conservative Governments' ambiguous attitude to civil liberties. It then, in search of a coherent alternative view of the constitution, scrutinises the views of the Opposition parties. Both are found wanting. In and around the Labour Party, there is increasing interest in radical ideas about 'market socialism' and institutional design. However, there is still a deeply entrenched hostility to law and constitutions within the Labour Party, illustrated by the response to the Human Rights Bill. By contrast, the Alliance parties, as we refer to them, are deeply committed to constitutional reform. Their problem is a nostalgia for an idealised nineteenth-century constitution, and their ideas largely ignore the consequences of the growth of the modern state and the forms of extended government for such a prescription. The implication is that, on all sides, a major rethinking of our approach to constitutional fundamentals is long overdue.

2

Economic Decline and the Crisis of Legitimacy

Andrew Gamble

The problem of decline

In the 1970s a deep-seated crisis of legitimacy developed in Britain. There was a loss of faith in political institutions and the effectiveness of government policies. This crisis had many causes but at its heart was widespread disillusion with the policies which successive governments had pursued since the 1960s to remedy the relative weakness of the British economy and render it internationally competitive again.

This crisis over policy came to raise major constitutional questions. The channels for representing interests and opinion appeared no longer capable of shaping a definition of the public interest that could preserve the legitimacy of the state. Much that was being done by governments could be justified in terms of general constitutional principle by the doctrine of Parliamentary sovereignty. But as is explained in the Introduction, there is a real practical tension between the doctrine of Parliamentary sovereignty and the doctrine of the rule of law.

The consequences of the steady growth of government programmes and responsibilities created a vigorous right and left reaction to what had become widely termed the 'new corporatism' in the 1950s and 1960s – the attempt to legitimate the growth of government by portraying it as the result of tripartite consensus between government, employers and unions.

The modernisation programmes of the 1960s and 1970s were launched amidst great optimism that they would allow Britain to eliminate the obstacles to more rapid growth. There was a broad consensus among all the political parties that a more interventionist role by government was required. Governments needed to spend more to boost demand and create essential new infrastructure; they needed to provide subsidies and incentives to firms and individuals to persuade them to act in ways that would promote growth; and they needed to act where necessary as a catalyst for change, identifying bottlenecks and obstacles, and setting up new public agencies to remove them.

This interventionist style was nothing new in British politics. The understandings about the role of the state in the economy which had been established in the 1940s at the time of the wartime coalition and post-war Labour Governments, made interventionist solutions seem the natural ones. The Conservative Government led by Harold Macmillan and including within its ranks R. A. Butler, Iain Macleod, Reginald Maudling and Edward Heath, led the way on this. The new public spending programmes, the new planning machinery and the new policy priorities gave few difficulties to a government whose leader and many of whose ministers believed in the state having a strong and positive role in the economy.

The policy innovations of the 1960s maintained broad continuity with the priorities of the post-war consensus. The problem of the relative economic decline was diagnosed as the pursuit of the wrong policies, which could soon be rectified by the adoption of the right ones. There was little disposition to question constitutional arrangements or the broad parameters of policy. The modernisation programme was regarded as building upon a foundation that was still largely sound.

This all changed very rapidly. The disillusioning of the expectations which the modernisation programmes had aroused discredited the political leaderships of both major political parties, and by polarising opinion within them weakened support for the consensus. By 1970 Enoch Powell and representatives of a New Right in the Conservative Party had launched a strong attack upon many of the assumptions of the consensus. They urged the party to repudiate them and reclaim its independence.

The failures of the interventionist policies of the Labour Government and pressure from this New Right brought important shifts in the presentation of the programme on which the Conservatives were elected in 1970. They emphasised the need for market solutions to Britain's economic problems, and advocated a policy of disengagement by the state (Holmes 1982). At the same time this 'competition policy', as it became known, was set in the context of two important constitutional changes: the successful conclusion of the negotiations to enter the EC, and the passing of the Industrial Relations Act. The first represented the achievement of a goal which had always been seen as crucial to a successful modernisation policy. Community membership had long been regarded as a way of compelling British industry to become more competitive. The second revived the unsuccessful attempt made by the Labour Government to alter those aspects of trade union behaviour which were now blamed as a chief cause of poor economic performance.

The alacrity with which the Heath Government reverted to a more interventionist style of government when market solutions failed to bring quick results outraged the New Right and showed how far the modernisation programme of the Heath Government remained within the ideological horizons of the post-war consensus. Heath's attitude towards the desirability of market or government solutions to problems was pragmatic, and was influenced by particular circumstances more than fixed principles.

The way in which the Heath Government lost office left the Conservative Party in considerable disarray. The Government had gone to the country on the issue of 'Who governs Britain?' following the miners' refusal to accept a pay offer within the guidelines of the Government's statutory pay policy. The inability to persuade enough voters to endorse the Government's stand made it seem that all its major policies with the exception of entry into the EC had ended in failure. The Government's relative lack of success in winning confrontations with sections of organised labour was viewed as an ominous erosion of its authority.

The failure of the Heath Government to check the relative economic decline coincided with the beginning of the generalised world recession in 1974. The dissatisfaction with domestic economic performance relative to other major competitors was intensified by the realisation that many of the old conditions that had sustained world prosperity and the remarkable increases in economic output during the long boom of the 1950s and 1960s were now much weaker or had disappeared altogether. What was now in prospect particularly for the older industrial economies was a period of painful restructuring – the abandonment of old industries and the search for new products and new services which could be traded internationally and could sustain employment and profitability.

The old international order did not break down all at once. The signs of strain had been multiplying for some time. Nevertheless, the oil crisis of 1973 does conveniently mark the beginning of a new era, a watershed in the world economy and in national domestic politics. A new politics and a new agenda was created.

The relative fluidity of the political situation in Britain, the apparent loss of competence and authority of both governing parties, and the signs of electoral disaffection, as well as a ferment of ideas on both left and right provided opportunities for those bold enough to seize them. Margaret Thatcher's success in ousting Edward Heath from the leadership of the Conservative Party in early 1975 opened the way for the dissemination of New Right ideas within the party and for the adoption of a programme and an orientation that fully embraced the concerns of the new politics.

The new economic programme

The conversion of the Conservative Party to monetarism and the adoption of many New Right ideas has sometimes been represented as the hijacking of the Conservative Party by an evangelical sect who imposed their own brand of high-minded doctrine on the party's economic policy (Keegan 1984). Such interpretations tend to give too much weight to ideology in the development of the new programme and too little either to the context of party manoeuvre and electoral calculation or to the way in which the changing realities of the world economy forced changes on all national policy-making and all parties. The responses of the Labour Government between 1974 and 1979 anticipated in several respects the policies later associated with the Conservatives.

The ideas of the New Right were important in the shift that took place in Conservative policy, but their influence was limited. Few Conservatives were interested in the constitutional changes necessary to put through a New Right programme and consolidate it. In New Right circles there was a lively debate about these constitutional conditions (Birch 1984), but this debate was almost entirely ignored by the Conservative leadership.

What the leadership seized upon in the New Right critique was the opportunity it offered for criticising the policies of the Labour Government and distancing the party from the policies followed by the Heath Government. It allowed the Conservative leadership to take up a distinctive position from which it could expose the mistakes of the incumbent government and indicate that it was making a fresh start and not returning to past Conservative programmes.

The main policy document which set out the party's ideas on the economy was *The Right Approach to the Economy*, published in 1977. This was very much a compromise programme to maintain the unity of the shadow cabinet. But the political need to challenge Labour dictated, as on previous occasions, that the party should move away from interventionist policies and assert the virtues of market solutions for problems of public policy. The problem for those Conservatives who remained attached to the policies of the Middle Way and pragmatic consensual government was that the proponents of economic liberalism within the party wished to go much further than mere electoral rhetoric.

Rethinking the consensus

The new thinking in the Conservative Party challenged several of the assumptions on which post-war economic policy-making had been based. The social-democratic or welfare consensus of the post-war years represented in the first place agreement on policies. But this in turn reflected a balance of forces in British society, an acceptance of the parameters within which policy-making was to be conducted, which was constitutional in character. This is why the consensus is often spoken of as the post-war settlement. What was 'settled' at that time was the claims of the Labour movement for an extension of citizenship rights. This involved

many new and important public spending programmes and the establishment of new public agencies. It entailed the recognition of the status and
legitimacy of the trade unions. But most important of all it was the
acceptance of the collectivist principle that government responsibility for
what happened in the economy should be considerably increased.

This was not a new principle in 1945. But it had had to make its way
against the assumptions of the old liberal orthodoxy which sought to keep
government as limited as possible. By 1945, however, the defences of *laissez-
faire* had crumbled and the ideas of New Liberalism and social democracy
were very much in the ascendancy. All parties now accepted an extended role
for government in a capitalist economy, and opposition, although present,
was muted.

The acceptance of the principle was most striking in the fields of
stabilisation policy and welfare. They were closely related. It is sometimes
suggested that the first was inspired by Keynes and the second by
Beveridge, but this overlooks the extent to which a major part of
Beveridge's schemes were policies to promote full employment. The idea
that it was possible to have Keynes without Beveridge would have made
little sense to the reformers of 1945.

Accepting that governments had a responsibility to use their power in the
modern economy to promote full employment was more radical than
merely substituting one economic policy goal for another. It involved a
substantial change in the way in which the relationship between
government and the economy was conceived. Keynes offered compelling
arguments as to why governments, now that they had it in their power to
intervene and reduce unemployment, should make it their duty to do so.

What Keynesianism recognised was that the interpenetration of public
and private sectors and the enlargement of the state's revenue base and
spending programmes made discretionary policies of economic management feasible and effective. Without seeking to replace the co-ordinating
function of markets or the private ownership of capital, the state could still
choose to 'steer' the economy to promote objectives such as full
employment, stable prices and faster economic growth.

In practice during the 1950s and 1960s governments found that the
problem for which they needed discretionary economic management was
not unemployment but inflation. What they also found was that indirect
manipulation of demand was insufficient to achieve many of their
objectives. The solution was to develop more direct methods of
intervention. The modernisation programmes of the 1960s were no part of
the original Keynesian prescription. But Keynesianism had helped to make
them possible by weakening the political and ideological obstacles to
interventionist policies. It had helped undermine the notion that only
policies that preserved the minimal state were legitimate and constitutional.

The problem with the modernisation programmes was not that they were
dirigiste but that they failed in their primary objective – reversing Britain's

relative economic decline. It was this failure which emboldened the liberal New Right to challenge the whole post-war orthodoxy and to assert that a major change of direction was now required. The programme that emerged was both a distinctive diagnosis and prescription for the ills of the British economy, and a response to the very different world economic conditions of the 1970s.

The monetary cure for inflation

The main elements of the New Right critique of the post-war consensus can now be examined. One of the earliest and most important battles came over inflation. The discrediting of Keynesianism in the 1970s turned a specialist debate on the causes of inflation into a badge of political identification. 'Technical monetarism', as it came to be called, involved propositions about the relationship between the growth of the money supply and the rate of inflation in the medium term. But, from the start, in the hands of able publicists like Milton Friedman it had a sharp political and ideological edge (Bosanquet 1983).

Friedman's assertion that inflation is always and everywhere a monetary phenomenon was hardly controversial. But from this starting-point he went on to argue that inflation can only be produced by an increase in the quantity of money that is more rapid than the increase in output. Since governments are responsible for the money supply Friedman concluded that governments must be primarily responsible for inflation. If governments desired it, they could always halt inflation by controlling the money supply (Friedman 1977). The cost would be some transitional unemployment. Monetarists disagreed about how high unemployment would have to go, and what the lags were between changes in money supply and changes in prices. But all monetarists agreed that control of inflation was possible if governments were prepared to introduce the correct policy.

The case for monetarism was often presented as a technical economic policy. But it was always more than this. It did not just offer another model of how the economy worked that was different from the Keynesian model. It provided an alternative political economy, an alternative conception of how state and economy should be related. For monetarists inflation was not a problem at a particular time that should be given priority in economic management. Their position is rather that the achievement of 'sound money' should always take priority over full employment and growth.

Monetarists criticised Keynesians not just for advocating a policy that could not halt inflation, but also for accepting a perspective on the economy that justified increasing state intervention to solve economic problems. The monetarists wished to limit state intervention to those functions which only the state could perform for a market economy, such as the control of the money supply. The level of employment or the rate of economic growth were placed outside the scope of legitimate government activity.

The basis for this judgement was the traditional liberal view that the economy worked best if government involvement and interference were kept to a minimum. If this were achieved markets would clear spontaneously and resources would be fully employed and rationally allocated. All economic problems such as inflation derive from governments intervening actively in market processes or suspending the market mechanism to achieve their objectives.

Monetarism therefore implied not simply a change in economic policy away from the management of demand towards the control of the money supply. Acceptance of the monetarist case signalled also a major constitutional change in the sense defined in Chapter 1. It meant governments accepting that they should refrain from intervention in the economy and that they should only accept responsibility for the things, like the control of the money supply, which were directly within their power. Employment and growth would be left to the working of the market economy.

Keynesianism as a form of political economy presupposed an active and interventionist state which expected the market to produce disequilibrium and which stood ready to correct such failures. Monetarism confined the role of government to protecting the conditions under which the market economy could flourish.

The control of public expenditure

The monetarist analysis of the causes of inflation placed the main blame upon government. The more sophisticated analyses, often drawing on the writing and ideas of economic liberals beyond the monetarist camp such as Hayek, went on to discuss the reasons why governments failed to control the money supply (Hayek 1972). In this way the critique of Keynesianism became a broad attack on the political assumptions and institutions that underpinned social-democratic politics.

By this means the failure of Keynesian policies in the 1960s and 1970s to control inflation was taken by monetarist critics to be symptomatic of what was wrong with the British economy. The decline could be explained by continual interference with the market economy practised by successive governments since 1945. The degree to which the market economy had been fettered by government controls and distorted by government interference became the key idea in explaining why the British economy had performed so badly in relative terms since 1951.

The reason why governments found it so difficult to control the money supply and restrain inflation was the level of public spending to which they had become committed and which created constant political pressures on government to expand spending further. In this way governments had become enmeshed in the coils of social democracy. Every new spending programme created a new vested interest to press for its retention and enlargement.

The key notion that the New Right challenged was the idea that the state was either enlightened or neutral. The Virginian school of public choice theory, for example, has argued that politicians and bureaucrats act rationally to maximise their own interests. In the situation in which they find themselves this means appeasing powerful lobbies and seeking by every means possible to enlarge the bureaus and the programmes which they administer. Social democracy with its endorsement of large-scale public spending creates irresistible pressure for further expansion of the public sector (Tulloch 1976; Buchanan 1978).

The New Right argued that public spending was inherently unproductive and a drain on the wealth-producing private sector because of the levels of the taxation required to fund it. Where public spending was financed by borrowing rather than by taxation, this was either inherently inflationary because it involved borrowing from the banks, or it crowded out private sector investment projects by driving up interest rates. Public expenditure programmes were more likely to be wasteful and inefficient and misallocate resources.

Governments which presided over large public sectors were therefore likely to be presiding over relatively inefficient economies, because they would be subject to political pressures for more spending and intervention. Such measures, however, would only distort the pattern of market allocation and unleash inflation through injections of demand in vain attempts to maintain prosperity and employment. To keep control of this situation governments would need to resort to ever tougher measures of control – over wages, prices and investment.

This is the road to serfdom which Hayek foretold in 1944. For Hayek there is no resting place on the road from moderate social democracy to totalitarian central planning (Hayek 1944). Since even moderate Keynesianism requires interference with the market order and credits governments in some situations with more wisdom than the market, it justifies an expanding public sector. In the end this must erode the prosperity of the private sector, because it requires ever more drastic interventionist measures to sustain it, and ever greater politicisation of economic relations.

It follows that if governments wish to break with the cycle of accelerating inflation, the adoption of monetarist policies to control the money supply must be accompanied by determined efforts to control public expenditure so as to reduce the political pressures on government to increase the money supply. The New Right view of how the political system works indicates that only a minimal state is compatible with the maintenance of a market order and therefore with prosperity. If the public sector is not reduced to a minimum, it will constantly create demands and pressures from special interests, and the bureaucracy itself, for relaxation of spending controls and new expansion of public programmes and public initiatives.

Transforming the supply side

Another political condition for the success of monetarism is an active supply-side policy. Monetarism will only lead to stable prices and full employment if all markets throughout the economy are free and competitive. This means that governments must actively intervene to ensure that obstacles that prevent markets clearing are removed. This kind of intervention by government is quite legitimate, indeed it is essential if a market economy is to succeed.

The biggest obstacle of all is the existence of monopoly groups such as trade unions. Enterprise monopoly is treated as a lesser problem, since with the growing openness of economies few firms can protect themselves against competition. Trade unions, however, as well as professional cartels, can exert significant control over the supply of labour in particular markets. The New Right argument is therefore that while trade union behaviour is not the cause of inflation, it is the cause of unemployment and slow growth (Joseph 1979).

Trade unions are the main reason why labour markets do not clear at full employment. They prevent wages falling far enough. By obstructing change and distorting relative prices trade unions prevent markets from working. A monetarist policy that was not accompanied by a supply-side policy to remove rigidities in labour markets would halt inflation only at the expense of a large rise in unemployment. Many monetarists feared that such a rise would create political pressures which might endanger the survival of monetarist policies since it would provide powerful ammunition for elements of the bureaucracy and opposition politicians to argue for policies of expansion and increased public spending.

To counter this threat, a monetarist government would be obliged to intervene in labour markets to reduce union power. Monetarism was not enough. A labour market without unions at all, or with unions that were organised at the level of the individual plant rather than the enterprise or the industry, would be ideal. If this could be achieved, if other obstacles to labour mobility such as housing tenure could also be removed, and if social security were lowered sufficiently so that it was never above the lowest market wage, any unemployment that remained would become voluntary. It would represent the individual's relative valuation of leisure and work. (For more detailed discussion, see Chs. 8 and 9.)

As with public expenditure, the supply-side vision of the monetarists and the New Right rests on a particular concept of a market order and the proper relationship between state and economy. Free exchange in competitive markets is accepted as a self-regulating and harmonious system. The task of the state is to uphold the general rules that are required for such a market order. It has to safeguard property and enforce contracts. It has to maintain the conditions for competition in all markets. It has to secure sound money. In upholding the conditions for a market order the state adopts a neutral policy stance. It abstains from detailed intervention; it does not substitute itself for the market; it does not interfere in market outcomes.

This does not, however, make the state a weak state. On the contrary, a market order is a highly artificial contrivance. The state has a constant role in intervening to remove the rigidities and obstacles that constantly emerge to threaten the conditions for free exchange. The need to stamp out private coercion and to limit public coercion to the minimum necessary to permit a market order to exist, requires an alert and active state.

The constitutional problem

The need for a neutral policy stance is central to the New Right conception of public policy. In the field of economic management this involves the pursuit of sound money policies as a top priority and avoiding either intervening in market processes or suspending them. To make such a policy viable, the public sector needs to be reduced to a minimum and obstacles to the working of markets removed.

The dilemma for the New Right which many of its theorists acknowledge is whether it is possible to move towards a neutral policy stance in existing social-democratic regimes with their swollen public sectors and entrenched special interests. This becomes in New Right discourse the 'problem of democracy'. One reason why public sectors have grown, special interests have become entrenched and governments have become prone to intervene is that a democratic political system facilitates all these things (Olson 1982).

Democracy creates a competitive struggle for power between interests organised in parties and pressure groups. Under cover of the slogans of popular sovereignty and the public interest, it establishes a policy-making process in which the most powerful and successful lobbies can gain privileged positions by prevailing on government to subsidise their activities or restrict the competition they face. Once such a system of special interests becomes established, political competition between the parties comes to mean competition to win the support and approval of these dominant blocs.

If this is so, how can a government, even one strongly influenced by the New Right, break out and restore the conditions for a neutral policy stance? Will it not be overwhelmed by the pressures of a democratic political system and forced to retreat? How can such an imperfect political system such as democracy safeguard the conditions for a market order? On the other hand, if democracy cannot be trusted to safeguard these conditions, what other system can?

There has been much thought devoted to these questions. A number of solutions have been canvassed. One idea is to remove certain functions such as the control of the money supply from government and give them to statutory bodies, like the US Federal Reserve, which are protected in their operational management from interference by elected politicians. An influential body of writing in the United States seeks constitutional controls on the amounts that governments can tax and spend. In Britain there has been some support from New Right writers for a written constitution that could protect the private sector from government interference, by making certain individual rights – ownership of property and inheritance, and the right to buy education and health – inviolable (Moss 1975). Another approach, advocated by Hayek and explored in Chapter 1, is to reform democratic institutions in ways that would drastically restrict the operation of popular sovereignty and the powers of the elected government. A second chamber would be instituted elected on a very restricted franchise and empowered to challenge and overturn government legislation (Hayek 1979a).

The intention of all the solutions is the same: to prevent democracy from threatening liberty and the replacement of the market by planning. But the paradox itself remains. How can such a major constitutional change be brought about in a political system which is itself the chief reason for the drift away from market principles?

This has been one of the major problems of Thatcherism, and accounts for the bitter disillusion that is sometimes encountered amongst New Right supporters of the Government. From the outset the Thatcher leadership was not inclined to consider the constitutional implications of the changes in economic policy it desired to see. It sought from the beginning to operate through the established institutions and procedures of the British state. It has not tried to alter the voting system, to introduce a Bill of Rights or any form of written constitution, to establish a Currency Commission or to reform the civil service.

But although the Thatcher Government has not introduced major constitutional changes formally, there have been major constitutional implications in many of the policies it has pursued. These do not add up to the kind of coherent New Right programme which many wanted to see and which some have interpreted the Thatcher Government as offering.

The record of the Thatcher Governments

If it is judged by the ideological criteria of the New Right, the Thatcher Government has been a failure. Monetarism was adopted and pursued vigorously at the beginning. A medium-term financial strategy was set out in the 1980 budget and the Government showed a surprising readiness at first to adhere to its targets and to take the necessary fiscal and monetary measures when it looked as though the targets would not be met. The decision in the 1981 budget to increase taxation at a time when the recession was at its deepest, was the most dramatic instance of this policy (Keegan 1984).

Monetarism, however, has not survived. Ministers have lost faith in it, and since 1984 it has been quietly buried (D. Smith 1987). Instead of a single unambiguous measure of money supply, the Treasury now uses a wide range of measures. This means any particular measure can be ignored and the Chancellor is free to manage the economy in a discretionary manner rather than responding mechanically to a single monetary signal. The framework of the medium-term financial strategy has been preserved, but its earlier significance has been lost. The targets have been overshot and revised too often. Monetarism has been discredited in the sense that hardly anyone now suggests that precise monetary targetting is necessary to bring down inflation.

Inflation has been sharply reduced under the Thatcher Government, but the OECD average has fallen still faster. Conditions in the world economy appear to have had more to do with first the acceleration then the deceleration of inflation than domestic monetarist experiments. The quest for sound money also appears to have its limits. Inflation in Britain has been stuck in the 3–5 per cent band since 1983.

The Government's record on public expenditure has been still more disappointing from a New Right perspective. The share of public expenditure as a percentage of national income rose substantially in the first period and only in 1987 did it begin to approach the levels inherited from Labour. The same was true of taxation. The Thatcher Government increased rather than reduced the tax burden as part of its early insistence on monetarist rigour. This brought reactions of incredulity from supply-side economists in the United States (Gilder 1982).

The Government slashed spending on many programmes but was obliged to increase it on others, particularly social security payments to the unemployed and industrial subsidies, while in other cases, such as defence, it was committed to increased spending. The result was a major restructuring of public expenditure but no reduction in the overall burden (Mullard 1987). Because of the monetarist principles of the Government, this meant no substantial tax cuts were possible.

The record on the supply side was no better. The programme of denationalisation, one of the greatest successes of the Government, became the most visible expression of the Conservatives' pledge to reduce the public sector, but the manner in which many of the denationalisations were organised severely restricted competition. This prompted criticism that the Government was merely creating private monopolies rather than creating new competitive industries.

The Government passed several new trade union laws, but to the dismay of many of its supporters it produced few radical reforms of the labour market. It relied instead on an interventionist agency, the Manpower Services Commission (MSC), inherited from Labour, to try to limit the impact of mass unemployment. Unemployment doubled to over 3 million under the Thatcher Government and remained at that level between 1982 and 1987. The monetarist faith that only a little transitional unemployment would be necessary to bring the economy back to full employment was shown to be ill-founded. But the Government proved reluctant to supplement its monetarism with an active supply-side policy.

On the Government's central policy, its desire to reverse Britain's relative economic decline, the results were also disappointing. The Government presided over a major shake-out of jobs in manufacturing industry and a wave of bankruptcies. Productivity subsequently improved, but many economists argued that it was due more to the much smaller manufacturing base and the contraction in employment than to a lasting improvement in British industrial performance (Pratten 1987). Investment in manufacturing industry remained very low, and in 1983 for the first time imports of manufactures exceeded exports, by £2.3 billion. By 1986 this had risen to £5.4 billion. The failure of British industry to win and hold a secure place in the new leading sectors of the world economy also looked gloomy for the future. The economic revival after 1981 was based on services, oil, banking and construction. A broad-based manufacturing revival looked unlikely to follow.

Nevertheless the decline was halted after 1981, even if no British economic miracle had appeared. The recovery and prosperity in parts of the economy was substantial, which made the contrast with areas of high unemployment even sharper. Despite the failures of Government policy in many areas, the stabilisation of the economy after the traumas and wild fluctuations of the previous twenty years appeared real. This became the foundation of the Tory appeal to the electorate. They appeared to have delivered to a majority of the electorate not just prosperity but reasonably stable prosperity.

Conclusion

The failure of economic policy under the Thatcher Governments to fulfil the expectations of its ideological supporters conceals the extent to which the policies represented an important consolidation of changes that had been gathering pace since 1973. If there was a watershed in policy it needs to be placed earlier than 1979 – in 1975–6. But the Thatcher Government ensured that what was begun reluctantly in those years and might only have proved temporary, was made lasting.

The momentum behind the Thatcher Government's policies was always political rather than ideological. The need to reassert state authority and disentangle government from the pressures created by special interests were paramount considerations which won support from all sections of the party. The moves to curb union power, the rejection of incomes policies and other corporatist policies, the emphasis on the need for sound money and control of public spending corresponded to New Right ideas but also reflected the interests of the party in rebuilding itself as a serious contender for government (Bulpitt 1986).

The same pattern can be observed in government. The actual course of policy was always *ad hoc*, rarely conforming to any pre-existing plan. Union legislation was improvised step by step. The privatisation programme was experimental and modest at first and only later acquired a greater scale and retrospective importance.

What New Right ideology provided was less a blueprint than a pool of ideas which were available to ministers either to justify policies or to seek new solutions. The climate of policy-making was very fluid under the Thatcher Government. What emerged was not a new consensus but a considerable widening of the parameters of policy-making so that many solutions which formerly would have been ruled out were now entertained. In this context the initiative came to be held by market and non-interventionist policies. Collectivist and interventionist ideas were placed on the defensive.

Britain has not progressed very far towards the minimal state under the Thatcher Governments. The balance of special interests may have changed but they still infest government. Public expenditure and taxation remain high and the end of inflation is not in sight. Union power has been weakened considerably but unions still possess significant strength, particularly at shopfloor level. Wage increases still run ahead of inflation. Meanwhile the bulk of welfare provision remains collectivist, both in its administration and its distribution.

Despite all this, the Thatcher years can plausibly be said to have produced a pronounced constitutional shift in the conduct of economic policy. The market and private power have been reasserted against the state and the public sector as the arbiters of public policy. One small but revealing sign of this are some of the questions now asked routinely by the Downing Street Policy Unit about every departmental paper that is sent to them. They include: is there a less interventionist solution which has not been properly considered or has been wrongly rejected? and is there a less expensive option. (Willetts 1987)

Practical difficulties may have hindered and frustrated the development of the Thatcher revolution, but despite its setbacks the line of development of policy is clear. The Government has repeatedly returned to the broad themes which it has used from the outset to justify its policies. It has been ready to experiment and to renew its commitment to find ways of reducing state involvement and setting markets free. The extent to which the other political parties have begun to follow it down this path and accept the assumptions of the new policy regime is already considerable. In this way many features of the Thatcher Governments' conduct of economic policy are likely to outlast the Thatcher Governments themselves.

3

Corporatism without Labour: The British Version

Ian Harden

Corporatism and the constitution

In the orthodox version of the constitution, 'public' and 'private' are distinct territories. The public sphere is legitimated by some combination of the common law and the will of a representative parliament. The private is the sphere of property and of voluntary market transactions between individuals, as well as of community-based forms of associative activity. Writing over a decade ago, Kamenka and Tay (1975) spoke of a 'crisis' of private law resulting from invasion by the state of market and community orders – especially the market. From the perspective of the late 1980s the message looks a little dated. A 'New Right' interpretation of Kamenka and Tay might accept that the growth of the public sphere had diminished the private, but envisages that the process can be, and is being, reversed. Public and private remain distinct, even if the border between them is disputed and shifting. Beyond bourgeois triumphalism, however, constitutional analysis needs to address the question of the proper scope and form of public accountability for decision-making in the light of modern developments that involve the *interpenetration* of public and private. The problem with the New Right approach as constitutional analysis is that it cannot come to terms even with pluralism (other than the most vulgar kind) let alone corporatism.

'Corporatism' is a notoriously protean, not to say tricky, concept. A review of the literature is impossible here (see e.g. Panitch 1980; W. Grant 1985; Birkinshaw *et al.* 1987) and it will have to be sufficient to say that in this chapter corporatism is understood to be a style of policy intervention rather than anything more all-embracing:

a process of interest intermediation which involves the negotiation of policy between state agencies and interest organizations arising from the division of labour in society, where the policy agreements are implemented through the collaboration of the interest organizations and their willingness and ability to secure the compliance of their members.

(W. Grant 1985: 3–4)

'Division of labour' might seem to restrict corporatism to situations where 'producer groups' are involved. From a constitutional perspective this narrows the field unduly and corporatism is here taken to encompass a large number of institutions and arrangements that fall within the area of social, or welfare, or 'consumption' policy.

It is not just corporatist arrangements that escape the traditional mechanisms of judicial and Parliamentary accountability, but a whole range of constitutionally significant processes, decisions and non-decisions (see Harden and Lewis 1986). Corporatism, though, is of particular interest for a number of reasons. First, it is commonly assumed that Thatcherism is antithetical to corporatism, which is supposed to be dead or moribund after its heyday in the 1970s. It will be argued here that, on the contrary, corporatism is alive and well in Britain and indeed, is a growing phenomenon. Second, corporatism involves a measure of institutional stability and formality: it is thus *a fortiori* of interest to constitutionalists who are concerned to map generally the patterns of interaction between public and private. Third, corporatism is at the sharp end of some of the economic changes which are presented ideologically in terms of the resurgence of the invisible hand of the market but which, in reality, mark a constitutionally important shift in the way the state conducts its business.

The economic dimension

Whatever changes may occur in the fashionability of particular economic theories, or in the level of economic expectations which governments seek to engender, the modern state seems irretrievably committed to the project of management of the economy (see e.g. Poggi 1978). The central problem facing economic policy-makers (actually a number of different problems rolled into one) can be stated as follows: the economic impact of the state is greater than its capacity to direct and control that impact. Some economists have argued, in a variety of ways, that the only rational public policy is, therefore, to minimise the impact of the state (see generally, Grant and Nath 1984, Ch. 5).

No modern state, and certainly not Britain, has sought to base its economic policies on such a prescription. All governments seek to plan, in the sense that they set objectives of policy and, guided by available indicators, use particular measures to bring into operation instruments to achieve targets. This does not imply that a *coherent* set of objectives exists, still less that policy consists of an instrumentally-rational maximisation of the achievement of objectives (Ball Committee 1978; Mosley 1984). Nor does it imply that all identifiable instruments can actually be wielded by government (Grant and Nath 1984: 13).

In the post-war period problems of macro-economic management gave rise to a perceived need for governments to co-operate with representatives of organised capital and labour in order to facilitate control of the economy and the development of trans-sectoral state policy. The centrality of neo-corporatist, as opposed to other state-interest group relations has been argued to be the outcome of the increasing threat potential or defensive strength of functional groups. The 'governability thesis' was that the degree of control which employer organisations and trade unions can exercise over key economic resources put them:

> in a quite different category from virtually all others in their ability to exert pressure on governments or simply to frustrate their initiatives. And in turn, it may be held, it is in the case of these organisations that corporatist developments, in the sense of governmentally guided attempts at the concertation of interests, have been most distinctive and have carried the furthest-reaching implications.
>
> (Goldthorpe 1984: 324–5)

Hence neo-corporatism has been associated with state intervention to integrate labour-market organisations into decision-making and administrative processes, a form of corporatist development on which Sweden, for example, ranked high whilst Britain was formerly rated as 'medium, on the borderline to weak' (McBride 1985; Lehmbruch 1982). Such a strategy underpinned the creation of the National Economic Development Council, and Office (NEDC and NEDO) in 1962. Similarly, in relation to the issue of pay the strategy of state action which emerged from the Donovan Commission was to increase the ability of unions to make binding national level bargains with employers which could not be outflanked by wage-drift caused by shop-steward-led action at plant level (Wedderburn 1986).

Macro-level concertation thus offered the promise of increasing 'governability': softening the incompatibilities of democratic politics and economic liberalism by taming both markets and 'pluralist' political action aimed at distortion of markets (Goldthorpe 1984; Streek and Schmitter 1985). It also offered the possibility of a facilitative framework for meso- and micro-level bargaining to act as a substitute for the adjustments that market pressures make necessary but which market mechanisms cannot themselves deliver (Zysman 1983).

In assessing the role of corporatist processes in Britain in the late 1980s it is important not to equate corporatism with *tripartism*, which Grant defines as:

> [a] weak form of liberal corporatism in which the state, capital and labour engage in macro-level discussions on economic policy which, however, only

result in general guidelines for the conduct of policy; impose no firm responsibilities on the partners to implement any policies to which they have agreed; and are not linked, except in the most tenuous way, to discussions at the meso or micro levels.

(W. Grant 1985: 9)

This identifies the *participants* in tripartism, but tripartism is not necessarily restricted to the macro-level. For example, a body such as the Manpower Services Commission (MSC), which remains tripartite in structure, operates primarily at meso-level (whilst being directed primarily to macro-level goals). Such bodies need to be distinguished from, for example, the Review Board for Government Contracts (RBGC), which operates at meso- and micro-levels, but in which only one 'producer group' – in that case capital – is involved in a bipartite relationship with the state.

Both the MSC and the RBGC need to be distinguished from the NEDC, which has operated not as a decision-making body but more as an 'educative' forum. The NEDO Economic Development Committees (EDCs), on the other hand, have played a more direct policy role at meso-level, albeit operating on a consensual basis (Middlemas 1983). The Chancellor of the Exchequer's decision in 1987 to reduce the number of NEDC macro-level discussion meetings from twelve a year to four was no more than a long-awaited political gesture. However, the decision to abolish twenty-two of the thirty-six EDCs represents a real downgrading of active tripartite meso-level institutions.

In general, the type of corporatism that is compatible with Thatcherism excludes traditionally-organised trade unions and also eschews any discussion of macro-economic policy, which remains the prerogative of the traditional governmental institutions of Treasury and Bank of England. Orthodox Keynesianism has been seen (though not, perhaps, by Keynes) as the state providing an organised framework for the operation of markets; 'formal support' in Jessop's terms (Jessop 1982), operable according to Offe's 'allocative' criteria (Offe 1975). Monetarism during its brief currency in official statements was often presented in similar fashion. The practice of economic policy, particularly with the shift of emphasis to 'supply side' concerns, has more and more involved government attempting to act as a *player in the market*, rather than as a rule-maker and umpire setting and monitoring a framework for autonomous economic actors. The concept of the state as player in the market was developed mainly to understand the phenomenon of corporatist meso-level industrial intervention but clearly has macro- and micro-level applications as well:

the government can be an economic regulator, an economic administrator or an economic player. As a *regulator* it is an umpire refereeing the behaviour of others in the hope that if they follow a particular set of rules, a certain set of outcomes will occur. ... As an *administrator*, the government executes certain operations based on a specific assignment or task, applying particular decision criteria and following set procedures. As a *player*, it pursues specific outcomes on a case by case basis, assembling packages of incentives which can be used to persuade or coerce. ...

To be a player in the market a government bureaucracy must be able to make its administrative or regulatory decisions contingent on particular actions taken by the firms it administers or regulates.

(Zysman 1983: 75)

Not all the mechanisms through which the state operates as a player are *ipso facto* corporatist. In relation to land-use planning, for example, bargaining over development control is frequently no more than a rational mechanism for the pursuit of public policy in discrete cases rather than a stable mechanism for sharing public power with private interests (Lewis *et al.* 1986; Davies *et al.* 1986). The potential contribution of specifically corporatist arrangements is that they may offer access to existing instruments in the hands of other economic actors; new instruments; a simplified and hence more predictable environment; or, at least, better information about the existing environment.

The concept of the state as a player in the market-place has not yet received adequate constitutional definition. It is clear, however, that to understand the modern economy we need to go beyond even a complex taxonomy of relationships between 'state' and 'market', because it can no longer be assumed that all economic systems are necessarily to be understood as some amalgam of ideal types of private economic ordering and public authority.

Streek and Schmitter (1985) have recently proposed that a fourth ideal type of 'associative order' needs to be added to the familiar trilogy of community, market and state in order to capture theoretically the emerging patterns of interaction between private interests and public authority. Associative order emerges from the unresolved conflicts of state, market and community and involves strategically interdependent organisations which satisfice rather than maximise, in a process of long-term concertation. As for the state, Streek and Schmitter conceive its role to be an active one, both in facilitating and authorising the organisational and institutional characteristics of interest associations and in regulating systems of self-regulation (Streek and Schmitter 1985: 25–6). A growing role for interest associations in public policy affects not only the form and functioning of 'the state' but forces re-examination of the concept of 'the market' itself. We need to distinguish between (1) markets as processes distinct from 'the state', and in which state activity is facilitative or supportive and; (2) markets in which the state is, in Zysman's term, 'a player'.

The nature of the state as player will depend crucially on the constitutional characteristics of the instruments it uses, and here the distinction between *imperium* and *dominium* types of power is useful. *Imperium* describes the government's use of the command of law in aid of its policy objectives, and *dominium* the employment of the wealth of government for policy purposes (Daintith 1985: 177-8). Although we cannot explore them in detail here, there are significant differences in the constitutional frameworks of the two types of activity and the traditional mechanisms of accountability are much weaker in respect of *dominium* powers. In particular, in so far as English law recognizes a principle of freedom of association, it does so through the absence of legal constraints on joint activity and the provision of a private law framework for the creation of suitable institutional forms. Central government is at liberty to make use of the private law framework in the same way as anyone else, subject only to the general principles of ministerial responsibility to Parliament (see Harden and Lewis 1986, Ch. 4). Governments can thus create quangos, in a variety of shapes and sizes, with no need for statutory authority.

One of the organisational forms available to government, as well as to private interests, is the company. Government may create companies as a step to privatisation (see Ch. 5 below) or for many other purposes for which a convenient non-statutory corporate form is required. It is important in discussing corporatism not to confuse the idea of a 'firm' (which may or may not be a single corporate personality) with the legal concept of a 'company'. Companies may sometimes be quangos. In some cases the structure of firms makes them in effect 'organisers of interests' and thus potentially corporatist actors. If production in a certain field is dominated by a single firm or oligopoly, this is, in effect, a cartel in a different organisational form. It is significant that the central focus of competition policy in Britain has shifted from the problem of cartels, which loomed large at the time of the Restrictive Trade Practices Act 1956, towards market dominance by large firms and the problem of mergers (Merkin and Williams 1984).

There is also a general trend for larger firms to deal directly with government and only secondarily to participate in group activity. This involves:

> the direct integration of large firms into the definition and development of public policy, working directly with Government Departments or, more commonly, with a governmental body of some kind.... Advanced technology, major capital investment schemes, and military procurement are the best-known fields for such direct co-optation.
>
> (Dunleavy 1982: 190-1)

Dunleavy also instances the organisation of the civil nuclear industry, but there are many other examples such as the Pharmaceutical Price Regulation Scheme in which firms deal directly with the DHSS (Sargent 1983a, 1983b); the offshore oil industry (see Daintith and Willoughby 1984; Daintith 1985); and applications for selective assistance under section 8 of the Industrial Development Act 1982. The effect of privatisation of state-owned enterprises can only be to increase the scale and significance of such contacts (Graham and Prosser 1987 and see Ch. 5 below). For example, the government has proposed, after lengthy negotiations and the initial offer of a much lower sum, to fund 65 per cent of the £750m British Aerospace costs for further Airbus development. It is also expected that government will continue to provide around 60 per cent of Rolls-Royce's R & D budget after privatisation, as well as remaining a major customer in the defence field.

The state and the 'private' sector

We can now identify a number of ideal-typical conceptions of the constitutional role of the state in relation to the 'private sector' (this is not meant to be an exhaustive classification):

(1) Regulation (limited) of autonomous markets using *imperium*-type powers. The state enters the market rarely and as an 'ordinary' player.
(2) The state organises authoritatively using mainly *dominium*-type powers.
(3) The state acts as a player in the market; both *imperium* and *dominium* powers are open to bargaining in a process of strategic interaction and concertation with other economic actors.

The implicit aim of Conservative economic policies has been to re-create some approximation of type 1, and thereby to solve the various problems (of legitimacy and rationality) created by the state's involvement as an administrator of economic processes (Offe 1975; Habermas 1976). The path of development mapped out by Winkler (1975) as 'corporatism' (type 2) has not been followed. For various reasons it may be doubted whether it is a theoretically coherent type in any event, though elsewhere in the book many examples are given of the accretion of powers to central government as a result of its efforts to 'roll back' the state (and see Lewis and Wiles 1984).

However, type 3 is also likely to involve networks of corporatist arrangements. Many aspects of Thatcherism itself, as well as some of the institutions and processes which have survived under Thatcherism, fit much better into this type than they do into type 1. It is important to emphasise that the corporatism which forms an attractive style of intervention for the pursuit of many Thatcherite policies is not new. It is characterised by preferential access for privileged groups, and a lack of accountability for the delegated formation and implementation of policy.

The contribution of Thatcherism has been twofold. First, there has been an increased willingness to devolve public responsibilities to private interests, legitimated by the rhetoric of markets and born of a desire to offload state responsibilities (especially in the welfare field) both for financial and ideological reasons. Second, governments since 1979 have not been prepared to accept societal organisations 'ready-made', as it were, in the way typical of 'liberal corporatism' (Lehmbruch 1979). Policies have been pursued which have been designed to encourage, directly and indirectly, the emergence of organisations willing and able to co-operate with government in its approach to social and economic problems and to assume delegated responsibilities accordingly. The balance of *dominium* and *imperium* in these policies has varied as between say, trade unions; City self-regulation; 'managing agents' for the Youth Training Scheme and the proposed City Technology Colleges.

Access to policy-making: quangos and corporatism

Numerous potential constraints upon a government's ability to act as a player in the market can be identified, some of which are general 'limits of administration', whilst others relate to a specifically British political culture or to its particular constitutional and legal arrangements. One of the most important factors in this regard is also one of the most complex. The terms and conditions of access to the policy process need to be understood as being (actually or potentially) an instrument of policy, a constraint on particular instruments and a subject for bargaining. Access to policy, furthermore, is a two-way process. We are talking not only of *private* access to public policy-making but of *public* access to *private* policy and decisions: indeed, this is the heart of both the concept of the state as player and of the concept of corporatism. It is also the focus of many pressing constitutional concerns: who has access, on what terms, and through what processes are they made accountable?

In Britain the tradition of secret 'efficient' government developing through *ad hoc* pragmatic adjustments and legitimated by a 'dignified' Parliamentarism reduces the need for participants in the process to have any sort of theory of corporatism. In addition, popular and political discourse largely equates corporatism with tripartism and, in particular, with trade union influence. We should especially expect corporatism to be a 'self-denying concept' in Britain (and the United States) in present circumstances because of the dominance of market ideology. This is likely to have greatest real effect at macro-level, where the incompatibility of corporatism with traditional Parliamentary and rule of law claims to legitimacy is most evident.

At the micro- and meso-levels there is less conflict with legitimation claims, because those levels are in traditional terms 'private'. As Winkler (1975) emphasises, whilst this 'privacy' is potentially in conflict with an active policy of state intervention, corporatist or otherwise, at the same time it facilitates 'voluntary' bargaining and co-operation. Despite the high degree of executive dominance of the legislature and the exclusion of the political opposition from policy-making, Britain does have highly developed mechanisms of quasi- and quasi-non-government ('quangos') for the involvement of interest groups in public policy-making and implementation (Barker 1982; Birkinshaw *et al.* 1987).

Because they have defined organisational forms (albeit of a number of different types), quangos make an obvious starting-point for the constitutionalist in search of corporatism. Quangos play a number of potentially overlapping roles in corporatist arrangements and the balance between different roles may change fundamentally over time, even within a stable institutional framework (as e.g. in the case of the University Grants Committee).

Not all quangos are involved in corporatist arrangements, but they may act:

(1) as sites of corporatist bargaining, the institutional framework of the organisation itself encompassing the relevant interests (this will not necessarily be an 'encompassing organisation' in Olson's [1965] sense);
(2) as government – the organisation acting as the public input into bargaining with private interests (e.g. the monitoring of self-regulation and bargained regulation);
(3) as bargainers with government (usually with a sponsor department).

Corporatism and Thatcherism

The Thatcher Government's early attempt at a substantial 'cull' of quango numbers was a failure (Hood 1981; and see Cabinet Office 1986). Most of any importance survived, including those with the greatest corporatist significance such as the Housing Corporation, the MSC and the RBGC. Not only did the Thatcher Government fail to reduce quango numbers, new policy initiatives have required the creation of new ones. Some of these clearly involve corporatist arrangements such as self-regulation in the City, others potentially so, such as Urban Development Corporations. Let us now examine some examples of the relationship between Thatcherism and corporatism, beginning with one of the less visible of our corporatist quangos.

The Review Board for Government Contracts

The RBGC is a bipartite corporatist body of a rather shadowy constitutional nature, which falls into quango category 2 above. It was established in 1968 by a Memorandum of Agreement (see RBGC 1984) between the government and the CBI following the scandal of 'excessive' profits made by Ferranti and Bristol Siddeley on certain defence contracts. The Treasury and CBI each nominate two candidates after consultation to make sure that the candidates are acceptable to the other party. There is also a Joint Review Board Advisory Committee comprised of representatives of the CBI and those trade associations with particular interest in government contracts, including the Society of British Aerospace Companies and the Defence Manufacturers Association.

The Board's main purpose is to oversee the formula for calculating profits and the target rate of profit on non-competitive government contracts, of which the largest user is the Ministry of Defence, which placed some £5 billion worth in 1983-4. The general principle is to give contractors a fair return on capital employed, equal on average to the overall return earned by British industry. Government is dependent on the goodwill of the CBI and the trade associations in order to ensure that sufficient information is made available to calculate general rates of return on non-competitive government contracts, and contractors have refused to give the Treasury access to information which they have been willing to supply to the RBGC (National Audit Office HC 243 1984-5; Public Accounts Committee HC 390 1984-5).

The Memorandum of Agreement binds the CBI and the trade associations to use 'best endeavours' to ensure that the relevant information is supplied to the Board. The only practical alternative to firms', trade associations' and the CBI's co-operation in the RBGC framework would have been wholesale nationalisation or an enormous, tremendously expensive – and certainly cost-inefficient – administrative effort to acquire the necessary information to make wholly 'arm's length' bargains. Nationalisation, of course, produces its own needs for information and co-operation which are in many ways very similar to the ones we are examining here; not least in the practical inapplicability of 'arm's length' constitutional solutions (Prosser 1986). The *quid pro quo* for contractors is not only that 'unconscionable losses' as well as excessive profits are remediable but that it is the Board rather than the Department which, in the last resort, can be called to adjudicate on whether the contract price was 'fair and reasonable'.

The Board establishes general rules of the game as a matter of negotiation between the Treasury and the CBI, guided by independent accountants, and taking into account the views and interests of trade associations representing contractors. It adjusts the conventions in the light of information provided by contractors as a result of the co-operation of representative bodies. It also deals with individual disputes, making sure that the subjective judgement needed to supplement the rules is not ultimately a matter of the unchecked discretion of one party, a situation which tends to destabilise the long-term concertation involved in associative order.

The present Government has made significant efforts to expand competitive tendering in defence procurement. This, however, does not solve the policy dilemmas with which the corporatist framework of the RBGC is designed to deal; rather, it represents a shift in the *relative* importance attached to different policies. The government's role as a player in relation to defence contractors requires a number of rather different goals to be pursued at the same time. First there is the goal of cost-effectiveness of public expenditure – getting defence equipment that works, as cheaply as possible. This has to be balanced against, second, the diplomatic and defence importance of security of supply and the retention of domestic capacity to produce weapons systems. Third, there is the economic importance of the defence industry and in particular its export role. Reconciling these different policy goals has caused problems in competition policy. For example, the proposed takeover of Plessey by the larger defence and electronics group GEC was blocked, despite reports that the Department of Trade and Industry (DTI) had itself promoted the proposed merger in order to retain a UK domestic electronic capability that could compete with US and Japanese firms. The Ministry of Defence argued that savings attributable to competition between Plessey and GEC on contracts where they had been competitors amounted to between 17 per cent and 34 per cent of the contract price (*Guardian*, 7 August 1986).

The different strands have proved equally hard for the RBGC to disentangle, and the rates of profit it has recommended have had to take account of the perceived need to retain a viable defence industry. Despite the tendency to claim market solutions as a panacea, the Government has not abandoned the long-term concertation, which enables it to juggle various competing goals, in favour of a 'maximising' strategy of the cheapest possible procurement of defence equipment.

Industrial policy

The same shift in the *balance* of the policy agenda has been at work in relation to industrial policy and, for example, the level of R & D expenditure by British industry. This is not simply the result of disenchantment with, or ideological dislike of the process of attempting to 'pick winners'. In the process of industrial adjustment, as in many other fields, traditional Treasury objectives have combined with the new political impetus to reduce or offload public expenditure wherever possible. Interestingly, the same does not apply to training. In the rapid expansion of policy measures, involving a highly corporatist style of intervention organised through the MSC, government seems largely to have abandoned the attempt to make employers pay for training (see Vickerstaff 1985; HC 46 1985–6).

Historically, the structural relationship between finance and industrial capital in Britain has resulted in a system in which investment finance is primarily sought and provided through the securities markets and retained profits, banks providing primarily short-term funding. There has as a result been no point of leverage for government in Britain to influence industrial structure through flows of credit for investment (Zysman 1983). This constraint is linked to a broader suspicion and mistrust of measures of selective industrial policy. The development of instruments for effecting selective measures in Britain 'has been brought about more by a process of elimination than as a result of any conscious design' (Sharpe 1979: 205–6). Over the past two decades a cumulation of experience has made the idea of governments seeking to influence the market behaviour of individual firms, and to discriminate between firms, familiar to 'insiders' even if un-acknowledged publicly (see Young and Lowe 1974; Noreng 1980).

Despite ideological opposition to selective intervention and the desire to restrict expenditure, Conservative Governments since 1979 have not abolished the machinery of assistance to industry originally established under the Industry Act 1972. Annual reports made to Parliament under the Industrial Development Act 1982 show that £584.45 million was paid under Parts I, II and III of the Act in the year to 31 March 1985 and £531.6 million the following year (HC 604 1983–4; HC 556 1984–5; HC 552 1985–6, Appendix 2 in each case). There is an Industrial Development Advisory Board (IDAB) to advise the Secretary of State on regional and national selective assistance under sections 7 and 8 of the Act, statutory Welsh and Scottish IDABs and Industrial Development Boards for each of the English regions with substantial assisted areas. The Department of Trade and Industry (DTI) also provides considerable finance to local development agencies which seek to attract inward investment.

The pattern of regional assistance was substantially recast in 1984 (Co-operative Development Agency and Industrial Development Act 1984 and HC 556 1984–5). Overall, the amount of resources devoted to regional policy has been considerably diminished. The number of schemes funded under section 8 of the 1982 Act (national selective assistance) has also been reduced (see HC 552 1985–6, paras. 19–38). The range of 'aids to industry' none the less remains very wide and includes support from central government departments other than the DTI, as well as tax relief in various forms (see generally Bienkowski *et al.* 1986).

In addition to the committees based on the NEDC, government has used *ad hoc* processes of industrial policy in relation to, for example, information technology (IT). The Alvey Research Programme, established in 1983 following an inquiry chaired by John Alvey, is a form of national support for advanced IT research, providing finance for collaborative research involving industry, academic and other research institutions and govern-ment in four main areas of work. Government funding is estimated at £200 million and meets up to 50 per cent of company expenditure and 100 per cent of academic spending on allowable items including labour costs (Bienkowski *et al.* 1986). A report in 1986 by Sir Austin Bide recommended a further £1 billion five-year programme to replace the Alvey scheme, which lasts until 1988. The Bide Report recommends a shift of emphasis from research to collaborative projects in IT application with variable public support for companies, depending on degree of risk. Also proposed is a board to run the programme and an executive group staffed by industrialists and civil servants. It was reported that the government established a six-man steering group (including the Deputy Secretary in the DTI with responsibility for IT; John Alvey; the head of OFTEL; and the managing director of Mullard) to advise the Secretary of State, and that a further committee was established in July 1987 (*Guardian*, 22 November 1986, 13 April 1987 and 2 July 1987).

An interesting example of a quango which acts as a player in the investment market-place is English Estates (EE), a statutory body whose function is to provide and manage sites and premises in England for occupation by industrial and commercial undertakings. It undertakes property development and estate management in assisted areas, drawing funds from the DTI, the Development Commission and the private sector. Directions given to EE by the Secretary of State require it *inter alia* to act to advance the regional and industrial policies of the DTI and at the same time to secure the maximum possible degree of private sector participation in its work. It is now England's biggest industrial and commercial landlord and has carried out partnership developments with major financial institutions. It has power to guarantee obligations, make loans, form and participate in forming corporate bodies and in other ways assist commercial interests in areas where they would be unlikely to operate without partnership with a public body. It has recently been reported that EE is to become heavily involved in the inner-cities programme (*Guardian,* 30 July 1987).

At local level, Chambers of Commerce are of importance in relation to the formation and implementation of public policy of support for industry and business. Unlike their continental counterparts, Chambers in Britain have no public law status and the Government has resisted proposals to give it to them made by the Association of British Chambers of Commerce. The Chambers are, however, the sole government-approved body for issuing certificates of origin for exporters and act as the DTI's agents. Members of Chambers receive this service at half the cost of non-members (R. King 1985). Furthermore, local authorities are required by the Department of the Environment (DoE) to consult Chambers before schemes to be included in the urban programme are sent forward to the DoE, which is almost certain to reject schemes of which a Chamber is critical. This requirement of consultation (imposed by administrative action through government circular, not by delegated legislation) and *de facto* veto has meant that the chambers are now in effect 'co-responsible partners' in the planning of the urban programme and not infrequently have representation on key local authority committees (W. Grant 1983).

Chambers of Commerce have also become managing agents under the MSC Youth Training Scheme and play an important role in relation to the development of local enterprise agencies, which have been encouraged as part of the government's policy to attract private sector investment to inner-city areas. Tax relief is available on contributions made in cash or kind to approved enterprise agencies, a number of which are located on Chambers' premises. The promotional body for enterprise agencies is Business in the Community, formed in 1982 with the sponsorship of a number of major industrial concerns, the DoE, MSC and the local authority associations (Bienkowski *et al.* 1986; R. King 1985).

The DTI is providing £1.5 million support for the Northern Development Company, recently formed by trade unions, industrialists and local councillors of all parties in the five northern counties of England (*Guardian,* 3 March 1987). This will be a much smaller operation than the Scottish

Development Agency, established in the mid-1970s but still retaining a wide range of powers, including loan guarantees and equity participation. Like other public–private partnership initiatives (such as the 'urban development agency' being set up by Birmingham City Council in conjunction with the Chamber of Commerce and five development companies), this form of local quango has considerable corporatist potential.

A highly corporatist form of industrial policy has emerged in the case of the Channel Tunnel, with government insistence that only private capital is to be involved. In fact, of course, without public facilitation through the exercise of both *dominium* and *imperium* power, no tunnel would be possible. Large amounts of public money, furthermore, are to be spent on supporting infrastructure (rail and road links especially). Considerable Bank of England pressure was also needed to ensure that the consortium eventually chosen by government to build the Tunnel was able to raise the first tranche of necessary capital from the City. An executive director of the Bank commented that he 'would not call it arm-twisting' but 'seeking to ensure that there is a common basis of understanding of the problem before final and definitive decisions are taken by those involved' (David Walker, *Pillars of Society*, Radio 4, 30 April 1987). It was also reported that the DTI put pressure on British Rail to agree eventually to pay 65 per cent of forecast revenues to EuroTunnel on a monthly basis (*Observer*, 10 May 1987).

What these examples illustrate is that, despite the ideology of marketism, neither a 'pure market' nor a 'social market' industrial policy (W. Grant 1982) operates in Britain. Industrial policy remains, though less visibly than at the time of the last Labour Government's Industrial Strategy, a matter of processes and institutions that partake strongly of the delegation of public functions to private or semi-private bodies, including selectivity between firms and sectors, and a degree of dependence on (quasi-) non-government bodies for information, expertise and co-ordination of private sector activity. This does not imply that a *coherent* industrial policy exists, directed to identifiable and achievable goals. In fact, the defining feature of Thatcherism in government–industry relations is not the demise of corporatism but the absence of clear and acknowledged public objectives. In relation to telecommunications policy, for example, it has been argued that:

> The British government dithers unable to decide whether Britain's best interests lie with the EEC or with the United States, paying lip service to the one, but deliberately increasing imports of companies, equipment and technology from the other.
>
> (Hills 1986: 190)

The financial sector

The form and style of Thatcherite corporatism is most clearly evident in the self-regulatory system based on the Financial Services Act 1986, which is discussed in detail by Moran in Chapter 4 below. Despite the antagonism of the City to tripartism (see Middlemas 1983: 58, 61) corporatism has been the traditional basis for the operation of City institutions. The reshaping of the City has not diminished the importance of corporatism in its structure, albeit that there has been a change in the nature of self-regulation and the forms of state involvement in the regulatory process. More hierarchical, more structured and more visibly clothed with the power of the state, the new system none the less retains many of the constitutional characteristics of the old.

The attribution of public status to interest groups under the provisions of the 1986 Act relating to designation of Self-Regulatory Organisations (SROs) involves a delicate balance of voluntarism, persuasion and compulsion: it is an experiment in regulated autonomy in which both the autonomy and its regulation are clearly apparent. However, to what extent and in what ways the Securities and Investments Board (SIB) will exercise its powers to restructure, or to discriminate amongst competing.SROs, are all matters that are unanswerable at this stage. It also remains to be seen whether the exclusion of the Takeovers Panel, and of Lloyds, from the SIB framework will be tenable in the longer term.

Corporatism and accountability

The last eight years of Conservative government have not reinstated a clear divide between the public and the private sectors, with relations between them governed by clear constitutional principles. Public–private inter-penetration has become more pervasive. Traditional mechanisms of accountability, already archaic and outflanked by the growth of the state, have not evolved so as to bring within the purview of the constitution institutions and processes that embody and foster corporatist arrangements.

The view of the executive itself about the constitutional nature of the extended state relies on the old framework of ideas about Parliament and ministerial responsibility (Cabinet Office/Treasury 1985; Harden 1987). The new system of City self-regulation, for example, has not been designed so as to involve a greater degree of public visibility and debate of key policy decisions and non-decisions. It seems likely, however, that the fact that key powers are formally delegated from the Secretary of State to the SIB under the Financial Services Act, will lead to greater pressure from Parliament, through select committees, questions and the like, on both ministers and the self-regulatory institutions themselves. The courts may also become involved.

Courts have adopted the language of 'public' and 'private' law (see particularly *O'Reilly* v. *Mackman* [1982] 3 All ER 1124) but have not so far engaged in any systematic attempt to define the boundaries of the state and to address the new constitutional problems. Sometimes the courts have even gone out of their way to disclaim administrative law jurisdiction over quasi-non-government and even over a quasi-government body such as the

Independent Broadcasting Authority, where the legal framework is the private law of contract (see e.g. *Cinnamond* v. *British Airvorts Authority* [1980] 2 All ER 368 at 374; *R* v. *IBA ex parte Rank Organisation, The Times* March 14 1986 and cf. *R* v. *National Coal Board ex parte NUM* [1986] ICR 791). On the other hand, although the Takeovers Panel 'operates without visible means of legal support', the Court of Appeal has decided that it is susceptible to judicial review, since its operations are essentially public and are backed indirectly and *de facto* by means of compulsion:

> Possibly the only essential elements [for the court to have jurisdiction] are what can be described as a public element, which can take many different forms, and the exclusion from the jurisdiction of bodies whose sole source of power is a consensual submission to its jurisdiction.
> (R. v. *Panel on Takeovers and Mergers ex parte Datafin*
> [1987] 1 All ER 564 at 577)

The court was prepared to recognise that deliberate non-decisions by the government in respect of the statutory regulation of takeovers, together with the Bank of England's role in appointment of the chairman and deputy chairman meant that the Panel was established by the act or quthority of government. However, the meaning of 'consensual submission' in the passage quoted above is unclear, and one judgement in the case denies that judicial review can take place of a tribunal whose source of power is *contractual*. Whether courts will be prepared to abandon formalism sufficiently to claim a general jurisdiction over quangos remains to be seen. Even if they do, there are reasons for pessimism over the ability of British judges to fashion an appropriate framework for a judicial role in processes of regulated autonomy.

Whatever may be expected of the judges in practice, there seems no reason in principle to assume that suitable accountability mechanisms cannot be devised for self-regulatory and similar quasi-public arrangements. Much of the corporatism literature assumes that there is a necessary tension between efficacy and accountability in corporatist arrangements, because corporatism involves the exclusion of affected interests and a degree of co-option of the leaders of organisations at the expense of the membership. As an *empirical generalisation* about corporatism, it is largely true that 'private interest government' works through lengthy deliberative processes, producing 'a series of second-best compromise solutions that are often difficult to justify on normative or aesthetic grounds'. Furthermore, 'deliberations are kept informal and secretive in an effort to insulate them as much as possible from outside pressures or from dissidents within the associational ranks' (Streek and Schmitter 1985: 13).

It is asserted in many public law contexts that secrecy, informality and absence of external accountability are necessary to effective and efficient decision-making. I do not wish to discuss here the abstract arguments that greater accountability impedes efficacy – arguments which I take to be fundamentally misconceived. At a concrete level, the interrelationship between efficacy and accountability is highly complex and depends on the type of accountability which is being discussed, as well as the policy objectives that are in question.

If government seeks to use corporatist arrangements instrumentally to achieve specific goals, then 'accountability' in almost any shape or form will seem to it to be a hindrance. This, however, implies nothing special about corporatism; it is simply a corollary of the fundamental truth that constitutions are corsets restraining those who seek to exercise power. The concept of regulated autonomy achieved through 'reflexive' law implies that, to some extent at least, the 'public interest' can and must be served through procedures that do *not* seek to dictate specific outcomes (Teubner 1983). Limitations on knowledge, and on the ability to assemble and deploy available knowledge, make it rationally necessary to abandon the idea that only *centralised* control of social and economic processes can serve collective goals effectively.

Despite this, there is nothing to guarantee that all corporatist phenomena do actually represent a move towards reflexive law or associative order. The state acting as a player may seek to use corporatim *ad hoc* and tactically to achieve specific goals rather than as a long-term strategy in which particular outcomes are regarded as beyond the proper reach of government. Or, more likely, it may do both in different circumstances and in relation to different social and economic actors. The chapters in this book on the trade unions and City self-regulation perhaps represent the clearest examples of the tactical and strategic approaches respectively.

Where government acts tactically, attempts to make it accountable for its own actions are justified even on a traditional view of the constitution – albeit that the traditional mechanisms of courts and Parliament are less than adequate. More problematic at first sight is the question of what forms of *public* accountability are compatible with 'regulated autonomy'. Provided that the procedures by which delegated public policy functions are performed, meet broader standards of constitutional legitimacy, no attempt should be made to draw a hard-and-fast line of demarcation between the public accountability of corporatist bodies and their accountability *to their membership*. This can be illustrated by the example of the setting of accounting standards, a vital matter for many facets of government activity such as selling state assets, contracting-out of services, competition policy and the award of grants to industry. Standards are set, however, not by government but by the accountancy profession itself.

The Accounting Standards Committee (ASC) of the Consultative Committee of Accountancy Bodies (CCAB) is the umbrella organisation which endeavours to speak for the accountancy profession as a whole on the issue of standards. Unlike members of the American Financial Accounting Standards Board (FASB), members of the ASC are part-time, unpaid and not wholly independent of the bodies to which they owe their appointment.

The ASC comprises twenty members, including five users of accounts, who need not be accountants. The remaining fifteen are members of the profession and preparers of accounts from industry. ASC meetings are also attended by observers, including the head of the Companies Division of the Department of Trade. Appointments to the ASC are made by the presidents of the professional bodies that form the CCAB (ASC 1983).

The absence of an equivalent of the Securities and Exchange Commission to provide backing for an independent body, and the cost of such a body, have been seen by the accountancy profession as decisive arguments against an FASB-type operation in Britain (Watts 1981, 1983). However, despite the differences between the FASB and the ASC in relation to the status of members, the latter body has adopted a highly American approach to the process by which Statements of Standard Accounting Practice (SSAPs) and Statements of Recommended Practice (SORPs) are set. SORPs may be prepared by the ASC itself for certain matters. 'Franked SORPs' though, are prepared by the industry or area of the public sector concerned and then approved by the ASC. The procedures used parallel some (though not all) of the best practices of American 'hybrid' rule-making (Harden and Lewis 1986, Chs. 8 and 9). For example, an 'exposure draft' of a proposed standard often contains a preface setting out the background to the subject and arguments for and against the proposed text. At a later stage efforts are made to identify those who may be affected by the proposed standard but who have not submitted comments, with a view to further consultative meetings (ASC 1983, paras. 4.16, 4.27, 4.28).

The sophistication of these procedures taken as a whole is almost unprecedented in a British context, although it is to be noted that the ASC has so far drawn the line at opening its own meetings to the public (ASC 1981, para. 6.3). Undoubtedly the example of the FASB was an important channel for the importation of US style notice-and-comment and 'hybrid' rule-making procedures. Perhaps the most significant factor though was the shock inflicted on the CCAB when proposals for inflation-accounting were rejected by the membership in 1977. The differences of interest between the six accountancy bodies represented in the ASC, and between the leadership and members, are resolved by methods that involve breaking down the barrier between intra- and inter-organisational concertation (Streek and Schmitter 1985: 21) and between accountability to the membership and broader public accountability.

The setting of accounting standards is an example of the way in which internal and external accountability may fuse together in practice. This particular empirical context also serves to highlight the fact that both 'associative order' and 'regulated autonomy' need to be placed in a broader constitutional framework. Streek and Schmitter, for example, claim that a 'central problem of public control over self-regulating groups is to make organised groups internalize as much as possible the costs of their self-interested behaviour for other interests'. (1985: 21)

As a matter of abstract theory, however, what counts as a 'cost' is by no means obvious. Even if we are prepared, for the sake of argument, to take actual or hypothetical market prices as a basis, we cannot logically escape the need for a theory of entitlements, or of legitimate constitutional authority to establish entitlements (see Kennedy 1981). (The subordination of basic constitutional questions to systems-theoretic formulations has also been one of the characteristic weaknesses of the 'reflexive law' literature.)

More concretely, the need for an 'external constitution' (Habermas 1985) as a framework for private interest governments can be illustrated by returning to the example of accounting standards. Although the ASC's procedures are akin to those adopted by the US Federal Agencies in response to court-imposed requirements to demonstrate that a 'hard look' has been taken at policy, there is no public body charged with monitoring the ASC's operation of and compliance with its own procedures. (By contrast, the ASC actually imposes *and monitors* its own 'soft' mechanisms for the preparation of 'franked SORPs', rather than relying on 'pure' self-regulation of the kind which it enjoys itself.) The largest of the accountancy bodies, the Institute of Chartered Accountants of England and Wales (ICAEW), has expressed concern that, despite nearly twenty years of efforts to standardise accounting practice, users are little better off. Particular areas of concern relate to takeovers and mergers ('the choice of accounting treatments allows an acquiring company to show either a gently rising trend of profits or a rapidly falling one'); off-balance sheet financing; depreciation; R & D costs; pensions surpluses and the oil industry (ICAEW 1987).

The courts are, for a variety of reasons, unlikely to take the initiative in imposing the kind of 'hard-look' requirements on corporatist institutions that could force a structured response to claims of the kind made by the ICAEW. The other traditional guardian of the constitution, Parliament, is unable itself to play such a role other than sporadically through the select-committee system. A constitutional response to the developments and processes that have been described in this chapter thus demands some institution-building towards the aspiration of *constitutionally* regulated autonomy.

A fundamental requirement is, of course, freedom of information (FoI), not just for central as well as local government but also for non-departmental public bodies and 'private' bodies that are affected with the public interest. Freedom of information that included a blanket and unconsidered exemption for 'commercial confidentiality' or which did not apply to self-regulatory structures, would simply provide a further stimulus to bipartite corporatism. Part and parcel of FoI is openness of meetings, both of public and semi-public bodies (for the United States see the Government in the Sunshine and Federal Advisory Committees Acts).

Institutions are also needed both to require that a 'hard look' be taken at policy and policy alternatives and to judge whether this has been done satisfactorily. These kinds of institutions do already exist; the Office of Fair Trading (OFT), for example, brings a critical eye to bear on the Securities and Investments Board (SIB) and criticised some of its first proposed rules as anti-competitive. Other bodies, such as the Monopolies and Mergers Commission and the Social Security Advisory Committee, perform similar tasks. However, the presence or absence of such bodies is largely a matter of *ad hoc* decisions, they share no common administrative jurisprudence of appro-priate procedural standards and, most significant of all, have no constitutionally entrenched role. The OFT report on the SIB rules, for example, was rejected by the Secretary of State and the rules were presented to Parliament for approval.

I have argued elsewhere for an Administrative Procedure Act that would establish general procedures and include standards for participation rights, and for a Standing Administrative Conference with a wide-ranging jurisdiction to examine the administrative structures through which public policy is developed and implemented (Harden and Lewis 1986). The definition of 'public policy' for these purposes would be complex and would certainly need to be more sophisticated than the provision establishing the jurisdiction of the National Audit Office (National Audit Act 1983, s. 7).

As a final quality-control mechanism, there is, however, no escape from the need for courts to enforce 'hard-look' standards. Despite the failure of the courts to develop the common law in appropriate ways, there is no reason to suppose that they would not apply an Administrative Procedure Act to the best of their abilities. The probability of any British government introducing such an Act seems small at the moment. The probability of a government led by Mrs Thatcher doing so can be confidently predicted to be zero.

4

Politics and Law in Financial Regulation *

Michael Moran

Thatcherism's constitutional settlement

'Thatcherism' was the most vigorous force in British politics during the 1980s. It drew its intellectual vigour from two sources: from its vision of a renewed economy, and from its vision of a renewed constitutional settlement. Economic renewal entailed constitutional renewal. Thatcherism argued that the nation's economic decline could only be reversed by taming sectional interests, by abolishing many of the state's economic responsibilities and by strengthening free-market forces.

These economic changes implied important alterations in key constitutional practices – in the way interests were represented, in the way the line was drawn separating public from private power, and in the significance of law as a source of legitimate authority. These constitutional changes were summed up in an ostentatious rejection of the perceived 'corporatism' of the 1970s – in the rejection of a constitutional design which endowed private interests with public capacities, blurred the distinction between public and private spheres and elevated bargaining with sectional interests over the impersonal formality of law.

*This chapter reports work done as part of a study of stock-market regulation commissioned through the ESRC 'Corporatism and Accountability' initiative. The analysis was influenced by interviews conducted in London over the last two years with practitioners in the markets, and I would like to thank the many busy people who gave their time to talk to me. I would also like to thank Cosmo Graham and Tony Prosser for their comments on a first draft of the chapter.

There is of course fierce argument about how far the economic policies pursued by Mrs Thatcher's administrations really do correspond to the economic visions of Thatcherism. Less attention has been paid to the question of how far the corresponding constitutional apparitions have endured. Harden's contribution to this volume (Ch. 3) surveys the changing constitutional significance of the publieprivate divide in the 1980s, but understanding the constitutional significance of the Thatcher years also demands a close examination of experience in particular sectors. The purpose of this chapter is to contribute to the latter task by describing the new constitutional settlement – for it was no less – which was reached in the financial services industry in the 1980s.

Three reasons make the experience of financial services particularly illuminating for any examination of the constitutional significance of Thatcherism. The first is that the industry in the 1980s underwent revolutionary economic changes, and these were quintessentially Thatcherite: restrictive practices were abolished, inefficient firms absorbed into multinational giants, and domestic markets – especially those in the City of London – were opened to foreign competition. For better or worse, the revolution in financial services has become an exemplar of Thatcherite economics.

The second reason is that these great changes in economic practices forced equally profound reforms in regulation – in other words, in the constitutional settlement governing the industry. We thus have a unique opportunity of seeing how fundamental constitutional reforms worked in reality. But the third reason is by far the most important: the new constitutional settlement in the financial services industry is utterly contrary to what we might expect, were we to take the constitutional rhetoric of Thatcherism at face value. The established system of regulation in the industry, especially in the City of London, was indeed corporatist. By the beginning of the 1980s these arrangements were in decay. Yet the response of the authorities was not to abolish corporatism but to make it stronger. If we can explain this unexpected outcome we will understand not only how an important industry is in future to be regulated but also how the constitutional vision of Thatcherism translates into reality.

I tackle this job as follows. The next section sketches the old system of regulation and describes the new arrangements with which it is now replaced. This is followed by a description of the economic and institutional changes leading to the new constitutional settlement. It shows how the solution inaugurated in the famous 'Goodison–Parkinson' agreement was shaped by internal City politics and by the desire to preserve the independence of key markets from public control. The succeeding section – Corporatism resurrected – explains why the new Financial Services Act adopts a corporatist – rather than any alternative, regulatory mode. The argument is that the choice was shaped by prevailing ideologies and by the desire to preserve the traditional autonomy of financial services from democratic politics. The chapter concludes by examining the problems involved in preserving this new corporatist constitutional settlement.

Politics and law in financial regulation

Until the 1980s the constitutional settlement in the financial services industry, especially in its most important part located in the City of London, was dominated by a system of self-regulation – involving in reality, as Harden and Lewis remark, 'a delegation of public functions to private control' (Harden and Lewis 1986: 60). In other words, under the banner of self-regulation the City practised corporatism: representation and regulation were performed by a series of semi-private institutions, like the Stock Exchange; entry to markets was closely controlled, with admission depending on willingness to observe severe limits on competition; authority was exercised with a maximum of discretion and a minimum of precise rules, especially of rules derived from statute; and the whole system was guided and protected against outsiders by the City's Guardian Angel, the Bank of England (Moran 1984; Ingham 1985).

Corporatism in the City originated during the last quarter of the nineteenth century, reached full maturity by the 1950s – and then decayed. The decay was marked by the destruction of what had been a private community, by the declining authority of corporatist institutions inside the City, and by the rise of markets and institutions outside traditional spheres of control. By the end of the 1970s a combination of scandal, economic crisis and market innovation had pitched the City's corporatism into crisis. The reforms contained in the 1986 Financial Services Act are a response to the crisis.

The new corporatism is embodied in that Act. The legislation creates a wide definition of an investment business, encompassing most present activities in securities markets and insurance markets (Financial Services Act, Schedule 1). Carrying on an 'investment business' without proper authorisation is now a criminal offence. The Act provides powers to establish the institutions which will license and monitor the behaviour of authorised firms. It is these institutions which make the legislation corporatist (Financial Services Act, chs. III and XIII). The Secretary of State for Trade and Industry is – subject to certain substantive criteria, reporting requirements and an appeals procedure – to delegate statutory power of authorisation and the monitoring to a designated agency. This agency now exists in the form of the Securities and Investments Board. The Board is incorporated as a private company, and is financed by a levy on the industry, but its Chairman is appointed by the Secretary of State, with the agreement of the Governor of the Bank of England. Members of the Board are appointed by the Governor with the agreement of the Secretary of State. The Board may either license an investment business directly or delegate its powers, subject to substantive and procedural criteria, to a range of Self-Regulatory Organisations (SROs) created by particular parts of the financial services industry

As I write, the Act is still being implemented, so the precise institutional arrangements are not yet clear. It is likely, however, that the Securities and Investments Board will directly license only a small number of businesses. Most of its energies will go into authorising and monitoring the SROs and into developing model rules for the SROs and for individual firms. The burden of authorisation will therefore fall onto the shoulders of the SROs, who will probably number five, covering the span of the securities and insurance industries. The most important SROs are likely to be the Securities Assocation (based on a merger between the regulatory arm of the Stock Exchange and an association representing the large multinational houses dominant in the Euromarkets) and the Financial Intermediaries Managers and Brokers Regulatory Association (FIMBRA), which hopes eventually to license and regulate as many as 20,000 enterprises involved in the growing mass market in investment advice and securities' sales.

The SROs are, like the Securities and Investments Board, private institutions joined by contract to their members, and funded by the subscriptions of those members. But membership of an appropriate SRO is legally obligatory, SRO rules have the force of law and the composition of governing bodies is in part prescribed by statute. SROs are, in short, a powerful new breed of half public, half private institution.

The new arrangements are conventionally described as practitioner-based regulation, and are presented as something naturally evolved out of the old system of self-regulation. But this is not self-regulation as traditionally practised, for as Gower remarks, 'Although the Securities and Investments Board is envisaged as being a private, practitioner-based, body, it will be exercising public functions and statutory powers ... its regulatory powers derive from the legislation, not from contract' (Gower 1985: 12). The Chairman of the SIB, Sir Kenneth Berrill, has made the same point (Berrill 1986).

The Securities and Investments Board and its subordinate SROs will – by the traditional standards of regulatory bodies in the City – have impressive resources and regulatory authority backed, in the last resort, by the law. The SROs will be licensed by the state to exercise a monopoly of regulatory authority over their membership and, in turn, will bargain with the state on behalf of that membership. In other words, a government which claims to reject corporatism has put onto the statute book a system which is uncannily like Schmitter's famous definition of corporatist representation:

> A system of interest representation in which the constituent units are organised into a limited number of singular, compulsory, non-competitive, hierarchically ordered and functionally differentiated categories, recognised or licensed (if not created) by the state and granted a deliberate representational monopoly within their respective categories in exchange for observing certain controls on their selection of leaders and articulation of demands and supports.
>
> (Schmitter 1979: 13)

The terms of the new constitutional settlement in the financial services industry can be summarised as follows. The traditional system of regulation was corporatist, but the controlling institutions were dispersed and fragmented, and they operated largely independently of the state. The new settlement creates systematically designed institutions, arranged in a clear hierarchy, wielding state-backed power. We have moved, to use Schmitter's terms, away from 'societal' corporatism towards 'statist' corporatism (Schmitter 1979).

The significance of this shift becomes clear when we remember the alternative models of reform to which the authorities could have turned. It is common to consider corporatism as one of three ideal-typical models of regulation, to be distinguished from *market* and *bureaucratic* regulation. Market regulation permits free exchange within a spare framework of law; bureaucratic regulation centralises directive power over markets in a public bureaucracy. These modes are associated in their ideal-typical form with different social systems and with different ideologies, but within a single community they emerge as different regulatory nuances (Cawson 1982; Cawson and Saunders 1983).

Most leading figures in the financial services industry subscribed in the 1980s to an ideology of deregulation. The 'City revolution' was commonly pictured as a way of allowing free competition at the expense of traditional restrictions. We might therefore have expected a corresponding response in the realm of regulation; in other words, a retreat from intervention, an insistence that investors should take their own precautions against risks, and a determination to confine the regulatory task to the enforcement of contracts. An equally plausible alternative existed in the form of a bureaucratic mode. In the banking industry, for instance, the crisis of regulation in the 1970s led to the development of elaborate administrative controls implemented by a distinct class of public regulators.

The reforms in the Financial Services Act are a puzzle. They reject the two obvious alternative responses to the crisis of corporatism in the City – bureaucratic control or market regulation. Why did the authorities respond to the collapse of the old constitutional settlement in the financial services industry by rebuilding corporatism in a more hierarchical and state-controlled form? And why was this done by an administration whose public statements suggested a contempt for corporatism? Part of the answer lies in the events which led to the present reconstruction. They are the subject of the next section.

The City revolution and the decay of corporatism

The system of regulation now being created by the Financial Services Act is inseparable from what is colloquially called the 'City revolution' – those changes in ownership and competitive practices which, originating in the securities markets, are causing fundamental alterations to the whole financial services industry. The City revolution involves three factors critical to understanding the character of the developing regulatory regime. They are the consequences of structural change for traditional interests and traditional forms of control; the particular regulatory problems raised by issues of investor protection; and the struggles for regulatory jurisdiction unleashed by the decline of the old corporatism. All those involved agree that the key revolutionary event occurred in July 1983 with the 'Goodison–Parkinson' agreement. In exploring this agreement we see the significance of our three key factors – structural change, investor protection and regulatory jurisdiction.

The origins of the 'Goodison–Parkinson' agreement go back to the introduction of Statutory Instrument 98 of 1976, laid before the House of Commons in January of that year. The measure, the Restrictive Trade Practices (Services) Order, extended the scope of restrictive-practices legislation from manufacturing to service industries. The Order thus immediately brought a wide range of financial institutions, the most important of which was the Stock Exchange, under the regulatory jurisdiction of the Office of Fair Trading, the agency responsible for implementing restrictive practices law. The effects of the Order were to oblige the Exchange to register its rule-book with the OFT; to require the reform of any offending rules; and, failing an agreement on reform, to require the OFT to bring the rule-book for judgement before the Restrictive Practices Court (Office of Fair Trading 1977: 133).

This sequence might almost have been designed to throw the Stock Exchange into an adversarial relationship with the OFT, involving as it did a number of features – intrusion by a 'bureaucratic' agency, control by statute and resort to the courts – to which the City was widely and intensely hostile. More substantively, the Exchange's rule-book manifestly contained major restrictive practices, of which two were the keystones of its regulatory structure. These were the requirement that members charge a minimum commission on bargains transacted, and the rule enforcing a separation between brokers, who act as agents for buyers and sellers of stock, and jobbers, who deal as principals. (The latter arrangement is conventionally called single capacity.) It was a common belief – and, events have shown, a correct belief – that single capacity could not survive without minimum commissions, and that the Exchange's traditional system of regulation could likewise not survive the abolition of the two restrictive practices.

The Stock Exchange Council's response to this challenge was twofold: to attempt escape from the clutches of the OFT, and in the event of that attempt failing, to mount a comprehensive legal defence of the rule-book. In the late 1970s the Council, supported at the highest levels by the Bank of England, lobbied the Labour Secretary of State for Prices and Consumer Protection, Mr Hattersley, for exemption from the 1976 Order (Stock Exchange 1979: 5).

This attempt was futile. It is a truism that affected interests have the best chance of influencing policy before government commits itself publicly. Once the original Order was published, hardly any administration was likely to agree to special pleading; was even less likely to retreat when it was a Labour administration suspicious of City interests; and less likely still when those involved in defending the original Order (Mr Hattersley, and Sir Gordon Borrie, Director-General of the Office of Fair Trading) were part of a social-democratic tradition hostile to the restrictive practices of business and the professions. The final acknowledgement that the Exchange's and the Bank's lobbying had failed came after a meeting with ministers on 8 February 1979. On the following day Mr Hattersley's Minister of State told the Commons that the Exchange would not be exempted from the Order, and in the same month the Director-General gave notice that he was referring the Exchange's rule-book to the Restrictive Practices Court (962 HC Debs col. 305 [written answer] 9 February 1979; Stock Exchange 1979; Office of Fair Trading 1980: 45).

The return of the Conservatives to office in May 1979 gave renewed hope that the Exchange might escape the clutches of the OFT. That hope was an illusion; despite a repeat of representations from the Council and from the Bank, two successive Secretaries of State – Mr Nott and Mr Biffen – declined to amend the original Order (Stock Exchange 1980: 5; 972 HC Debs col. 230, 23 October 1979). By June 1983, when the Conservatives were of course returned with a greatly increased majority, the Exchange had turned most of its energies to preparing a detailed defence of its rule-book for the Restrictive Practices Court. The first hearings were scheduled for January 1984, and at the moment of the Conservatives' victory witnesses' proofs were in the final stage of preparation (Stock Exchange 1984: 3). Mrs Thatcher's choice as Secretary of State for Trade and Industry in the new administration, Mr Cecil Parkinson, lasted only until the following October, when private troubles forced his resignation; but his brief tenure was momentous for the Exchange and for the future of London as a financial centre.

One of Mr Parkinson's first acts was to see, in quick succession, the Director-General of the OFT and Sir Nicholas Goodison, the Chairman of the Stock Exchange. At the meeting with Sir Nicholas, the Secretary of State offered the concession for which the Exchange had long lobbied: exemption from the jurisdiction of the OFT. In return the Exchange was to amend key rules to which the Office of Fair Trading had objected. After discussions with Council members, Sir Nicholas in turn offered a set of concessions which, adopted unanimously by the Council on July 22, were announced by Mr Parkinson in the House of Commons four days later. The critical proposals were as follows: minimum commissions on bargains were to be abolished by December 1986; there were to be lay representatives on the Council of the Exchange; a new appeals procedure against rejections of applications was to be established; the substance of rule changes was to be decided in agreement with the Bank of England; and the implementation of the whole package of reforms was to be monitored by a group drawn from both the Bank and the DTI. In return the government committed itself to seek Parliamentary approval exempting the Stock Exchange from the restrictive practices legislation (46 HC Debs cols. 1194–203, 27 July 1983; Stock Exchange 1984: 3–4; Office of Fair Trading 1984: 9–10).

The reaction to Mr Parkinson's announcement was astonishingly hostile: the Government's friends were dismayed, its enemies inflamed and the Office of Fair Trading outraged. *The Times* denounced what it called the 'corporatist' manner in which the decision was taken. Labour's Front Bench described it as a deal done by 'cronies in a smoke filled room' (46 HC Debs col. 1195, 27 July 1983). A stream of Conservative backbenchers in the Commons and Lords expressed anxiety about both the substance of the agreement and the manner of the negotiations. Sir Gordon Borrie bitterly protested against the 'blow to the Office' (of Fair Trading), declined voluntarily to withdraw the Office's case against the Exchange, and thus obliged the Government to introduce highly contentious legislation exempting the Exchange from restrictive practices law (Office of Fair Trading 1983: 9; 49 HC Debs col. 246, 22 November 1983).

These responses were astonishing because they bizarrely misjudged both the way the Goodison–Parkinson agreement was concluded and its substantive consequences. The bargaining was anything but 'corporatist'. On the contrary, Mr Parkinson proceeded by unilaterally making the Stock Exchange an offer it couldn't refuse – and making it in such a way that the ruling Council of the Stock Exchange could do little more than accept terms with which it was suddenly presented. Contrary to partisan accusations, there was no collusion between the Conservative Party and its friends in the City. The initiative came from discussions between a small number of individuals involved in the high politics of Whitehall. Some informal accounts say that Lord Cockfield, Parkinson's predecessor, had already decided to offer the Exchange exemption in return for reform. There was certainly a departmental briefing paper on the issue awaiting the new minister in June 1983. But Mr Parkinson himself says that in advance of discussing the issue with Sir Gordon Borrie he spoke only to fellow members of the Government (46 HC Debs cols. 1198–9. 27 July 1983).

The notion that we are here witnessing the result of collusion between the Conservatives and the City is wrong. The idea that the agreement was a victory for traditional interests on the Stock Exchange is even more mistaken. On the contrary, it was catastrophic for the traditional practices and regulatory structure which the Exchange had been publicly defending. As we noticed earlier, two practices provided the keystones of regulation in London: minimum commissions and the separation of broker and jobber. The agreement itself prepared a timetable for abolishing the first; and within a few months the ensuing structural changes produced a similar timetable for abolishing single capacity. Nor was this unexpected; Sir Nicholas told Mr Parkinson at the time of the agreement that the separation of brokers and jobbers would not survive the abolition of minimum commissions, though ministers for several months afterwards publicly insisted that single capacity could be preserved (Stock Exchange 1984: 3). They likewise argued that the Stock Exchange rule prohibiting outsiders from owning more than a minority holding in member firms would be maintained (49 HC Debs col. 188, 22 November 1983). Yet within a few months Council had announced that the prohibition was to be abandoned, thus precipitating the most important structural change in the City revolution – the absorption of most important member firms into multinational financial conglomerates, many of them foreign owned. It is small wonder that shortly after his bruising at the hands of Mr Parkinson, the Director-General of the OFT could console himself with the observation that 'by the end of 1983 it was clear that events had moved towards eliminating the very restrictions and practices which our litigation had challenged' (Office of Fair Trading 1984: 10).

The Goodison–Parkinson agreement is thus one of the many puzzling episodes in the story of the City revolution. It conceded every point of substance in the OFT's case, with the exception of the attack on single capacity; and single capacity, we now know, was swept away in the ensuing structural changes. Why incur the criticism of allies, the odium of opponents, the fury of the OFT and the expense of scarce Parliamentary time on contentious legislation when the same substantive result could have been reached in a quiet bargain with the OFT?

The official Stock Exchange answer to this question is that the Office of Fair Trading was not intent on a negotiated settlement but, in the characteristic manner of a bureaucratic agency, had launched a wholesale attack on the rule-book, thus petrifying the structure of the Exchange for the duration of the case (Goodison 1985). The OFT's adversarial character does indeed seem to be suggested by the fact that it identified 165 restrictive practices in the Exchange's rule-book, of which it proposed to challenge fifty-nine in court.

But this account is nonsense. The regulatory style of the OFT has been anything but adversarial. In a characteristically English manner it stresses bargaining and compromises in dealings between regulators and regulated. By the end of 1980, for instance, it had registered 495 agreements in service industries under the original 1976 Order; by the time of the Goodison–Parkinson agreement only six of these had been brought to the Restrictive Practices Court (Office of Fair Trading 1980: 46; 1983: 32). In the Stock Exchange's case the apparently draconian character of the Office's examination appears less severe when we realise that of the fifty-nine challenged rules, fifty-two covered minimum commissions, membership and single capacity (446 HL Debs col. 382, 15 December 1983). The first two issues were settled in the Goodison–Parkinson agreement; the third was resolved in its aftermath. In short, the notion that the Exchange failed to negotiate a settlement because it was faced with a bureaucratic, inflexible adversary is a fantasy. To understand why 'Goodison–Parkinson' was necessary we have to recall some of our general themes: the impact of structural change on different interests in the financial services industry; the effects of structural change on the regulation of investor protection; and the contest for regulatory jurisdiction.

By the beginning of the 1980s structural change had produced a 'reform tendency' in the City – a loose alliance of leading individuals and important institutions convinced that deregulation of the securities industry was desirable. Of these structural changes, the most important included the increasing control of huge blocks of shares by a small number of institutions; the domination of the jobbing system by a handful of firms; growing competition in all financial markets; the appearance of markets operated on a global scale; and the associated rise of markets communicating and dealing electronically. (For a general account of change, Sir H. Wilson 1980.)

These changes stimulated desire for reform in a variety of quarters, on a variety of grounds. Large multinational banks, and US and Japanese brokerage houses, were anxious to destroy barriers to entry to the British securities industry as part of a world-wide expansion of their operations. Big institutional investors wanted to end minimum commissions in order to cut the huge, effortless profits enjoyed by brokers transacting the institutions' orders. The big jobbing and broking firms saw integration with large multinational conglomerates as their only hope of competing in the world securities industry, a view shared by senior officials at the Bank of England. Those concerned with the institutional health of the Stock Exchange became increasingly concerned about the robustness of the jobbing system. As early as 1977, for instance, the Committee of Senior Partners (on the Exchange) had warned that the reduction in number of jobbing firms, problems of maintaining adequate capital and pressure on profit margins all made the system highly vulnerable (Stock Exchange Council 1984). From the late 1970s onwards there were frequent debates inside the Stock Exchange Council, with supporters of the reform tendency urging change in a wide range of restrictive practices (Goodison 1985).

The pressure for reform intensified with the abolition of Exchange Controls in 1979. Abolition was both a response to the increasingly global character of markets, and a further contribution to the process of global integration. After 1979 the British securities industry no longer operated in a protected, domestic arena; it was a small declining part of ferociously competitive world markets (Leigh-Pemberton 1984a). London's survival as a significant trading centre depended on full integration into these markets, and that in turn entailed the destruction of traditional regulation.

It might be thought that, in the circumstances, the OFT case presented the ideal opportunity for reform. Yet there existed two great obstacles: the internal politics of the Exchange, and the battle for regulatory jurisdiction which reform would inevitably prompt. We can examine each of these in turn.

The reforms required by the OFT, and the structural changes which reforms would in turn bring, promised substantial benefits to members of the biggest firms on the Exchange. (Huge personal fortunes have indeed been made from selling out partnerships.) By contrast, small and medium-sized brokers had only to look to the carnage in New York after the abolition of minimum commissions in 1975 to see the unpleasant consequences of fierce competition. Yet the reforms on the Exchange could only be implemented by changes in the constitution requiring, in most cases, a 75 per cent majority. This gave the smaller brokers a veto; reform could only be introduced if they were prepared to support changes harmful to their own interests. This is precisely what they were induced to do after the Goodison–Parkinson agreement. Sir Nicholas's considerable powers of persuasion, aided by the public perception of the agreement as a 'Stock Exchange victory', did in the crucial cases produce the necessary majorities for the constitutional amendments needed to implement the agreement. But the process was accompanied by bitterness, by doubts among Exchange members, and by some reversals for the Council élite (*The Banker*, July 1985: 5). The Goodison–Parkinson agreement was accepted because it could be represented as a victory wrung from the Government, at the expense of the OFT; a 'Goodison–Borrie' compromise could never have been sold to the membership in similar terms.

The substance of the reforms represented a great victory for the OFT – or rather, for the reform tendency of which it was a part. But there is one critical sense in which the Office was indeed defeated: the Goodison–Parkinson agreement partially rebuffed its claim to a say in the regulation of the securities industry. Had Goodison negotiated the same substantive terms with Borrie, the OFT would, by contrast, have acquired a permanent right to intervene in issues of regulation. A senior official of the Exchange has put the point exactly: 'Had the exemption [in the Goodison–Parkinson agreement] not been granted the Stock Exchange would always have had to submit its rules for OFT approval, a process entirely incompatible with the principle of self-regulation' (L. Jones 1984). This, then, is the second reason why no compromise with the OFT was possible: a bargain would have recognised the Office's claims to regulatory jurisdiction over the industry. It was almost universally agreed in the City that intervention by 'bureaucratic' agencies like the OFT should be resisted. (Even here, however, the OFT's defeat was not total. Under the Financial Services Act it has the right to scrutinise regulation for anti-competitive effects.)

The forces shaping the Goodison–Parkinson agreement – notably the struggles for regulatory jurisdiction – warrant close examination because they are also critical to understanding the system of regulation now under construction. To this we next turn.

Corporatism resurrected

Corporatism as traditionally practised by the City approximated Schmitter's model of societal corporatism: it grew out of the institutions, culture and social structure of the London markets, and operated largely independently of government. By the end of the 1970s it was in decay; the structural revolution inaugurated by the Goodison–Parkinson agreement completed the process of dissolution. The end of single capacity; the entry of powerful multinational firms; the creation of complex, multi-functional financial conglomerates; the conscious decision to intensify competition – all these made imperative the creation of a new regulatory order. That order is embodied in the Financial Services Act. Understanding why the legislation solves the problem of reform by creating a more hierarchical and statist system of corporatism has to begin by recalling the other possible routes to reform. They are, as we saw earlier, market regulation and bureaucratic regulation.

The new proposals by no means utterly reject market regulation. It would, indeed, be odd if such were the case since the whole City revolution is being legitimised by an ideology of deregulation. The Financial Services Act puts substantial limits on the extent to which the new SROs can impose restrictive practices. It also exempts from many of its 'investor protection' clauses dealings between 'professional' investors, who are presumed to be sophisticated enough to know the risks they run.

Yet these measures, though important, are exceptional. The Act largely rejects the notion that regulation should only create a legal framework within which contracts can be made by actors obliged to form their own estimation of risk. The reason is straightforward: hardly anybody is now prepared to defend the doctrine of *caveat emptor* as a cardinal principle of financial regulation. The reasons are fourfold.

First, small investors, whose numbers have grown greatly as a result of privatisation, demand special protection. The drafting of the Financial Services Act was greatly influenced by Professor Gower's review of investor protection – a review commissioned by the DTI in part because of losses suffered by small investors in a series of high-risk investments in the early 1980s (Gower 1982, 1984, 1985).

Second, even the most sophisticated institutions can only tolerate the doctrine of *caveat emptor* to a limited degree. The character of the most important advanced securities markets – their impersonality, global reach and speed of transaction – mean that high levels of trust are necessary if exchanges are to take place. Yet *caveat emptor* is a low-trust doctrine. Even the most sophisticated firms need assurance that an independent regulator is policing the behaviour of their competitors and those with whom they deal. The way markets seize up at the first hint of crisis shows this need for a high-trust environment. The demand for a regulator is reinforced by the complexity of modern markets – the institutional complexity of the biggest firms, the complex range of services which they offer and the complex financial instruments which they trade. The great modern financial crises are marked by the failure of even the most sophisticated and wary market actors accurately to estimate the risks involved in trading. One of the most striking features of the Financial Services Act is the extent to which its restrictions on market regulation command support from the élite of the largest institutions.

To the demands of small investors, and the need of the most advanced institutions for a high-trust environment, we can add a third reason for the rejection of market regulation: the anxiety of the financial élite to curb competition deemed unfair or unethical. The Act – like most measures of regulatory reform in the financial services industry – is aimed at 'the fringe', as it is conventional to describe small entrepreneurs struggling for survival at the turbulent edge of markets. The most vital SRO in the new system will be that organisation – probably the Financial Intermediaries Managers and Brokers Regulatory Association – licensed to represent and to regulate investment managers and advisers operating outside established City markets. The Act considerably increases the extent to which the marketing of securities and investment advice by such small operators is subject to control.

Market regulation has been rejected, therefore, because neither investors nor financial institutions are prepared to live with its high-risk, low-trust consequences. To this we may add a fourth consideration: public regulators are not prepared to live with its prudential consequences. Change in the financial services industry has, in creating new financial conglomerates, produced significant problems of prudential control, especially in banking. The growing involvement of banks in activities like securities trading and underwriting poses regulators with constant difficulties in assessing the capital adequacy of the banking system. Since the stability of banking is vital to wider economic stability, regulators inevitably presume that they have a duty to intervene. The discussions about regulating the new markets have therefore involved detailed debates about the disposition of capital inside the new banking conglomerates, coupled with general expressions of worry about prudential control by bank regulators (for instance see Leigh-Pemberton 1985).

In the debate about the shape of the financial services industry, appeals to market principles have been commonplace, but the function of such appeals is to legitimise changes supported by the reform tendency, or to help opportunistic cases made in arguments about the details of the Financial Services Bill. (The biggest firms in the Eurobond market, for instance, appealed to the market mode in their successful efforts to secure exemptions from many of the investor protection clauses of the legislation.) But a significant shift in the direction of market regulation was never a likely outcome of the reconstruction of controls.

A change towards the bureaucratic mode was, by contrast, an obvious possibility. Across the Atlantic, the Securities and Exchange Commission provides (though in highly adulterated form) an example of regulation with a large bureaucratic content. But in truth the bureaucratic mode was barely considered because hardly anybody of significance thought it merited consideration. Throughout the markets 'bureaucracy' is a term of abuse.

The OFT was disposed of precisely because it was seen as a bureaucratic body, and therefore as a threat to the City's regulatory autonomy.

Hostility to bureaucratic regulation also pervades the public agencies. The public body with most experience of the securities markets is the Bank of England, and it shares the City's distaste for bureaucratic solutions. The only other public institution with a potential claim to regulate securities, the DTI, never wanted such a task. It has little experience of regulating the markets, and correspondingly few resources to exercise control. (For instance, in 1984, when the proposals were being prepared, the relevant part of the Companies Legislation Division of the DTI had no lawyer or accountant, and only four staff who had been in post since 1980 [Gower 1984: 21].) To equip the Department, or to establish a free-standing regulatory commission, would have required a substantial investment of money and staff under a government nominally hostile to increases in public spending and public employment. Even if the particular outlook of Mrs Thatcher's Government was no obstacle, adopting a bureaucratic mode of financial regulation in a country with a weak tradition of control by government would require an administrative and cultural revolution as profound as the City's own revolution in market practices. Prevailing cultural assumptions made a bureaucratic solution almost literally unthinkable.

The rejection of the market and bureaucratic modes meant that the reconstruction of regulation had to proceed by building a strengthened and more tightly disciplined corporatism. Reaching consensus about the details of this new system was greatly helped by the activities of Professor Gower. His review of investor protection – originally commissioned by the Department partly in response to the collapse of firms advising on high-risk investments – helpfully illuminates the evolution of thinking in the industry. Gower's first report, published in 1982, received a hostile reception in the City, despite the fact that it proposed (albeit reluctantly) only modest reforms, which would have left the City's own Council for the Securities Industry with the key regulatory role (Gower 1982; Stock Exchange 1984). Gower's second report, published in 1984 after extensive consultations, resembled much more closely the corporatist pattern of the Government's 1985 proposals. The change in attitudes wrought by the 'City revolution' is indicated by the favourable reception received by his final report. Only one of his proposals was widely rejected: that there should be a public agency – either the DTI or a Commission – to oversee the control of the whole system. This rejection typified the commonest City view about regulatory reform. The City was prepared to undergo many major changes, but not to subject its activities to the control of a 'bureaucratic' institution – in other words, to control by a body which could have transmitted influences from Whitehall and Westminster.

Eliminating the 'bureaucratic' threat in Gower's proposals was not difficult. The Goodison–Parkinson agreement had left the City dominant in the discussions about the new system, with the Bank of England playing a key orchestrating part. In May 1984 the Governor of the Bank announced the formation of an Advisory Group, drawn from the great and the good of the markets, to advise him on the details of reform. It is clear from the Group's terms of reference that the industry was to be given a veto over any proposal for a public agency, for it was to advise on a structure which would 'attract sufficient support from potential participants to be capable of early implementation' (Leigh-Pemberton 1984b). Every important factor – the content of the Goodison–Parkinson agreement, the prevailing ideology of regulation in the industry, the DTI's lack of expertise in securities regulation – thus worked to kill the proposal for control by a public agency. By October 1984 the Government had publicly committed itself against a public agency, and in the following February a White Paper confirmed that control would be 'practitioner based' (Department of Trade and Industry 1985).

The Securities and Investments Board, and the associated self-regulatory system, is an attempt to solve the problem of how to provide a disciplined system of regulation without submitting the markets to public control. The SIB will, through delegated powers, enjoy many of the coercive powers of the state. It will also be able to transfer power to its subordinate Self-Regulatory Organisations. Yet it will be largely controlled by the markets: located in the City; paid for by the markets; its governing body drawn from the élite of the financial services industry; and its staff largely recruited from the City, at City salaries.

The SIB and the Self-Regulatory Organisations are thus the key parts of the new system of control. The object of the exercise is to resurrect corporatism in a more disciplined and hierarchical form. But accomplishing this involves a precarious balancing act, the object of which is to use public powers while minimising public accountability. The next section examines the problems which this exercise creates.

From corporatism to bureaucracy?

Modes of regulation – corporatist, market or bureaucratic – never exist in pure form in the real world. The practise of regulation is conditioned by a complex range of forces: the object of the activity, the administrative culture in which it occurs, the characteristics of the regulated – to name but the three most obvious. Actual modes of regulation are therefore hybrids, in which corporatist, market and bureaucratic 'strains' are crossed in diverse ways. To continue the image: the distinctive feature of the new system of financial regulation in Britain is the unexpected degree to which a vigorous corporatism has been 'bred in' at the expense of market and bureaucracy. But the process of regulatory evolution never stops. It is not at all certain that the corporatist strain can maintain its present dominance. Three sources of difficulty can be detected: democratic politics, the role of the courts and the problem of settling jurisdiction between competing SROs. I deal with each in turn.

The Financial Services Act attempts an extraordinarily difficult task: to appropriate the power and legitimacy of the democratic state in order to support corporatist arrangements, but at the same time to minimise the extent to which corporatist institutions are accountable to democracy's representatives in Parliament, and to its agents in Whitehall. Some of the problems can be seen in the fate of the original proposals. Appropriating the power and legitimacy of the state has, of course, necessitated legislation. The discussions on the Bill showed the consequences: Parliamentarians, once their assent was required, began to take a close interest in the details of regulation. In committee, for instance, the Government was obliged to strengthen the position of the SIB under pressure from an alliance of its own backbenchers and Opposition members. More generally, there has been an increase in the 'transparency' of regulating institutions because of the processes of consultation associated with legislation. More ominous still was the degree to which the industry and the new regulatory bodies were drawn into the lobbying process surrounding the legislation. Most ominous of all, the tradition of bipartisan silence on securities regulation was broken. The issues involved are now a standard part of adversary politics, used by government and opposition to abuse each other. In everyday language, the reforms have 'politicised' the industry. This is, for instance, why insider trading, once an accepted City practice, became a major source of public scandal during the passage of the Financial Services Bill through Parliament, and why a whole section of the Act now deals exclusively with that problem (Financial Services Act, Part VII). The change in turnover is remarkable: before the new legislation there existed the little enforced, mild prohibitions against insider trading enacted in 1980. It is not possible to appropriate the power and legitimacy conferred by legislation without incurring some attendant dangers – to wit, that democratic institutions might begin to take an interest in those doing the appropriating. It may be that the complex delegation of powers prescribed in the Act will guard against the danger. At the very least, however, the authorities will have to practise some highly successful constitutional mystification to keep Parliament at bay.

Their chances of success in this respect are diminished by the growing importance of the courts. To use the language of legal theory, the securities industry is becoming increasingly 'juridified'. The SIB and its SROs are not private bodies. As Gower has forcefully pointed out, they exercise statutory powers. Their operations are subject to judicial review. The amendments conceded to the Financial Services Bill increase their powers, especially in the case of the SIB. Already, the bill itself has had to create safeguards and rights of appeal; complex argument and intense lobbying has taken place concerning the powers and immunities of the new organisations.

The apparently inexorable advance of the law is well illustrated by the case of the Panel on Takeovers and Mergers. Although the Panel successfully resisted attempts to put it under the jurisdiction of the SIB, it has nevertheless now been endowed with a quasi-legal status. In December 1986 its decisions were held to be subject to judicial review, and in May 1987 the DTI announced that compliance with Panel decisions would be one of the conditions of SRO membership (*Business Law Review* 1987). The Act thus entangles the City not only in the democratic process but also in the judicial process. The City's instinctive suspicion of law was sound. Courts are highly public places, and their decisions often lead the parties to even more public arenas – notably to Parliament.

The possibility of growing legal entanglement is heightened by the problems of settling the jurisdiction of the various SROs. Competition in the industry now extends beyond the usual scramble for business, to a struggle for institutional power. The Financial Services Act confers large benefits, because designated SROs enjoy great rights in regulation and representation. The struggle to control these is generating fierce institutional jostling. The Investment Management Regulatory Organisation (IMRO) was, for instance, created to ensure that élite City institutions were not subject to the same regulatory regime as the smaller operators. The International Securities Regulatory Organisation (ISRO) came into existence to lobby for the great Eurobond houses, and then persuaded the Stock Exchange into an amalgamation to form a new Securities Association.

The Securities Association itself will certainly be a leading SRO, but initial recognition is only the starting-point in the struggle for institutional authority and prestige. To take a single instance, the wide range of services and products offered by a typical financial services conglomerate will oblige many firms to join more than one SRO. A clear division of regulatory responsibilities will be established, it is hoped, by designating a single SRO as a 'lead' regulator. Establishing criteria to help identify the appropriate 'leader', and arbitrating between the competing claims of ambitious SROs, will be tasks of some delicacy and complexity. The potential institutional complexity of the new system is perhaps the greatest threat to the new corporatist design. Corporatism in the City has traditionally been used to keep 'bureaucracy' at bay. Yet the new arrangements inadvertently introduce features – administrative hierarchies, complex rules, struggles for institutional jurisdiction – which are characteristic features of bureaucratic regulation.

There is thus a double irony about the Thatcherite constitutional settlement in financial services. Thatcherism was distinguished by its hostility to both corporatism and to bureaucracy. Yet in financial services it has created a corporatist structure which is evolving into a system of bureaucratic control.

5

'Rolling Back the Frontiers'? The Privatisation of State Enterprises

Cosmo Graham and Tony Prosser

The privatisation programme

The programme of privatisation of nationalised industries would at first sight appear to be the clearest example of the implementation of a full-blooded strategy of reducing the role of the state and replacing it with the discipline of market forces. Thus by the end of the second Thatcher Government, the state's involvement in production had been reduced by almost half; moreover, the number of individual shareholders in Britain had doubled or trebled, one survey suggesting that almost a quarter of the adult population now owned shares (*Guardian*, 21 September 1987). Moreover, the scale of the programme had continually increased from fairly modest beginnings to achieve a scope beyond the wildest dreams of most early advocates of privatisation. In autumn 1986 the target for the net proceeds of privatisation was raised to £5 billion per annum in each of the following three financial years. The 1987 Conservative Election Manifesto promised sales of the Water Authorities and electricity industry, and a bill to pave the way for these was introduced almost immediately Parliament reassembled (Public Utility Transfers and Water Charges Bill). Indeed, it appeared that the target of £5 billion pounds per year was likely to be overshot.

Recently some of the lustre has rubbed off the privatisation programme, in part because of the mounting criticism of British Telecom's performance. Perhaps more importantly, the fall in share prices on the world stock markets raises questions about the feasibility of further sell-offs. The sell-off of the Government's remaining shares in BP was clearly a failure and only went ahead through the Bank of England supporting the share price by a special buy-back scheme for BP shares (*Independent*, 3 November 1987; *Financial Times*, 6 November 1987). However, the Government remains determined to press ahead: indeed, shortly after the stock-market collapse the Financial Secretary to the Treasury pledged that the programme of £5 billion per year would continue for the following three years (*Financial Times*, 18 November 1987). In the following weeks plans were announced for the sale of British Rail Engineering Ltd and of the British Steel Corporation.

If the scale of the privatisation programme is extraordinary, so are the claims made as to its effect on political and industrial life. According to the then Financial Secretary to the Treasury, who had played a major role in preparing the programme:

> In the course of two Parliaments, we ... have nearly halved government involvement in state-owned business and liberated a substantial portion of economic activity from suffocation by the state. I have no doubt that the successful conclusion of this Parliament's programme will produce an irreversible shift in attitudes and achievement which will bring lasting benefits to the United Kingdom.
>
> (Moore 1986a: 97)

As is apparent even from this brief quotation, the privatisation programme has been associated with what are essentially constitutional claims in that they are based on a particular view as to the legitimate role of government. To quote the Financial Secretary once more:

> Less government is good government. This is nowhere truer than in the state industrial sector. Privatisation hands back, to the people of this country, industries that have no place in the public sector.
>
> (Moore 1986b: 93)

Indeed, privatisation's justification as cutting back the state as a matter of principle has grown in importance as the programme has proceeded. In the early days justifications for privatisation concentrated on the disciplines to be provided by exposing the industries privatised to a competitive environment: indeed, most of the enterprises privatised under the first Thatcher Government existed in an environment in which there was some degree of competitive pressure. However, this has now changed; the enterprises sold in the second term do not necessarily face any real competition in important markets, as is notably the case with the British Gas Corporation. Moreover, opportunities to increase competition have in important cases not been taken up on privatisation (see e.g. Beesley and Littlechild 1983; Vickers and Yarrow 1985; Hammond, Helm and Thompson 1985). Indeed, in two cases privatisation has served to reduce competition; the acquisition of the Royal Ordnance Factories by British Aerospace, thereby creating the largest Western defence manufacturing company outside the United States, and the takeover of the airline British Caledonian by British Airways.

Instead of the virtues of competition, two linked themes have come to prominence as the new justifications for the privatisation programme. The first is that privatisation will free the industries from the governmental intervention which had bedevilled the nationalised industries. In one sense, this is used to mean that the industries will be able to raise finance for their extensive investment programmes of the next few years outside the artificial constraints of the Treasury's external financing limits. In another sense it refers to the freeing of the industries from bureaucratic constraints on their commercial judgement: the first reason given for the proposed sale of the water authorities was that 'the authorities will be free of Government intervention in day to day management and protected from fluctuating political pressures' (Cmnd 9374 para. 3).

The second theme in this argument is that ineffective mechanisms of political accountability will be replaced by accountability to shareholders. This forms part of one of the central presentational themes of the programme: the promotion of wider share ownership. This is not, of course, an argument based on a more equal distribution of wealth, but rather that individual responsibility, independence and freedom will be increased through ownership of a stake in a major industry and that a more direct form of accountability can be exercised through the capital market and the company meeting. This will be more effective than diffused and indirect political control (see e.g. the Secretary of State for Trade in relation to the Telecommunications Bill at 48 HC Debs, cols. 26–38, 18 July 1983). The encouragement of wider share-ownership suffered something of a battering with the fall of the stock market and the failure of the sale of the government's final stake in BP, 'in which the only significant new recruits to wider share-ownership turned out to be the Bank of England and the Kuwait Investment Office' (*Financial Times*, 7 December 1987), and it remains to be seen how central this theme will become in future flotations. Our major aim in this contribution will be to assess the claims that privatisation will free the industries from governmental intervention and that democracy through share ownership offers a more direct form of political accountability than does public ownership.

It is worth reminding ourselves, however, that these claims feed on a real and justified dissatisfaction with nationalisation in Britain. At the time of the major examples of nationalisation in the late 1940s it had been assumed that government could remain mainly at 'arm's length' from the industries, which could discover an unproblematic 'public interest' to provide an objective once the profit motive had been removed. This unsurprisingly proved a will-o'-the-wisp and instead governmental intervention on a range of matters (especially pricing) came to dominate industry decision-making. The intervention, however, did not provide coherent objectives over anything but the shortest of terms, and later attempts to rationalise government intervention through the provision of financial targets or, more recently, external financial limits, have not resolved the problems (Prosser 1986, Chs. 2–4; for a recent assessment see the Public Accounts

Committee in HC 343 1985-6).

Nor did nationalisation provide effective public accountability. Government intervention was not implemented through published directions but through informal and usually secret processes. As a result, accountability was attenuated to vanishing-point: who could be accountable if it was not clear whether responsibility for decisions rested with the industry boards or with government? Parliamentary accountability has been deliberately limited by ministers and industry chairmen (Prosser 1986, Ch. 10; for a recent critical assessment see the Public Accounts Committee, HC 26 1986-7). Moreover, the consumer councils established to protect consumer interests were generally weak, unimaginative and hampered by an inability to gain information from the industries (Prosser 1986, Chs. 8-9).

As with so many other themes within Thatcherism, then, the dissatisfactions on which privatisation draws are real and the failure to develop effective and accountable structures for nationalisation has been a source for much of the attraction of the programme. However, whether the privatisation programme will solve the problems is a different matter. In a complex and interdependent economy with an inevitable role for government, privatisation does not solve the problems characteristic of nationalisation simply through change in ownership. Rather, it merely provides the opportunity for the design of fresh institutions which may or may not be superior to those of public ownership. We will now assess the extent to which the claims made to justify the privatisation programme can be justified.

Privatised industries and government

It is quite clear that the Government possesses enormous discretion in the actual process of privatisation, for example as regards pricing and timing of disposals. This discretion is largely unscrutinised, at least until after the event (for descriptions by the National Audit Office of the sales of British Telecom, the Trustee Savings Banks, British Gas and British Airways making this clear, see HC 495 1985-6; HC 237 1986-7; HC 22 1987-8 and HC 37 1987-8). Even as regards the recent BP sale, the major negotiations took place in private between the lead underwriter, the Treasury and BP after which, in the absence of agreement, they were contractually obliged to seek the Bank of England's advice, the final decision resting with the Treasury (see 121 HC Debs col. 169, 27 October 1987). However, pricing of issues has become a major issue of political controversy with allegations of underpricing and, as a result, substantial premiums being available to share purchasers (see e.g. Mayer and Meadowcroft 1985; Buckland 1987; Public Accounts Committee in HC 35 1985-6). In other cases the Government has actually taken added powers to compel the nationalised industries to dispose of assets or subsidiaries (this is something that has also occurred in relation to local government). The most notable example would have been the power proposed in the Treasury Consultative Proposals on Nationalised Industries Legislation of December 1984. This would have given the sponsoring minister power to require the privatisation of any assets and activities, and would have had the power to amend any statute applicable to a nationalised industry by statutory instrument to facilitate the exercise of his powers (Treasury 1984). These proposals were shelved, but there are nevertheless such powers in other statutes. (See e.g. the British Telecommunications Act 1981, s. 62(3), providing such powers in relation to the Post Office, the British Shipbuilders Act 1983, ss. 1–2, and the Iron and Steel Act 1982, ss. 2 and 5. For fuller discussion see Graham and Prosser 1987: 24–30.)

However, disposal does not end the Government's role. Whilst a major theme in the justification of privatisation has been that once denationalised the industries will be free from political intervention and able to concentrate on their own commercial interests, the history of nationalisation should give us immediate pause here. It was precisely the objective of keeping the nationalised industries free from extensive governmental interference that led to the adoption of the Morrisonian model in which the industries were to be at 'arm's length' from government. As outlined above, this was a manifest failure: political intervention became extensive but largely *ad hoc*. It could be argued that this was because the nationalised status of the industries made the temptation to intervene irresistible, but it is not hard to think of a variety of situations in which governments of any political complexion might wish to intervene in the affairs of privatised industries. These include the threat of bankruptcy (particularly of industries with a major defence role such as British Aerospace or occupying a strategic role in the economy such as British Telecom), unwelcome takeover bids either by the privatised industry or for it, the threatened curtailment of socially desirable services or abandonment of British suppliers, industrial action threatening the rest of the economy, pressure from foreign governments party to contracts with the privatised firm, and other types of political pressure (see Steel 1984: 105–8). Given such temptations, the key question must be whether government possesses the tools by which it can successfully intervene in the affairs of privatised concerns. The answer to this must be a firm 'yes', and indeed it has taken care to provide itself with the necessary legal powers for intervention.

Government and regulation

It must first be stressed that a number of the most important privatised industries will necessarily be surrounded by a pattern of strategic decisions to be taken by government. For example, despite some liberalisation of gas import and export policy, important governmental powers remain, and these are likely to be crucial in the future strategy to be adopted by the British Gas Corporation. Imports will be allowed subject to consent for laying pipelines across the Continental Shelf (paraphrased by one commentator as, 'if we don't like your next gas import, you will only be able to get the stuff into the UK in balloons' (*Financial Times*, 11 March 1987) and in appropriate cases the conclusion of inter-governmental treaties: British Gas has given the Government an assurance that it will be consulted on its import plans. As regards exports, the Government will consider waiving the requirement to land gas in the United Kingdom on a case-by-case basis (83 HC Debs cols. 211–12 [written answer], 6 March 1986). Even more importantly, the Department of Energy retains control of the allocation of licences for the development of North Sea oilfields, and the Department of Transport has an important role in the allocation of route licences to airlines, in addition to the role of government in international negotiations for the designation of air carriers. As we shall see, these powers are central to two key areas of controversy involving recently privatised industries. In other contexts, privatisation has been accompanied by the provision of new regulatory powers directly in the hands of government. Examples are the promulgation of traffic distribution rules at airports and the limitation of aircraft movements after the sale of the British Airports Authority (Airports Act 1986, ss. 31–4). In the case of the water authorities, current plans are for a Director-General of Water Services, whilst the powers of environmental regulation previously held by the authorities themselves will be transferred to a National Rivers Authority. However, river quality objectives will be set by the Secretary of State and he will have the power to direct the Authority to implement specific policies of an environmental nature (Department of the Environment 1987, paras. 4.6 to 4.8).

Planning competition

In the telecommunications and gas industries, new regulatory bodies independent of government have been established. This has served to disguise the fact that government has retained important powers and the operation of the regulatory bodies is to a large degree dependent on prior decisions of the Secretary of State. Thus in telecommunications, the previous British Telecom monopoly has been replaced by licensing of telecommunications systems by the Secretary of State (after consultation with the Director-General of Telecommunications, the new regulator). This means that the development of competition is effectively in the hands of government, and there has already been criticism of 'the government's illiberal policies on the licensing of public networks and resale' (Vickers and Yarrow 1985: 45, and see generally Ch. 3 and pp. 81–3 therein). This may or may not be justified (and there are in fact forceful arguments in favour of initial restrictions on competition to prevent 'cream-skimming' of the most profitable services and to protect 'infant industries' as potential forces for increased competition). What it makes clear, however, is that paths to greater competition must be *planned*; as the Director-General of Telecommunications has put it:

> although I believe that a presumption exists in favour of competition, and careful consideration must be given to the justification for any inhibitions of competition, nevertheless some planning of the path to competition and some limitation of the ultimate scope of competition is likely to be in the public interest.
>
> (HC 457 1984-5)

In Britain, such planning has been retained firmly in the hands of government. As regards the gas industry, similar powers for the licensing of public gas suppliers have been given to the Secretary of State, though here the extent of competition is bound to be far less than in telecommunications.

Apart from such special provisions for the regulation of privatised industries, the industries are subject to the normal provisions of competition law. The point must be firmly made that the operation of British domestic competition law has *not* been privatised. Under domestic law the right to bring a private action arises only in narrowly defined instances, although it is possible to invoke European law in the domestic courts. Nevertheless, the central characteristic of UK competition law remains the extent of the discretion given to the Department of Trade and Industry, the Office of Fair Trading (OFT) and the Monopolies and Mergers Commission (MMC). As would be expected, the enforcement of competition law depends on a complex network of bargaining between these institutions and the affected parties. Two examples will suffice: anticompetitive practices and merger references to the MMC. The former are policed by the OFT which conducts preliminary investigations, such as that on the complaints by industrial users about British Gas's charges, negotiates undertakings after MMC investigations and supervises adherence to undertakings. All these activities involve bargaining between the OFT and the affected firms. O'Brien (1982) has argued that there is a built-in incentive to co-operate with the OFT at an early stage, in order to avoid referral to the MMC, although the pricing policy of British Gas in regard to industrial customers is currently under investigation by both the MMC and the European Commission.

On merger references, the Director-General of Fair Trading advises the Secretary of State, but before doing so the advice of a mergers panel, consisting of representatives of the OFT, the MMC and interested government departments is sought (Fairburn 1985). The MMC has a wide discretion as to the procedures it adopts. For example, it was reported that the Commission indicated that BA's original bid for British Caledonian was likely to be seen as against the public interest; BA therefore produced new proposals to meet the MMC's fears (see Cmnd 247 1987 paras. 5.36 to 5.38, 8.70 to 8.71). Other interested parties were not given sight of, nor opportunity to comment on, these proposals, which convinced the MMC the bid was not against the public interest. One participant then unsuccessfully challenged the Commission's decision through an action for judicial review on the grounds of procedural unfairness (*Financial Times*, 12 November 1987; *Guardian*, 21 November 1987). The Secretary of State need not accept the advice of the OFT nor of the MMC that a merger is against the public interest, and this discretion is structured by the most rudimentary of guidelines (see HC Debs vol. 63, cols. 213–14, 5 July 1984 [written answer]; s. 84 Fair Trading Act 1973) and there are no requirements of openness.

The role of the Secretary of State in deciding whether to make a reference to the MMC has already become the central issue in one case involving a privatised concern. When the Royal Ordnance Factories were sold to the recently privatised British Aerospace there were a number of complaints to the OFT from other defence contractors that this would inhibit competition in key areas of military procurement and, in particular, would give British Aerospace a near-monopoly in the United Kingdom in making major missile and munitions systems. The sale had been made conditional on non-referral to the MMC; to no one's surprise the Secretary of State did not make such a reference, and instead assurances were received from the company that the Ministry of Defence would have the right to inspect British Aerospace's books to check the price of items supplied by Royal Ordnance. It was hoped that this would enable the ministry to detect whether British Aerospace was using its Royal Ordnance subsidiary as a preferred source of supplies at below market rates (see *Financial Times*, 23 April 1987).

Although the Secretary of State for Trade and Industry played a less prominent role in the takeover of British Caledonian by British Airways, the troubles of British Caledonian, leading the way to its takeover, seem largely to stem from the earlier decision of the government not to follow the recommendations of the Civil Aviation Authority that the company be awarded some of British Airways' route licences before the latter was privatised (see Cmnd 9366 1984). This decision has been widely attributed to a preference for a successful flotation over increased competition. In any event, it is indeed nonsense to talk of decisions determined simply by market forces in an area in which government has such a major role on competition issues and in the allocation of such basic assets as route licences and designation for international flights (see *Financial Times*, 12 November 1987).

Regulatory controls

The licence issued by the Secretary of State to telecommunications and gas operators will also contain the key regulatory provisions in the form of licence conditions: the most important of these is that controlling price increases (for the complexities of the practical operation of these formulas, see Helm 1987). The formula adopted is to relate certain prices to the retail price index; thus in the case of British Telecom a basket of charges cannot be increased by more than the retail price index minus three points (the latter figure representing the desired efficiency gains) each year until 31 July 1989. The negotiations on the actual figure to be set and on the range of prices to be covered were treated as a private matter between the Department and British Telecom, and, for example, the Post Office Users' National Council, representing consumer interests in telecommunic‍ations, was not allowed to participate.

The price formula appears straightforward and near-automatic in its application. In practice, however, its operation has proved highly controversial. Although total tariff increases have remained within the formula, its terms have permitted extensive 'rebalancing' of prices at the expense of rentals and some local calls. This was clearly envisaged when the licence was issued, and was indeed an inevitable result of the form of economic regulation adopted in an industry where prices did not directly reflect costs and where a degree of cross-subsidisation existed. Nevertheless, it does represent in effect a direct redistribution of resources from domestic and small-business users to the larger telecommunication users, and reponsibility for this lies strictly with the Government (see Hills 1986, Chs. 5 and 7). Criticism of the Director-General of Telecommunications over the scale of the tariff rebalancing is beside the point as his basic responsibility is to enforce the formula as included in the Licence, and he has (quite justifiably) decided only to seek a modification of the formula if British Telecom were making an excessive return on capital not attributable to increased efficiency. After 1989 a new formula is likely to be agreed through a licence amendment involving a report from the Monopolies and Mergers Commission. However, by then the rebalancing process is likely to have been completed, so the most controversial result of telecommunications privatisation will have been the result of direct governmental decision-making rather than deriving from principles drawn up by any independent regulator.

In the case of the British Gas Corporation, the pricing formula is more complex. As well as permitting the company to increase its domestic tariffs by a figure 2 per cent below the rise in the retail price increase, it is allowed to take into account in full the average cost of gas acquired during the year. This appears to assume that British Gas is a passive price-taker in gas purchase, but in fact it will remain the dominant buyer: the formula appears to remove the incentive for British Gas to minimise the cost paid for gas, thus creating the familiar problems associated with profit regulation by the regulatory agencies in the United States without the means available to US regulators for the scrutiny of efficiency (see Littlechild 1983, 1986; cf. Henney 1986). It would also be possible in principle for British Gas to purchase expensive gas to satisfy demand in more competitive areas of its markets and then to cross-subsidise it from consumers within the captive tariff market. Because of this possibility the Energy Select Committee of the House of Commons recommended that the Director-General of Gas Supply, the new regulatory authority for gas, should have the power to satisfy himself that contracts for the purchase of gas were prudently incurred to meet the needs of tariff customers and to disallow any costs not so allowed: the Government firmly rejected this proposal (HC 15 1985-6, para. 37: Cmnd 9759, paras. 46-9). The problem has rather disappeared from view because of the fall in oil prices and a resulting decrease in gas tariffs, but it can be expected to reappear in the future, and the question of cross-subsidy will be central to the MMC investigation into the corporation's pricing policies for industrial users.

A related difficulty can be anticipated as regards the electricity industry, because over 75 per cent of the CEGB's fuel input is purchased from British Coal. The purchase costs are the result of negotiations between the CEGB and British Coal which are embodied in an unpublished Joint Understanding. The Understanding has been criticised for limiting imports and forcing the CEGB to pay a higher than necessary price for coal, which is due, in part, to the Understanding being a mechanism for the implementation of government policy towards the coal industry (Electricity Consumers' Council 1987).

It is clear, then, that government remains at the heart of the regulatory process which has been created after privatisation. It is true that once licences have been issued, there is a separation of functions between the Secretary of State and the new regulatory authority, enforcement of licences being for the latter, and modification against the will of the licensee being the task of the regulatory authority after a report from the MMC. However, the initial licence is to run for a considerable period of time (twenty-five years in the case of British Telecom), and the procedures for amendment are cumbersome. Indeed, the procedure for licence amendment has already been bypassed in relation to the merger between British Telecom and Mitel, where the majority of the MMC recommended that anti-competitive practices be restrained by undertakings rather than licence modifications because the 'provisions of the Telecommunications Act which govern amendments are such that in the short term it would be difficult to make the necessary changes to the licence without involving further delay and a risk to the future of Mitel'. This has raised doubts as to the enforceability of the undertakings (Cmnd 9715: paras. 10.79, 10.82; see also Gist and Meadowcroft 1986) and British Telecom has already asked for them to be withdrawn (*Financial Times*, 21 October 1987). The really important aspects of regulation have been retained in government hands, and as the examples above show, this has effectively determined the major directions of strategy of privatised enterprises on such important matters as pricing.

'Golden' shares

The discussion so far has concerned government involvement in the affairs of privatised industries where regulation has been deemed necessary. The most important reason for regulation is that competition in the market-place for the sale of the industry's products is limited, and so intervention by a public agency is necessary as a surrogate for market forces, or to protect interests which would not be adequately protected by the free play of market forces, for example the provision of emergency telephone services. We now move from consideration of the product market to the market for corporate control. What powers has government taken to intervene in this market after privatisation?

In the early examples of privatisation, residual shareholdings were retained by government. Although these were accompanied by under-takings that the Government did not intend to use them to intervene in company decision-making, the right to do so was reserved, and the undertakings were anyway so vague as to be unenforceable (see e.g. the Secretary of State for Energy at 16 HC Debs col. 171, 19 January 1982). This inevitably led to speculation that such shareholdings could be mobilised as a means of intervention if the need arose: indeed, the Labour Party in Opposition announced a clear intention of doing so (Labour Party 1986: 6). However, as the target for asset sales has increased in size, such residual shareholdings have been sold off, and in more recent sales, such as that of British Gas, no residual shareholding has been retained. The most important example, the 49.8 per cent of ordinary shares of British Telecom left in government hands, is subject to a pledge that it be retained only until April 1988, although some recent reports have indicated that it is unlikely to be sold in the wake of mounting criticism of British Telecom (*Financial Times*, 29 September 1987; *Financial Times*, 4 November 1987).

In several cases, government directors are to be appointed to the boards of privatised companies. In the past such directors in other companies have had a very limited role as a means of government intervention. Thus in the case of BP there were both government directors and a substantial shareholding, yet it was widely recognised as possessing an extreme independence from governmental influence, though this was no doubt due largely to its market position and financial success. In the wake of the De Lorean affair, in which the presence of government directors had not prevented serious loss of public funds, the Public Accounts Committee recommended strengthening their monitoring functions, but this is unlikely to herald any major change. Anyway, company law at present places restrictions on the ability of such directors to represent interests other than those of the company as a whole (see HC 33 1985–6 and Cmnd 9755). It thus appears unlikely that government directors will play any important part as a means of influence on privatised companies; at most, they will ease the communication process between company and government.

Thus residual shareholdings and the appointment of government directors do not appear to provide important means for government intervention in privatised concerns. The next technique is, however, of the greatest importance. This is the retention of 'special' or 'golden' shares giving government a veto over major decisions – in particular, the power to block unwelcome takeovers. Aside from the product market, the other major form of market discipline is theoretically exercised through the market for corporate control and the threat of takeover. Golden shares replace this discipline by limiting shareholdings and preventing undesirable takeovers. This is accomplished through a variety of devices written into the articles of association of the privatised companies. Why different forms were used is not always obvious, and there has been little public debate over the choice of devices.

When a special share is created, held by a government nominee, the effect is to ensure that certain parts of the company's articles of association are only alterable with the consent of the special shareholder. The object is to prevent the limitations on shareholdings being avoided by altering the articles. In five cases (Amersham International, British Airports, Jaguar, Cable & Wireless, Rolls-Royce) the disposal of a material part of the assets of the group of companies, roughly 25 per cent of the assets, is also deemed to be a variation of rights of the special shareholder. In these cases, any substantial restructuring of the company can only take place with the consent of the government, and how such negotiations will be conducted is left entirely to the discretion of the parties involved.

The central object of the scheme is the prevention of undesired takeovers. As regards Britoil and Enterprise Oil this is accomplished in a relatively simple way. In summary, if any person, alone or acting in 'concert', controls more than 50 per cent of the votes then, from the date that occurs, the special share has, on any resolution in a company general meeting, one more vote than the total number of votes which are not controlled by the Secretary of State. So voting control remains with the government.

Subsequent flotations have utilised different special share arrangements which operate at a lower level of shareholding, domestic or foreign. Whenever any person, alone or in 'concert', obtains control of more than 15 per cent of the voting shares, then the directors shall (may, in Cable & Wireless) serve a notice on such a person requiring them to dispose of their excess shares. If this is not accomplished within a specified time limit, then the directors shall arrange for the disposal of the excess shares. After service of the first notice, the excess shares confer no voting rights at general meetings, these rights vesting, usually, in the chair of the meeting. Due to problems with European Community law, British Airways has a unique provision, as regards foreign shareholdings.

The significance of these provisions is that they replace the market for corporate control with the protective presence of government. The logic of the corporate market argument is that if managers are inefficient, the share price of a company will be lower than it could be with an efficient management. This provides the opportunity for an outsider to make a takeover bid and, if successful, to reap a profit. The mere threat of takeover is enough to encourage efficiency among managers. However well or badly this market may work in the ordinary case, it is simply non-existent when a golden-share scheme is in operation.

This is illustrated by the Enterprise Oil and Britoil experiences. When Enterprise Oil was floated, oil prices were depressed and the issue was undersubscribed. Rio Tinto Zinc (RTZ) applied, in secret, for 49 per cent of the shares, which meant that they would have gained *de facto* control without bringing into play the special share. This proved politically embarrassing for the Government, which had promised that Enterprise Oil would remain an independent company. It refused to allocate RTZ more than 10 per cent of the shares but, following the allocation, RTZ established a 29 per cent stake in Enterprise Oil. In the ensuing Parliamentary debate it was clearly stated that the special share would be used to block any takeover bid (62 HC Debs col. 20, 2 July 1984).

More embarrassment has been caused by BP's takeover bid for Britoil, which demonstrated that golden shares *will* be used as a means of policy intervention. Although the Treasury, and later the Chancellor of the Exchequer (125 HC Debs cols. 13–16, 11 January 1988) announced that the golden share would be used to prevent a takeover bid, this did not discourage BP, which has launched a full bid, after receiving clearance from the Takeover Panel, apparently hoping that either the Government will back down out of embarrassment or that company law will prevent the board acting against BP's interests. The problem has been exacerbated by the build-up of the Kuwait Investment Office's stake in BP which, according to one report (*Independent*, 8 January 1988), received the tacit blessing of the Government. BP has no protection in its articles of association because it declined the Government's offer of a golden share (*Observer*, 20 December 1987). Although the Government has powers under the Industry Act 1975 to limit foreign control of BP, it is not clear why the Government should be hostile to the BP bid for Britoil and yet, at worst, neutral about the Kuwait stake. There seems to be a lack of clarity about policy aims and, in particular, a lack of thought about the purposes for which the protective provisions of the golden share should be used (*Financial Times*, 15 December 1987 and 5 January 1988).

Other means of government intervention

The Government has retained, or created, important means of intervention in relation to privatised industries. These operate to modify the product market through government involvement in the regulatory process and in the market for corporate control through possession of golden shares. There are, however, a number of other ways in which government will be intimately involved in the affairs of privatised concerns. The first of these is through contracting. We have dealt with this issue at greater length elsewhere and will briefly summarise it here (Graham and Prosser 1987: 41–9).

Many of the most important privatised concerns are necessarily dependent on government contracts. Thus government is British Telecom's largest customer, but contractual relations are of particular importance in the defence field where particularly close links will continue to exist in the case of the warship yards of British Shipbuilders, Rolls-Royce, British Aerospace and the Royal Ordnance factories. Indeed, the saga of the Royal Ordnance sale illustrates the close interdependence of privatisation and contracting. Originally the company was to have been floated as a single entity. However, at a late stage the flotation was abandoned; it appears that this change of plan was for two reasons. First, it seems that the Ministry of Defence had refused to allow Royal Ordnance's accounts to be published or to provide an opening balance when it had become a limited company some months earlier: the inevitable lack of information as to its potential would hardly have produced a successful flotation (Veljanovski 1987: 125). Secondly, strong protests had been received from its sole British competitor in tank manufacture about the non-competitive award of a contract for the supply of tanks to Royal Ordnance shortly before the proposed flotation.

When the flotation was called off, it was decided to sell the tanks factory to the competitor at a price based on a confidential formula, thus creating a domestic monopoly in tank manufacture. Bids were invited for the remainder on the basis of a selling memorandum, and eventually the company was sold to British Aerospace, itself only recently privatised, thereby creating the largest Western defence manufacturing company outside the United States. In addition to the placing of the tanks contract, the Ministry of Defence had intended to prepare the company for flotation by placing with it all small arms ammunition contracts for three years, and virtually all explosives and propellant orders for seven years. After the cancellation of the flotation, the exclusive supply arrangements were retained, although the duration of that for explosives and propellant orders was scaled down to three years (*Financial Times*, 5 March 1987). The sale was heavily criticised both because of allegations that the method of sale had resulted in a serious undervaluation of the company, and because of the competition implications discussed above.

In other examples of privatisation, it has been alleged that the award of contracts has been used by government to 'fatten up' firms about to be privatised and to ensure their continued existence after sale, notably in warship procurement (Graham and Prosser 1987: 44–5). The key point is that, as we have seen in the case of Royal Ordnance, both before and after privatisation major links exist between government and the industries concerned through contracting. This would be less important if the contracts in question had any resemblance to the classic private law model of bargaining between equal parties in a competitive environment. In fact, such a contract – for example, the Joint Understanding between British Coal and the CEGB – will be 'more than a technical device for securing the wanted goods and fixing the reward of the supplier; it is also a kind of treaty, by which the conditions of a relationship of interdependence are established' (Turpin 1972: 264).

Despite the current moves towards a greater use of competitive tendering and fixed-price contracts in defence procurement, much contracting in the defence field is by its nature not susceptible to competitive bidding; currently, about 60 per cent by value of the Ministry of Defence's purchases are non-competitive, and this is expected to reduce only to about 40 per cent as a result of the current reforms. Where competitive tendering is not possible, a profit formula based on recommendations from the highly-corporatist Review Board for Government Contracts is employed (for more details see Ch. 3 above). This formula and its application have recently been subject to heavy criticism from the Public Accounts Committee as allowing the defence industry to fare much better than the rest of British industry during the recession: 'we feel bound to conclude that the profit formula has, in recent years, been applied in a very one-sided manner in favour of defence contractors'. The Committee has concluded that control of expenditure on defence equipment has been 'one of the most conspicuous records of failure in the whole field of Public Accounts' (HC 390 1984–5; HC 56 1985–6; HC 406 1985–6).

Apart from the question of whether contractual arrangements are such as to maximise value for money, contracting may provide a means of effective government involvement in private industries. In the 1960s the ship-building industry was reorganised largely through the use of government contracts (B. Hogwood 1979: 79, 87, 168, 171, 189–90 and esp. 264–5). More recently, a Public Accounts Committee Report on the supply of gases to the National Health Service revealed a process of negotiation over price setting very similar to that between government and nationalised industries, but without the equivalent minimal requirements of outside consultation (HC 67 1984–5). In the United States, government through contract is more fully recognised as a means of control; after a major Anglo-American conference on areas of public and private interdependence it was reported that there was 'general agreement that the US Government has achieved a greater degree of *de facto* management control over the aerospace industry through the contract device than the British Government has achieved by nationalising certain industries' (B. Smith 1971: 19). The danger is that a network of links between government and privatised concerns might develop through private law techniques largely immune to public law scrutiny.

Other opportunities will doubtless arise for the exertion of informal pressure by government on privatised concerns. A well-known example occurred during the Westland affair, when it is quite clear that the Secretary of State for Trade and Industry expressed considerable concern to the Chairman and Chief Executive of the wholly privatised British Aerospace about the company's involvement in a rival rescue plan for Westland to that favoured by the Secretary of State. Accounts of the key meeting between the Secretary of State and the Chief Executive differ, but it is clear that, at mildest, pressure, both explicit and implicit was exerted by the Secretary of State in an attempt to persuade British Aerospace to withdraw. It was assumed by, amongst others, the Chairman of the company, that behind this lay a threat to withdraw Government financial support necessary for the company to participate in the separate airbus project (for the different views see HC 519 1985–6, paras. 206–12; HC 169 1985–6 paras. 365 and 369 and Qs 781–800, 833–5; HC 193 1985–6 para. 121 and Qs 144, 869–83, 546–53, 558–85; Linklater and Leigh 1986: 145–8).

Openness and accountability

It is thus clear that there are a variety of legal devices available through which government can intervene in the decisions of privatised industries. In other words, to see privatisation as a straightforward example of the rolling back of the state would be misleading; although it limits the ownership of industry by the state, it is compatible with an extensive governmental role in the economy. Indeed, in an economy as complex and interdependent as that of modern Britain, it should not surprise us that no government can stand aloof from strategic industrial decisions.

This raises a new question of the greatest importance. If state intervention in industrial matters is inevitable even after privatisation, what degree of openness and accountability exist in relation to such intervention? This of course far transcends the issue of privatisation. Two central issues are the effectiveness of ministerial responsibility to Parliament and the degree of openness in government generally. In this sense the problems raised by privatisation are part of the more general problems endemic in British government, and are discussed more fully in Chapters 1 and 10. However, there are particular problems of openness surrounding privatised concerns, and these will now be examined.

Openness in regulation

The first issue is the openness of the regulatory arrangements. In particular, is regulation by government and the new agencies likely to be more open to public scrutiny than regulation by government (and to an extremely limited degree, the consumer councils) under nationalisation? It must first of all be said that privatisation has in some respects the potential to increase openness. For example, where licensing has been chosen as the mode of regulation, the licences must be published (see e.g. Department of Trade and Industry 1984; Department of Energy 1986) and these will set out the key regulatory provisions. In addition, the central problem to plague the consumer councils was their inability to acquire information from nationalised industries. Arrangements for obtaining information by the new Directors-General of Telecommunications and of Gas Supply are in principle superior, both by virtue of statutory provisions and through licences issued to regulated industries (Telecommunications Act 1984, s. 48; Department of Trade and Industry 1984, conds. 16, 20, 52; Gas Act 1986, s. 38. Department of Energy 1986, cond. 7). However, the arrangements for the provision of information to the Gas Consumers' Council also established as part of the privatisation of the British Gas Corporation retain many of the deficiencies of the nationalised industry consumer council provisions (Department of Energy 1986, cond. 8; for problems under nationalisation, see Prosser 1986, Ch. 8).

Nor has the acquisition of information by the regulatory bodies always proved easy in practice. The reason lying behind this is that, despite the apparently liberal powers to acquire information given in licences, there are limited requirements for the regulated industries to collect information in a form which will be useful to the regulator. As one commentator has put it:

> It was open to the Government to diminish the risk of regulatory capture by defining in legislation or licences the type of information required – identifying the form of accounts by laying down principles and by defining cost categories and cost centres. In the case of both British Telecom and British Gas, these opportunities have been largely overlooked. Detailed reporting requirements have not been specified with the monitoring functions of OFTEL and OFGAS in mind. As a result the ways in which the industries allocate their costs are not as transparent as they ought to be.
>
> (Helm 1987: 51)

This can be partly attributed to the decision not to enforce the splitting of the industries into separate cost and profit centres on sale which would have enabled the performance of different regions to be compared (Helm 1987: 48).

The Director-General of Telecommunications has expressed himself satisfied with his access to information from British Telecom, though he would prefer more information to be provided as a matter of course rather than on request and has criticised the lack of regular accounting information to enable him to deal effectively with pricing complaints (HC 15 1985–6, Minutes of Evidence Q254; HC 461 1985–6 para. 1.15; cf HC7 1987–8 paras. 2.17–2.19). His major problems have occurred in relation to performance indicators. The nationalised industries had been encouraged to publish such indicators as a central means of accountability and, although their quality varied, they provided one of the most important tools through which consumer councils could assess performance. After privatisation, British Telecom refused to provide them. The Director-General then took steps to monitor services and commissioned public opinion surveys. At this point, British Telecom agreed to provide indicators, although there has been lengthy wrangling about the timing and form of publication; almost a year after the agreement to publish the indicators, the Director-General was reported as complaining that British Telecom had not yet 'agreed a plan of action with me, nor has it made any public statement about its intentions' (*Guardian*, 7 July 1987). Shortly afterwards, British Telecom started publishing performance indicators (*Financial Times*, 27 October 1987; OFTEL 1987).

The major problem of the supply of information to the regulator has arisen in gas. A lengthy wrangle occurred between the Director-General of Gas Supply and the British Gas Corporation over the information supplied to justify its first tariff change after privatisation. The Director-General considered that insufficient information had been given to satisfy him that forecasts forming part of the process had been properly prepared, and had to threaten court action to obtain more details, which were handed over the day before the company's annual general meeting (*Financial Times*, 29 July 1987; *Guardian*, 28 August 1987).

As regards access to information, then, the provisions for disclosure are wider than under nationalisation, but in practice licences have been drafted, and privatisation has taken place, in such a way as to limit the amount of information actually available. What about the procedures adopted by the regulators? The Director-General of Telecommunications has already shown an impressive degree of openness in approaching his task. He has:

> made a commitment, in public statements, to be as open as possible in the discussion of issues arising out of my functions and duties. I intend to make public statements about major issues under review and to invite representations from any interested parties; I intend to establish contact with individuals, companies and representative bodies with interests in telecommunications so that I may become fully aware of their views on important issues; and I intend to give the fullest possible explanation of the basis for my conclusions, subject only to the need to respect commercial confidentiality.
>
> (HC 457 1984–5, para. 1.27)

He has taken a variety of steps towards implementing this commitment, for example by publishing a number of consultative documents and receiving representations on them, and taking the initiative in establishing a Telecommunications Forum representing a variety of interests and organisations for consultative purposes. He has also committed himself to making public his advice to the Secretary of State in so far as matters of commercial confidentiality do not arise. This degree of openness is most encouraging, especially in comparison to the dearth of information available under nationalisation, though it is unfortunate that it is dependent on the liberal instincts of this particular Director-General rather than being required from all regulators.

When one examines the regulatory functions exercised directly by government, the picture is less impressive. In some areas procedural duties are attached to powers given to ministers; for example, in drawing up traffic distribution rules for airports, the Secretary of State is obliged to consult the Civil Aviation Authority, which in turn is to consult airport and aircraft operators and organisations representing them, and similar provisions apply to rules limiting aircraft movements and allocating airport capacity

(Airports Act 1986, ss. 31–3). This no doubt reflects the tradition of relative effective participative provisions in civil aviation (for which see Baldwin 1985). As regards the licensing of telecommunications systems and gas suppliers, the procedural duties are minimal. Thus in the case of telecommunications licensing, all that is required is that the Secretary of State must consult the Director-General of Telecommunications, and in the case of public telecommunications systems (the major operators such as British Telecom and Mercury), the Secretary of State must give notice that the licence is to be granted, state reasons and consider representations and objections. Originally, the Telecommunications Bill did not contain any provision for the laying of licences before Parliament, but eventually an amendment was accepted providing for the laying of licences for public telecommunications systems (Telecommunications Act 1984, ss. 8(5), 9(2)). The provisions are similar for gas, except that no authorisations need be laid before Parliament. It has already been noted above that the vitally important price-restraint formula for British Telecom was the product of private negotiations between government and the company. Such lack of procedural constraint stands in marked contrast to the arrangements for regulation of the United States utilities, where a range of devices including open hearings and highly sophisticated provisions for disclosure of information have been adopted (see e.g. Henney 1986).

Shareholder accountability

Thus the arrangements adopted for regulation after privatisation have on the whole produced limited improvements as regards the openness and accountability of the regulated industries. However, a major argument offered by government to justify privatisation is that it introduces a new and more direct form of accountability – accountability of the privatised companies to their shareholders:

> The existence of large numbers of shareholders who have both paid for their shares expecting a reasonable return *and* are customers interested in good service at a fair price is an irresistible combination and a powerful lobby in favour of both efficiency and price restraint.
>
> (Moore 1986a: 95, original emphasis)

However, when one comes to examine the mechanisms of shareholder accountability which actually exist, the claims seem less impressive. First, the number of individual shareholders in privatised industries has often declined rapidly and markedly (Buckland 1987: 254). Second, on the basis of the reports of the first few annual general meetings of the privatised companies, the scrutiny of management performance can only be described as perfunctory (for British Telecom see *The Economist*, 13 September 1985, 89–90; for TSB, *Financial Times*, 2 May 1987; for British Airways, *Financial Times*, 30 June 1987). In the case of British Gas, an attempt by industrial customers to have Sir Ian MacGregor appointed to the board of directors as their representative was heavily defeated at the annual general meeting (*Financial Times*, 28 August 1987). Indeed, the TSB has complained that it costs too much to send out its annual report to shareholders and is seeking permission to send out a shorter, less informative, document to them. As for private legal action by a disgruntled shareholder, this is unlikely given the current state of British company law (see Graham and Prosser 1987: 39–40).

As for takeovers, we have already discussed the effect of 'golden' shares on them. Even ignoring golden shares, there must be some doubts about the openness of the market for corporate control. Under certain circumstances, takeover bids are potentially subject to a reference to the MMC. It is worth re-emphasising what a discretionary and secretive process this is, particularly on the question of whether to refer or not. Although the present guidelines, for the exercise of the Secretary of State's discretion, state that references will primarily be made on competition grounds, this is not an inflexible rule. The Elders IXL bid for Allied Lyons was referred because of its unique financing (109 HC Debs col. 373, 28 January 1987). This can give rise to controversy. When BTR made its bid for Pilkingtons there were rumours that three of the ministers in the Department of Trade and Industry were not consulted and did not approve of the non-referral. Given our current constitutional conventions, only one side of the case was presented to Parliament (*Financial Times*, 16 January 1987).

Even when government is not directly involved, the takeover process can be very secretive. One of the best recent examples occurred in the proxy fight over Westland. At the last minute some 20 per cent of the shares were acquired on behalf of six unnamed beneficiaries, three operating through Swiss banks. This assistance proved crucial to the success of the Sikorsky bid. At the end of their investigation the Stock Exchange's committee concluded:

> [We] found it difficult to understand why overseas buyers should consider it worth their while in order to gain voting rights to pay substantially above the prevailing market price. It is not beyond the bounds of possibility that there are six such ingenuous foreigners in the world, but [our] credibility was sufficiently strained to be sceptical as to the absence of a concert party of some sort.
>
> (Stock Exchange 1986: 7; HC 176 1986–7)

The Council of the Stock Exchange accepted the committee's view that the law should be changed so that companies should be empowered to disfranchise shares registered in nominee names but where the ultimate beneficiary is not disclosed – a proposal which has not been implemented.

The notorious Guinness affair revealed equal problems with the operation of the takeover system. In its bid for Distillers Guinness offered its own shares in exchange for shares in Distillers. Therefore the higher the

Guinness shares price, the more valuable and attractive the bid. It was arranged that allies of Guinness should purchase its shares, having been given an indemnity against any subsequent loss, thus raising the price and creating a false market (and being in breach of the Companies Acts) (Kochan and Pym 1987).

The point we wish to make is not that the takeover process can never be open and above board (indeed, this is the aim of the myriad of rules surrounding takeover bids), but that there are grave doubts whether the present regulatory mechanisms will ensure fair procedures (see Ch. 4 for an overview). These doubts appear to be shared by the Government as a review of the Takeovers and Mergers Panel's work has taken place.

Accountability and contracting

Finally, accountability for government contracting with the industries is attenuated in the extreme. The complex systems of review of contracting by Federal Government in the United States are notable by their absence here, as is the sophisticated regime for the review of government contracts by the administrative courts which exists in France. In the United States the Federal Government's discretion is structured by procedural devices, and its decisions are subject to review by a complex network of independent institutions, including the federal courts. There are procedural protections for the debarment and suspension of prospective bidders, and a formal disputes procedure exists for dealing with grievances over awarded contracts (Nash and Cibinic 1977, Vol. 2, Ch. 30; Calamari 1982; Steadman 1976). In the making of procurement regulations, although not subject to the 'Notice and Comment' requirements of the Administrative Procedure Act, the Office of Federal Procurement Policy requires that the views of interested non-governmental parties be given due consideration in the formation of federal procurement policy (Nash and Cibinic 1977, Vol. 1:42). In France there is a large case-law on review of government contracts by the public law courts (Brown and Garner 1983: 125–30). More recently, the increasing intervention of the state in the economy through contractual and quasi-contractual devices has given rise to a lively debate on whether the traditional methods of control and conceptualisations of the problem are adequate (Delmas-Marsalet 1969; Truchet 1980; Nitsch 1981).

The major constraint in Britain on central government is the work of the Public Accounts Committee in conjunction with the National Audit Office, and the Committee has undertaken extensive work in this area. However, it only examines individual cases on an *ex post facto* basis. For example, the report referred to above, on the application of the profit formula in defence contracting, came too late to prevent the payment of 'windfall profits' to contractors of between £220 million and £360 million. In a different context, the highly critical report on payments to De Lorean Motor Cars Ltd came too late for the recovery of over £70 million of wasted public money (HC 390

1984–5; HC 127 1983–4). Very recently, the Committee has complained about the failure to learn from previous experience and from its own reports, going back to the Ferranti affair of the early 1960s, in the development of major equipment for the Ministry of Defence from outside contractors (HC 104 1986–7). Moreover, the Comptroller and Auditor-General will not have access to the books and records of contractors but only to information in departmental files; this lack of access has been criticised by the Committee in relation to the books of the contractors who will manage the Royal Dockyards under the privatisation arrangements (HC 286 1985–6). (Compare these limitations with the remedies given to private contractors under the Local Government Bill.)

Conclusion

On close examination, then, the privatisation programme does not represent so major a change as appears at first sight. Of course, important and no doubt irreversible changes have been made to the ownership of British industry, but this has not achieved the fundamental cutting back of governmental powers suggested by the advocates of the programme. This means that major problems still remain concerning the openness and accountability of governmental intervention in the economy. The major stumbling block is still the secrecy characteristic of British government and the inadequacies of ministerial responsibility as a means of effective governmental accountability; inadequacies illustrated vividly during the Westland affair, which after all, concerned relations between the Government and companies which were privately owned. Thus privatisation does not offer a new constitutional departure, replacing inadequate mechanisms of political accountability with direct accountability to consumers through the play of market forces and to shareholders. Rather, the privatisation programme is one more example of the deficiencies of current British constitutional arrangements.

6

The Transformation of Central–Local Government Relationships

Steve Leach and Gerry Stoker

The cumulative impact of the actions of the Thatcher administration in relation to local government over the past eight years has been to transform the relationship between the two levels of democratically elected government in Great Britain. The 'unwritten constitution' which has governed the relationship between central and local government over the last century has been ignored and in effect radically (and unilaterally) changed. But the constitutional importance of the change which has taken place has been masked by the fact that the individual elements of change which comprise it have proceeded in a piecemeal and (initially) *ad hoc* fashion. The world of local government has become destabilised by the sheer volume of legislation directed at it, the perceived irrationality of much of its content, the fundamental challenge to many of its taken-for-granted assumptions and domains of responsibility, and the intensifying un-certainty about the scope of its responsibilities and indeed its future role.

We explore below the transformation of central–local relationships under the Thatcher administration. We begin by examining the broad composition of the attack on local government and move on to consider four specific illustrations dealing with local government finance, inner-city policy, the abolition of the GLC and the six metropolitan counties, and the Widdicombe Inquiry. We have not focused on the issue of privatisation and contracting as this is dealt with elsewhere in the book. In the concluding section of the chapter we consider what the transformation of central–local relations tells us about the nature of Thatcherite politics and what the future of local government is likely to be under the Conservatives' reform package.

The nature of central–local relations, 1979–87

It is important to emphasise that the current crisis in central–local relations is something which has developed only gradually over the 1979–87 period. The local government emphases of the first Thatcher administration were very different from those set out in the 1987 manifesto. Indeed, one of the first actions by Michael Heseltine, then the Secretary of State for the Environment, was to *reduce* the number of central government controls over local government and to reduce the number of quangos (Hood 1980) mainly on the grounds of their lack of public accountability. These actions reflected a strong and influential long-term strand in Conservative thinking about local government, namely that the more local authorities can be left to go about their business unhindered by central government, the better (Gyford and James 1983). Little trace now remains of that position however, at least within the Parliamentary Conservative Party and Conservative Central Office.

To see the local government-directed actions of the Conservative Government over the past eight years in terms of the planned implementation of a coherent philosophical position, is a mistake. Although the germs of the current anti-local government stance were present in 1979, and indeed in some cases well before that, they had not then been thought through properly nor interconnected conceptually and, at that time co-existed with a range of values more supportive of local government. What has happened since is best characterised as a process of (often fairly arbitrary) action and reaction, rather than the cumulative application of a clear ideological standpoint. As Ian Aitken has pointed out (*Guardian*, 27 July 1987), 'the most extraordinary feature of the process of Thatcherism has been the extent to which a supposedly ideological government has evolved its alleged principles of action by accident rather than design'. This is certainly true of the field of central–local relations, where much of what has happened reflects the failure of ministers (and civil servants) to comprehend the nature of the differentiated polity in which they operate (Rhodes 1988).

What has happened over the period in question is that a series of often misconceived and *ad hoc* centrally imposed changes have been resisted with a greater or lesser degree of (temporary) success by a world of local government increasingly dominated by the Labour Party (particularly in Inner London, the provincial conurbations and the large cities) and increasingly influenced by the Alliance parties (particularly in Shire counties and districts). The strength and in some cases the effectiveness of the resistance has further polarised the positions of the two governmental levels and resulted in the subsequent introduction both of retrospective legislation (to deal with unforeseen ambiguities or loopholes in previous attempts) and new more drastic legislative measures (in terms of the central controls involved, and/or the restriction on local government autonomy).

The initial driving force behind the Thatcher administration's concern with local government undoubtedly rested on its concern to achieve restraint in public spending. The Government argued vigorously for cuts in public expenditure, a reflection of their rejection of Keynesian economic management and their commitment to monetarism. 'Within weeks of taking office local government was strongly criticised by ministers who claimed it was wasteful, profligate, irresponsible, unaccountable, luxurious and out of control' (Newton and Karran 1985: 116).

But the Thatcher agenda is about more than fiscal austerity. It is about restructuring the pattern of spending. Further, it has been increasingly concerned with redirecting local policy-making to meet its perception of what is required in a changing industrial society. As we shall see, this emerges clearly in the case of inner-city policy, but we shall argue it has become the dominant factor in the Thatcher approach to local government. The Conservatives have moved beyond fiscal austerity to a concern to intervene in policy and redefine the purposes and role of local authorities.

A combination of these policy concerns and a desire on the part of the centre to impose its will on unco-operative local authorities has led to significant changes in the pattern of central–local relations. The transformation of the relationship is reflected in the intensity of the centre's interventions, the aggressive use of the law, the breakdown of traditional procedures of consultation and policy formulation and the increasingly dismissive language used by government ministers when referring to local government.

The form of central–local relations has changed substantially in a number of respects in the Thatcher years. First, the intensity of the Government's concern with the behaviour and performance of local authorities is more marked. This finds expression not only in the volume of legislation, circulars, advice and in some cases abuse directed at local government but also in the willingness of the centre to interfere with particular authorities through, for example, rate-capping. Second, the strength and force of the weapons that central government has given itself marks a departure from earlier years. The range of strategies used as we shall see is considerable. Legislation and other measures have been used to reduce local authority discretion and choice in education, housing, finance, transport, land-use planning and many other policy areas. This contrasts with enabling and empowering legislation which characterised much of central–local relations during the years of growth in local authority service delivery. In contrast to the negotiation and compromise which underlay much of post-war central–local relations, the Thatcher Governments have developed a style of setting for local authorities arbitrary and non-negotiated goals and targets.

During the first two Thatcher Governments over forty major Acts were passed with significant implications for local government. Legislation, plainly, has formed a vital element in central–local relations during the period. Loughlin argues that the Conservatives have sought to structure local authority action through formal legal procedures (Loughlin 1986:

195). At the same time, legislation has extended the discretionary powers of central government. Local government law has been reformalised to direct and control local authorities and give greater freedom to the centre to enable it to pursue its objectives.

This aggressive use of the law has led to the collapse of the traditional legal relationship which provided a flexible structure within which central and local authorities could bargain and negotiate. The result has been the 'juridification of the central–local relationship' (Loughlin 1986: 193). The legal relationship between centre and locality which in the past was a matter of minor concern has become a critical issue, as both parties have sought to establish the other's legal powers and duties. Given the uncertainties of the law in this sphere, local authorities and central government have used the courts to promote or defend their interests (see M. Grant 1986). Again this has caused difficulties given that the courts were relatively ill-equipped in terms of design and culture to cope with these new demands.

Indeed, it would appear that central government has increasingly attempted to place itself beyond judicial review. Where local authorities have won victories, the Conservatives have been prepared to pass new legislation to nullify the decision and often specifically exclude any further challenge through the courts. A striking example, as noted in Chapter 1 above, is provided by the Local Government Act 1987.

In general traditional procedures have broken down. First, established patterns of consultation have been eroded. Rhodes (1986) describes in detail how the Conservatives shunned the networks of consultation established in earlier years in England. The local authority associations 'saw their special position slip away'. The Consultative Council of Local Government Finance became a forum not for negotiation but for ministers to announce hard and fast decisions about local spending. Indeed, 'virtually all of the local government organisations at national level have been permanently on the defensive, stigmatized by Whitehall as promoters of profligacy rather than as potential allies or partners' (Rhodes 1986: 377). The Thatcher Governments have shown little faith in consultative mechanisms.

As Stoker (1988, Ch. 6) argues, a breakdown in relations has occurred in a range of policy networks. Educationalists, housing officials and planners have found their domination of specialist policy debates challenged. Thatcherism has in a number of policy areas created a fluidity of ideas and challenged the consensus-style of many policy networks linking central government, quasi-government and local authority officials.

A further change is the extent to which the Conservatives have been prepared to engage in major constitutional changes with the minimum of consultation or of other procedures typically associated with such changes. As we shall see, the proposals to abolish the GLC and the six metropolitan counties were pushed through without any public inquiry, let alone the Royal Commissions and public debate which had accompanied previous reforms of local government. The setting-up of the Widdicombe Committee provides the sole exception to this general trend. But even here, as we shall see, the Committee's existence and findings were treated by the government in a cavalier way.

These changing patterns of consultation and enquiry have been accompanied by a significant change in the tone and language which Conservative ministers have used to describe local government. Statements including virulent criticisms, questioning of competence and contempt have become commonplace, particularly in the public utterances of Nicholas Ridley (see e.g. his contribution to the debate on the Queen's Speech: 105 HC Debs cols. 332–9, 17 November 1986).

The battle over the control of local spending

The Conservatives came to power in 1979 committed to a restructuring of public expenditure patterns. They wished to spend more on defence and social security (as a cushion for the rise in unemployment) and less on areas such as housing, education and social services. But as Travers explains:

> Therein lay a difficulty which plagued the Government from 1979 onwards in its relationship with local authorities. The Conservatives were committed to. cutting spending on services which were not under direct central control. Local authorities had the power to raise any rates they chose within the law, and could if they chose, spend more than the new administration wanted.
>
> (Travers 1986: 80)

In addition to this organisational dilemma, the Conservatives increasingly faced sustained ideological and behavioural opposition from a range of radical Labour councils, committed not just to protecting local government provision but determined to develop new policy responses to social and economic ills in direct challenge to the Conservatives' approach.

Two phases in the battle over local spending can be identified. The first, 1979–83, may be summed up as a 'dishonourable draw' the second, 1983–7, can be characterised as a retreat (on the part of local government) from campaigning to creative accounting. Major financial problems are now being faced, following the 1987 election result, by those Labour-controlled authorities which have relied heavily on 'creative accounting'.

1979–83: a dishonourable draw?

In the 1979–83 period the Conservative attack on local spending came in three waves. First, the Government introduced a new system for allocating central government financial support as part of the 1980 Local Government Planning and Land Act.

The 1980 legislation replaced the old system for supporting local authority current expenditure by a new Block Grant. Simplifying our description of the old system greatly, it operated on the basis of existing patterns of expenditure among local authorities – in other words, on the basis of local assessments of what is needed to be spent. The new Block Grant was distributed according to centrally-determined grant-related expendi-ture assessments, or GREs for short. Grants were to be distributed on the basis of an assessment of local need made by central government. This was a constitutional change 'of fundamental importance' (Newton and Karran 1985: 117). It was accompanied by a provision for 'grant taper' to discourage local authorities from spending much above the central assessment of their spending needs. This was soon followed by an automatic penalty-zone for authorities which spent more than 10 per cent (on average) above their assessed need figure. The 'extra' expenditure would have to be financed to an increasing extent out of the rates rather than from central government funds.

The Government's strategy soon encountered substantial difficulties. Government ministers even in the first year in which the new Block-Grant system operated (1981–2) decided that the controls it offered over local spending were insufficient. This led to a second line of attack.

The second wave in the Conservative offensive involved the introduction of an extremely complicated system of targets and penalties, as an additional element grafted on to the Block-Grant scheme. The first targets for spending were set for every authority in England in January 1981. The targets were established on a different basis from GREs and were backed by a system of penalties: if an authority chose to spend above target, its Block Grant would be cut. These penalties were known as 'hold-back'. The penalties were made increasingly severe each year so that by 1983–4 many authorities were in the position of receiving less grant in absolute terms, at higher spending levels. Some, for example, ILEA and the GLC, managed to spend their way out of any entitlement to grant. However, more typically the shifting system of targets and penalties made it extremely difficult for local authorities to plan effectively (Audit Commission 1984).

The third wave in the Conservative attack was signalled by the 1982 Local Government Finance Act. This Act followed the failure of an earlier Bill which had proposed that local authorities should hold a local referendum if they wished to raise a supplementary rate. Conservative backbench MPs and others expressed concern about the constitutional implications of such a proposal, and the Bill was dropped. The Act which replaced it contained three important elements. First, it legalised *retrospectively* the system of targets and penalties introduced in 1981 by the Government, and discussed above. Second, it dealt with the issue of supplementary rates and precepts by simply abolishing the right of local authorities to undertake those activities. Third, it established the Audit Commission to oversee the auditing of local authority finances and encourage 'value for money' from local spending.

This Conservative attack was greeted in a number of quarters by a spirited defence of democratic local government (see especially Jones and

Stewart 1985). The Local Authority Associations were highly critical and complained bitterly about the centralisation and loss of local autonomy associated with the Government's proposals. There was stiff opposition to major elements of the Local Government Planning and Land Act, even when the Associations were Conservative controlled. The 1982 Act was also vigorously opposed, with some minor concessions wrung from the Government (Travers 1986: 86–90, 111–12).

The main weapon adopted in practice by local authorities wishing to resist cuts in services during the period 1979–83 was to increase their rates. In addition, some authorities in 1981, including the GLC and Lambeth, used supplementary rates in order to enable them to fulfil their programmes. It was such strategies which stimulated the abolition of this option in the 1982 Act. Individual rate rises were often spectacular, especially if an authority was badly hit by 'hold-back'.

Local authorities putting up their rates were able to limit the electoral damage by blaming central government cuts in grant for high rate demands. The electoral fortunes of the Labour Party in such authorities indicated that raising of rates was not as electorally unpopular as some had feared (see Blunkett and Jackson 1987; Weir 1982).

In addition to putting up their rates, the other main weapon used by local authorities in this period was 'creative accounting'. From 1981–2 onwards, in order to protect themselves from the uncertainties of block grant, targets and penalties, local authorities began to build up their rate-fund balances (Travers 1986: 133). This gave them some room for manoeuvre. Special funds were also established and are described by Douglas and Lord (1986: 38) 'as the most widely-used kind of creative accounting'. The advantage of special funds lay in the fact they enabled local authorities to manipulate the incidence of spending as between years, thus avoiding penalties as far as possible and maximising income from central government grant. As Blunkett and Jackson (1987: 155) put it, creative accounting 'became a major form of political opposition'.

The struggle between central government and local authorities in the years 1979–83 has been described by a senior local authority officer as 'a dishonourable draw' (quoted in Travers 1986: 145). Capital spending was reduced, but current spending was not significantly cut. The Government did, however, succeed to an extent in transferring the burden of paying for services from central government to local ratepayers.

1983–7: from campaigning to creative accounting

The Government retained its commitment to controlling local authority expenditure on its re-election in June 1983. Indeed, it stepped up its propaganda against the overall level of local spending and the behaviour of particular Labour authorities seen as 'overspenders'. The system of targets and penalties, first introduced in 1981–2 was maintained and tightened.

This period also saw the introduction of a further weapon in the Government's armoury: rate-capping.

The 1984 Rates Act gave the Secretary of State for the Environment the power to limit both the rates of named authorities and reserve powers to limit the rates of all authorities. It is the former power, however, that was used, and in June 1984 the Government published a list of eighteen authorities who were to be rate-capped in 1985–6. All but two of the councils were Labour-controlled.

The rate-capped Labour authorities together with Brent, and supported by some heavily penalised but not rate-capped authorities (in particular Liverpool), launched a major campaign against rate-capping. With the option of raising rates to cover the loss of central government grant no longer open, these authorities decided that the time was ripe for concerted and public mobilisation against the Thatcher Governments' policies. Local campaigns aimed at drawing together three elements – the council, the workforce and the community. This was by no means a smooth exercise as the description of Sheffield's campaign by Blunkett and Jackson (1987: 176–81) makes clear. Nevertheless, a wide range of community groups and local authority workers were drawn into the protest.

By November 1984 the threatened local authorities had decided to adopt the 'no rate' rather than the 'deficit budget' strategy. But behind this apparent unity there was growing evidence of division (Lansley 1985; Blunkett and Jackson 1987). There was uncertainty about the objectives of the struggle. Some were looking to wring substantial concessions from the Government in the application of the Rates Act; others wanted to force the Government to withdraw the Act and restore central government financial support to previous levels.

In July 1984 the involved authorities agreed 'a strategy of non-compliance' and committed themselves to adopt one of two tactics: either refusing to make a rate for the next financial year or deficit budgeting (which involves deliberately planning a level of expenditure which cannot be met by known income). The campaign had both national and local dimensions.

Nationally an unprecedented degree of co-ordination was achieved by the campaigning authorities. Over the autumn of 1984 and the winter of 1984–5 the leaders of rate-capped authorities and other sympathetic councils met regularly. In public an impressive degree of unity was displayed and a number of highly successful campaign activities were launched.

Although in total fifteen authorities deferred setting a rate on 7 March, the collapse of the precepting authorities (GLC, South Yorkshire, Merseyside and ILEA) marked the beginning of a disorderly retreat. By 5 June all the authorities had set a legal rate, with the exception of Lambeth and Liverpool. These authorities finally set their rates in July, and their Labour councillors were served notice by the District Auditors that they were to face surcharges and expulsion from office (in both cases this occurred). The defiant stand of the councils had collapsed.

The campaign against rate-capping failed because of miscalculations about what could be achieved, both in terms of denting the resolve of the Government and maintaining unity and commitment among the Labour authorities. The Conservative Government was able to stand firm behind its legislation and its mandate. It maintained a reasonable degree of information about the state of the local authorities' campaign. And crucially in February 1985 it revised upwards the rate limits of six authorities – thereby lessening the necessity for the councillors from these authorities to maintain a position of outright defiance in order to protect their local spending levels.

The weakness of the Labour authorities revolved around two factors (Lansley 1985; Wheen 1985). First, there was the failure of the Parliamentary party leaders to provide effective leadership to the campaign. Second, there was a considerable lack of frankness and honesty among the local government leaders. On the one hand, it soon became clear that most of the Labour councillors involved were extremely unwilling to act illegally and thus incur surcharges, loss of office and possibly an end to their political careers. On the other, the dire consequences of rate-capping were greatly exaggerated for the purposes of the campaign. Jobs and services could be maintained, at least in the short-term, by a combination of creative accounting and other techniques.

The Conservatives kept the pressure on in terms of rate-capping. In 1986–7 twelve local authorities were selected plus ILEA and the joint boards established after the 1986 abolition. For the financial year 1987–8 the list of rate-capped local authorities swelled to nineteen. The Government also moved to outlaw various creative accounting techniques. The 1986 Local Government Act, for example, restricted the sale of mortgage debts. With the Conservative victory in the 1987 general election many Labour authorities, in London and elsewhere, believe they have reached the limits of creative accounting and are faced by the prospect of having to implement substantial cuts in jobs and services.

Despite their determination and legislative action, the Thatcher Governments of 1979–87 found themselves constrained by their lack of direct control over local government. Many local authorities – through their manipulation of financial information, creative accounting and by raising their rates (subject to selective limitation) – were able to fight a sustained rearguard action against central government.

The Thatcher Governments were able to pass more of the burden of paying for local government on to local ratepayers and away from central government, but they did not succeed in substantially reducing local current spending. Indeed, on the contrary, local authority current expenditure has continued to slightly increase in real terms.

The Conservatives have kept capital spending under control, continuing the trend established by the Labour Governments of the 1970s. Capital spending on housing, schools and road maintenance by local authorities remained at a low level compared to the pre-1975 period. Some minor shifts in the pattern of local authority current expenditure have occurred in line with the Conservatives' priorities. The proportion of current spending devoted to law, order and protection services for example, increased from 12 per cent to 14 per cent in England between 1978-9 and 1984-5. Yet the Government itself claims that overall it has only achieved modest success in holding back local spending and that its efforts have been 'accompanied by a worsening of the relationship between central Government and even the moderate and responsible local authorities' (1986 Cmnd 9714: 5).

A recognition of these factors, plus concern over the problems associated with the rate revaluation in Scotland, led the Conservatives to commit themselves to a further wholesale reorganisation of local government finance. This time the main target was the abolition of domestic rates. The Green Paper *Paying for Local Government* (1986 Cmnd 9714) proposed that domestic rates would be replaced by a 'community charge' which, in practice, would be a poll tax levied from every adult in the authority. A community charge proposed by an authority could be subject to 'capping' if central government felt that it was excessive. Non-domestic rates would be set by central government rather than local authorities. The yield from this rate would then be handed back to local authorities as a payment per adult. Further changes to the Block-Grant system and more far-reaching controls over capital expenditure were part of the package. Finally, there was a proposal that people supported by welfare payments should be obliged to pay at least a proportion of their community charge themselves. Legislation to introduce the new community charge and other associated measures in Scotland was passed during the 1986-7 session. To provide a similar scheme in England and Wales was a Conservative manifesto commitment for the 1987 election, despite considerable professional and other criticism concerning the impracticability and distributive consequences of introducing those financial reforms.

Inner-city policy

The Thatcher Government's approach to inner-city policy can be divided into three phases. In the 1979-82 period there was a maintenance of the status quo, modified only by a tightening of central controls and an early period of experimentation with Urban Development Corporations (UDCs). During the 1982-6 period there was a growing perception at the centre of the inadequacy of local authority dominated approaches to tackling inner-city problems, and signs of an increasing predisposition to by-pass local authorities. From 1986, and particularly following the 1987 general election, 'inner cities' have been high on the Government's policy agenda, and more radical changes both of policy and in the allocation of responsibility for inner-city action are anticipated.

After the first Thatcher Government was elected in 1979, there was an initial period of uncertainty over their attitude to the only recently initiated Labour policy for the inner cities. Peter Shore had in 1977 designated seven inner-city partnerships and fifteen inner-city programme authorities. An annual budget of £100 million (1979 prices) – 75 per cent grant-aided by central government – was established to finance projects aimed at revitalising inner-city areas. The underlying concept was one of 'partnership', with central government departments, county and district authorities, health authorities and the voluntary sector all involved in drawing up 'inner-city programmes'.

After a few months of deliberation, Michael Heseltine, then the Secretary of State for the Environment, decided to continue with his predecessor's new initiative, but modified it significantly in two ways. First, he reduced the level of local direction over the content of inner-city programmes by emphasising the importance of projects aimed at regenerating inner-city economies, at the expense of projects designed to plug gaps in social provision (see Leach *et al.* 1983). Second, he decided that in two areas – the obsolescent docklands areas of Liverpool and London – a new institutional device was needed to facilitate regeneration: the Urban Development Corporation.

The 'Urban Programme', the funding source used to support the new inner-city partnerships and programmes, has increased its size in real terms. Local authorities in inner-city areas have lost rate-support grant but have had the opportunity to make up some of the difference through this targeted funding. Parkinson and Wilks (1986: 300) estimate that within four years of 1979 the percentage contribution of urban programme funding to the budgets of partnership local authorities had doubled. This led to increasing conflicts over priorities, with central government attempting to encourage projects which stimulated an enterprise culture or supported business, and local authorities favouring, other groups and interests or looking to plug gaps left by cuts in rate-support grant.

The setting-up of the two dockland UDCs in 1981 provides an example of by-passing. In both cases, but particularly in London, the local authorities concerned opposed the change, especially in the light of the loss of planning control over large tracts of land ripe for development. The UDCs were appointed by central government and directly funded by the centre. They took over the task of ensuring urban regeneration from local authorities and have pursued private sector investment in tune with central government's policy approach. The London Docklands Development Corporation has been more successful in achieving a revival of private investment interest. In its first five years of operation it spent over £300 million of public money on land reclamation, infrastructure and site preparation. It claims to have attracted considerable private investment as a result. Parts of London's docklands have been transformed. But most observers agree that the local residents have not been the main beneficiaries of the changes. The jobs created have not been available to them and the houses built are too expensive for locals to afford (see Brindley *et al.* 1988).

Towards the end of Heseltine's time at the DoE there occurred the two periods of inner-city rioting (1981 and 1982). For a time it seemed as though these disturbances would provoke a reassessment of government inner-city policy and the injection of new resources into inner-city areas. Although these changes did not materialise, Heseltine's experience of inter-authority working in Merseyside, the area in which he personally became most involved, convinced him of the need for further 'by-pass' measures.

In 1983–4, 'task-force' teams of civil servants were established in a number of inner-city areas, following the adoption of this approach in Merseyside in 1982. In 1985 City Action Teams were established in the seven inner-city partnership areas to co-ordinate and target government effort. And in 1986 a programme of small task-forces within particular inner-city communities was launched with projects in the Highfields area of Leicester, Moss Side in Manchester, St Paul's in Bristol, and Handsworth in Birmingham, among other places.

By 1987 it was clear that the new Government had discounted the potential contribution of local authorities in inner-city areas and were determined to extend the process of by-passing and build up its own role in such areas. Five further UDCs were declared in 1986–7 in Teesside, Trafford, the Black Country, Cardiff Bay and Tyneside. The Conservatives' 1987 election manifesto contains a commitment to set up a series of 'mini-UDCs' in the near future, with a low level of funding but with the same objective of taking-over the process of urban regeneration from local authorities. Likewise the manifesto commits the Government to establishing a number of Housing Action Trusts to take over the renewal and management of rundown local authority estates. All of these new institutions will be appointed and funded directly by central government.

Local government structure and the abolition of the GLC and the metropolitan county councils (MCCs)

During its eight years in office, the Thatcher Government has never seriously considered a comprehensive restructuring of local government along the lines of the 1974 reorganisation, despite the profound cumulative effect of the various measures which it *has* introduced upon local government. Indeed, such a restructuring with its implications of Royal Commissions and rational reappraisals of existing and alternative systems would have few attractions to a government of conviction and action. None the less it did, in 1982, from a very different and quite atypical starting-point, embark on a reorganisation of local government structure in the metropolitan areas (including Greater London), which turned out to be one of the most problematical features of its 1983–7 legislative programme.

The origins of the proposal to abolish the GLC and the MCCs provide an illuminating example of the policy-making style of Thatcherism in relation to local government. (The details are usefully set out in Forrester *et al*. 1985, Ch. 4.) The idea of abolishing the GLC, although first mooted by a handful of Conservative MPs in the mid-1970s (K. Young 1984) was certainly not on the Government's agenda between 1979 and 1982. Then a Cabinet Committee – MISC 79 – which had been set up in 1982 to investigate alternatives to the rates as a source of local government finance, and was finding it impossible to identify any viable alternatives, produced a proposal that the GLC and the six MCCs should be abolished, the detailed justification for which appears to have been negligible. The Committee's proposal was well received by the Prime Minister, who had by then developed a profound antipathy to the activities of the Labour-controlled GLC, and to Ken Livingstone personally (although MISC 79 was required to re-attempt the search for an alternative to the rates). The proposal and its reception soon found its way into the press. It appeared that a system of local government which had existed in Greater London for only seventeen years, and in the metropolitan areas for a mere eight, was suddenly vulnerable.

Forrester and his colleagues also relate how the abolition proposal found its way into the 1983 Conservative manifesto (Forrester *et al*. 1985: 64–6). It seems that it was a little-discussed, last-minute insertion, bearing the personal stamp of the Prime Minister and reflecting the paucity of manifesto content concerned with local government issues. Michael Heseltine and Tom King, the DoE Secretaries of State in the 1979–83 period were known to regard the policy as counter-productive. Several other leading Conservatives were surprised by its appearance. However, the subsequent inclusion of the proposal in the 1983 Queen's Speech made it apparent that the new Government intended to implement the policy as a matter of high priority.

The spate of problems which were experienced by the Government in the legislative process which ensued can be seen partly as self-inflicted wounds. As O'Leary argues, controversy over the 'democratic' content of the proposed reorganisation, and in particular a proposal to cancel the GLC and MCC elections, which were due one year before the date earmarked for abolition, brought the Government's case into disrepute (O'Leary 1987: 197). The 1984 Local Government Paving Bill, which included this proposal, was defeated in the House of Lords in the summer of 1984. Concessions were made to the Department of Education and Science (resulting in the preservation of ILEA with a directly elected status) and to the arts and voluntary sector lobby (resulting in a series of one-off or tapering grants to safeguard its position). In the House of Commons debates over the 1985 Local Government Bill, which introduced the substantive abolition proposals, the Government (and Patrick Jenkin in particular) was given a harrowing time not only by the Opposition but also by several of its own supporters. Jenkin's own ministerial career was ended by his understandable difficulties in maintaining a convincing defence of the Bill's proposals. None the less, abolition eventually reached the statute books, as it was (almost) inevitable that it would, given the size of the Government's majority. One commentator referred to it as 'the most disgraceful act in seven years of Conservative rule in Britain' (Ascherson 1986).

There are several aspects of the policy-making style of the Thatcher Government which are vividly illustrated by the abolition process. First there is an unprecedented failure to embark on the collection and analysis of detailed evidence prior to a major constitutional change of this kind. Several elements of the origins of abolition have already been discussed: the throwing-up of an unsubstantiated proposal by a cabinet committee whose *raison d'être* lay in a quite separate field; the failure to set up any kind of Royal Commission or committee of inquiry; the reliance for the legitimacy of the proposal upon the briefest of manifesto statements, inserted at the last minute by the Prime Minister herself, against the advice of many in her cabinet, including the DoE ministers with direct experience of the field. In all these ways the normal constitutional procedures for introducing major changes of this kind were ignored or by-passed.

Second, there were a number of features about the way in which the legislative process progressed from White Paper to Act of Parliament which raise issues of constitutional concern. The extremely poor quality of the White Paper *Streamlining the Cities* was widely commented on. The case for abolition was asserted rather than demonstrated. Where evidence was used, it was used selectively and in ways which it was not difficult to discredit (Wheen 1985: 28–32). *Streamlining the Cities* clearly failed to meet the traditional criteria governing the quality of White Papers. But then given the origins of and basis for the proposal, it is difficult to see how it could have been otherwise. There followed a consultation period, in which the large number of responses, overwhelmingly critical in character (Forrester *et al.* 1985: 118), were subsequently almost entirely ignored. The Government, its mind made up, was clearly not going to be swayed by reasoned argument. In addition, the considerable doubts about the proposal which existed and indeed grew within the wider body of the Conservative Party, were summarily swept aside.

Throughout the process, the Government regularly departed from the normal canons of rational argument in taking forward the proposals. The main justifications for abolition in the public arena were switched opportunistically from politics to finance to arguments about superfluous tiers of government (Wheen 1985: 8–11) as circumstances changed. In so far as the justification was primarily a financial one (and that is certainly where the emphasis has been in the *post hoc* ministerial statements on abolition) there were always much simpler and more straightforward remedies available to the Government, to control 'wasteful expenditure', namely rate-capping and the trimming of s. 137 powers. Also unusual was the extent to which the Government ignored the wide array of detailed technical and financial arguments about the consequences of abolition stemming not just from the 'suspect' world of academics and professional bodies but also from management consultants frequently used by the Government itself (Coopers and Lybrand 1984, PA Management Consultants 1985) and ultimately from a House of Lords Select Committee on Science and Technology (1985). It is easy of course to hold unrealistic expectations about the role of rational argument in government policy-making and legislation. But normally at least the motions are gone through, and a minimum level of consistency and responsiveness to consultation and evidence displayed. Abolition was remarkable for the extent to which even this level of rationality was absent from the Government's stance.

Why then was all this thought to be worthwhile? As O'Leary has put it:

> Thatcher's Cabinet's refusal to bend to cost–benefit analysis on GLC abolition, and its willingness to send ministers out to defend the indefensible were fascinating folly. Firmness, the resolute approach, is considered essential, even in defence of the indefensible; consensual, rational approaches to decision-making . . . are regarded as excuses for doing nothing. . . . The price of such a style is repeated unintended and counterproductive outcomes for its supporters.
>
> (O'Leary 1987: 214)

Thus perhaps the most significant feature of abolition was the way in which the Government embarked upon (and sustained) a major policy initiative as an unintended and ill-considered byproduct of its other policies, particularly those concerned with local government expenditure and the subsidisation of public transport.

The politics of local government and the Widdicombe Committee

One of the more perplexing decisions of the 1983–7 Conservative Government was the setting-up of a committee of inquiry into 'the conduct of local authority business' – the Widdicombe Committee – at the 1984 Conservative Party Conference. The impetus for this action was widely recognised to be the increasing level of concern felt within the Conservative Party about the use being made by increasing numbers of local authorities of publicity – or 'propaganda' in the Government's view – campaigns against proposed central government actions. There were two areas of particular concern: the highly effective publicity material issued by the GLC (and to a lesser extent the MCCs), epitomised by the whole-page advertisements in leading daily papers featuring photographs of leading Conservative ministers, and the similar type of material used in the anti-rate-capping campaign. These publicity campaigns represented a further stage in the action–reaction chain of central and local behaviour, and a further heightening of the level of central–local conflict and the widening of its scope in the second period of Thatcherism.

In addition, concern was expressed at the 1984 Conservative Party Conference about the apparent abuse by certain (predominantly Labour-controlled) authorities of their powers. So-called 'abuses' such as 'one-party committees', 'political' appointments of senior staff, 'twin-tracking' (the increasing (?) phenomenon of councillors in one authority becoming officers in another, and vice versa) and the role of party groups, were highlighted. The activities of the Labour-controlled Liverpool council already constituted a *cause célèbre*. Measures to constrain the right of local authorities to engage in publicity, and perhaps also of a wider nature, were by autumn 1984 confidently anticipated.

Yet the form of the Government's response was a surprise. First the decision to set up, if not a Royal Commission, at least a departmental committee of inquiry, was for this Government unprecedented in relation to local government matters. In the climate of 'conviction politics', such measures had not previously been seen to be necessary, even in relation to so fundamental a structural change as the abolition of a whole tier of local government.

Second, in a situation where it was clear that the Government's main preoccupation was the use of publicity/propaganda, the terms of reference announced for the Widdicombe Committee were surprisingly broad, and indeed on the face of it, to some extent supportive of local government, namely 'to make any necessary recommendations for the strengthening of the democratic process' (Widdicombe 1986: 17). Third, the Committee appointed was fairly conventional in character, and with its inclusion of two ex-local government officers offered no guarantee of a perspective which would match the Government's own.

Having for once respected the unwritten constitution of central–local relations, the Government in its subsequent behaviour returned to its more familiar 'politics of conviction' style, in its disregard of the traditional rules of operation of such committees. The quality of the DoE submissions to the Committee both in relation to the interim report on publicity and the much more wide-ranging final report, was a good deal more politically partisan than is normally the case, being high on assertion and low on evidence. It has been described by Ken Young, the Widdicombe Committee research adviser, as 'a pastiche of any plausible critique of local government' (K. Young 1986: 27). When the Committee's relatively mild and unremarkable interim report was published in July 1985, with its main recommendation that local authorities should continue to be prevented from using publicity for the purposes of furthering the interests of a political party, as they already were anyway, the Government press statement proclaimed that the Committee's interim report had justified their concern about the use of publicity and the need for action. The release of this statement had the unusual consequence of a government-appointed committee denying that its report could reasonably be interpreted in the way its sponsoring department had claimed. The Committee had to issue a similar disclaimer statement in December 1985, when the then Secretary of State for the Environment, Kenneth Baker, made a speech in which he announced the Government's intention to legislate upon a number of local government 'abuses', some time before the Committee's report was published, and almost certainly without prior knowledge of the Committee's developing stance. The attempts to deal with local government publicity and propaganda, inserted into the 1985 Local Government Bill, but subsequently withdrawn because of drafting difficulties and the ground-clearing operation in the run-up to the 1987 general election, bore little relationship to the Committee's interim report, in terms either of the Bill's (implicit) analysis of the problem or of the content of its clauses on local government publicity.

When the Committee's final report was published, together with four substantial volumes of research evidence, in June 1986, it was referred to by Baker's DoE successor, Nicholas Ridley, as 'radical', and a four month long consultation period established. In the middle of this consultation period, during the 1986–7 session Queen's Speech, Ridley in an immoderate and polemical attack on 'abuses' supposedly being carried out by Labour-controlled councils made hardly a single reference to the major report his own department had published four months previously, and made a number of assertions which were inconsistent with the report's analysis and research evidence (e.g. the claim that such abuses were concentrated within a limited number of left-wing Labour authorities). In all these ways the traditional practices typically observed in the operations of committees of inquiry were departed from.

In the months following the consultation period, there was no evidence that the Government intended to take any action on Widdicombe. Then quite unexpectedly the 1987 Conservative manifesto turned out to contain *inter alia* a brief and undeveloped commitment to 'implement Widdicombe'. At the time of writing (January 1988) there is no indication of what this commitment is likely to involve, or when it is to be translated into action.

Conclusion

It is clear from the four examples discussed above that the climate and nature of the relationship between central and local government has changed radically over the period 1979–87. The Thatcher Government now perceives and reacts to local government in a way quite different from that of its predecessors – Conservative or Labour – in the previous half-century. In this concluding section we argue that the transformation of central–local relations reveals some of the key characteristics of Thatcherite politics and potentially provides the overture to a radical restructuring of the role of elected local government.

The Conservatives' dealings with local government have often taken the form of conviction politics. One of the difficulties with 'conviction' politics is that the predisposition to act quickly and decisively often proves incompatible with the need for careful analysis of the possible repercussions of proposed actions. The advantages of traditional consultation processes (including the use of committees of inquiry) is that they do provide 'early warning' of the unforeseen consequences of hastily concocted proposals and the opportunity both to persuade initially unwilling local authorities to co-operate and to refine and revise policies in the light of the further information gathered. In both the proposal to abolish the GLC and the MCCs, and the series of attempts to control local government expenditure, the Thatcher Government may conceivably have benefited, in the achievement of their objectives, from a reliance on traditional constitutional procedures.

A major element of this distinctive conviction politics has been the attitude of the Prime Minister herself. Her tendency to intervene personally in decisions which would traditionally have been either left to individual ministers or agreed collectively in cabinet, has already been discussed in connection with abolition and rate-capping, and is becoming apparent currently in the field of inner-city policy and in the decision to replace domestic rates with a community charge. In addition, the policy style of the Government has increasingly come to resemble that of the Prime Minister. O'Leary characterises that style in the following terms:

> The end of the GLC is better illuminated by social psychological insights... Thatcher has never been an impartial leader of her colleagues, and her government has consistently refused methodological procedures in policy formulation... academic images of Thatcherism play up interests, ideology or policy consistency... and omit the irreducible stylistic aspect of Thatcher's policy-making [which is] Nietzschean policy-making, heroic and designed to transform values.
>
> (O'Leary 1987: 214)

As illustrated elsewhere in this volume (see Ch. 1) the 'irreducible element of personal style' is an important component of analysis in understanding Thatcherite policy-making processes.

The metaphor of a 'chain reaction' is appropriate to describe the way that policy has developed. Within the specific field of local government finance, as we have seen, there has been a series of actions and reactions as (some) local authorities have tried to evade or manipulate the sequence of attempts by the centre to control their expenditure levels. But just as important, it is clear that experiences in one policy area have sparked off changes in another. For example, the proposal to abolish the GLC and the metropolitan county councils was *inter alia* a response to the perceived 'overspending' of (some of) these councils, both in general and with particular reference to the subsidisation of public transport. The decision to set up the Widdicombe Committee was in turn partly a response to the effectiveness of the campaign organised by the GLC (and to a lesser extent the MCCs) to preserve their existence in the light of the abolition proposals.

Central intervention in local government has increased – that is the sheer number of times that Whitehall interferes – but it is far from clear that central control has been achieved in the sense of the centre achieving its objectives. The successes and failures of central intervention in finance, inner-cities policy, and abolition have been considered in this chapter. What emerges is a picture of increased control but over a narrow range of matters. Moreover, along with control has come unintended consequences, ambiguity and uncertainty. Resistance from local authorities has also been stiffened and politicised.

Indeed a recognition of the limits and contradictions of their earlier interventions lies behind the major programme of reforms launched by the Conservatives after their third election victory in 1987. The restructuring of local government finance and the abolition of the rates are an admission that the manipulation of central government grants and rate-capping have not achieved the regulation of local spending which the Conservatives desired. Legislation to force a range of local authority services out to competitive tender – including refuse collection, street and building cleaning, school meals and vehicle maintenance – indicates that earlier efforts at persuading local authorities to choose this option were, by and large, a failure. The major reforms of housing and education services are premised on the view that previous interventions have only tinkered with the perceived inadequacies of these services and that what is required is a root-and-branch reform. Again the development of inner-cities policy to the point where its rationale is to by-pass local authorities through UDCs and Housing Action Trusts, represents a Government perception of the failure of past policies which have worked through local authorities.

There appears also to be a growing confidence in a New Right vision associated with the post-1987 election package. Out of the Government's experience of piecemeal action and reaction has come a new coherent view of the role of local government in Britain. It is a minimalist vision of local government, in which the market is relied upon for an increasing number and range of services previously regarded as appropriate for direct provision by local authorities. Housing, education and welfare needs, it is contended, are better met through the private sector. Private enterprise and investment are seen as offering a better future for our inner cities than state intervention and planning.

Where the private sector cannot provide there is a commitment to approximating market conditions to guide the remaining public provision. Market mechanisms to be developed within the public sector involve particular forms of competition, choice and accountability. Competition between local authority producers and private contractors underlies the competitive tendering legislation. Choice is on offer in the reforms of education and housing. It is a market form of choice premised on the ability to go somewhere else if a particular service is perceived as unsatisfactory. For such exit options to be offered, existing local government bureaucracies have to be reconstituted on a fragmented, mutually competitive basis. Thus tenants on local housing estates are to be given the right to pick a landlord other than the local authority, with the aim of creating a greater diversity of provision within the public sector. Parents are to be offered increased choice over which school to send their children to, and local education authorities are to have their 'monopoly' position challenged by allowing schools to opt out of local authority control, through the development of City Technology Colleges and, in the case of Inner London, the break-up of ILEA. The final watchword of the reform programme is 'accountability', and what is offered is a particular form of market accountability premised on the view that we should pay for what we get. This is the rationale of the community charge and underlies the commitment to higher rent levels in housing provision and the increased use of charges for other local authority services.

The reform package has major implications for local government. It fundamentally challenges the role of the local authority as a large-scale, dominant service provider. If the Thatcherite vision becomes a reality, elected local authorities will be just one element in a fragmented, competitive system of local administration. The reform package also implies depoliticisation: local government political and electoral mechanisms for making choices are to give way to the superiority of market mechanisms for allocating goods and services. There is a strong possibility that by the end of the third term of Thatcherism, local government will have become transformed from a significant political institution, playing a major 'checks and balances' role premised on the value of diffusing power, to an emasculated and increasingly apolitical adjunct to the centre. The capacity for local choice through collective action, directed by the processes of representative democracy, will be lost. The ability of local authorities to raise substantial local revenues will be undermined by the removal of business rates from local control and the dominance of central government grant and targeted funding. The capacity for local strategic choice will be undercut by the fragmentation of existing service delivery on a competitive basis.

The transformation of central–local relations, described in this chapter, could be followed by a comprehensive restructuring of the role of elected local government.

The material impact of the Government's reform package on jobs, services and household incomes has rightly attracted considerable attention. The debate surrounding the community charge alone has produced a multitude of competing claims about who will be winners and who will be losers. We would argue, however, for some consideration to be given to the political and constitutional implications of the Government's reform package. Do we want to see the capacity for effective collective action at a local level ebb away? Are we prepared to see the opportunity for political and electoral choice reduced to determining the composition of the national government every four or five years? Jones and Stewart comment, 'Our belief is that local government is a vital part of our constitution, worth defending and worth reforming so that it can fully realise its potential as a major component of truly democratic government' (Jones and Stewart 1985: Intro). In broad terms the present authors share this view. The challenge, as we see it, is to develop the argument for effective and responsive elected local government. We need to clarify the respective roles of central and local government and allow scope for local discretion and choice. We need to consider how to improve the capacity of local authorities for collective intervention and provision in a way that maximises their responsiveness to the public both as customers and citizens.

7

Privatisation: Local Government and the Health Service

Bruce Wood

Introduction: defining privatisation

Privatisation as the wholesale disposal to the private sector of public sector assets (the focus of Ch. 5 on the nationalised industries) is not the dominant characteristic in the cases of local government and the health service. Instead, we need a broader definition, centring on various alternative means by which local authority and health services have been exposed to market forces. Sometimes that exposure has been voluntary, sometimes involuntary. Councils and health authorities, more than 700 quite separate institutions, have varied in their attitudes towards privatisation. Some have refused (in the case of councils) or dragged their feet (health authorities), whilst others have been enthusiastic in their pursuit of 'privatisation' in the 1980s.

Definitions of, and methods of, privatisation abound. A full-length study might well examine all of Stephen Young's sevenfold classification. This ranges from the selling-off of public assets (discussed in Ch. 5 above), through contracting-out, to increased charges. All seven are designed to alter the balance and relationship between the public and private sectors (S. Young 1986: 236–45). Pirie goes further, giving twenty-one methods, the majority of which apply to local government and the health service (Pirie 1985).

Space alone makes it necessary to concentrate on a small section of Young's or Pirie's approach. It is important, however, to understand that a comprehensive study would embrace a whole range of policies not always seen as 'mainstream privatisation'. The twelvefold increase from 20p to £2.40 in prescription charges between 1979 and 1987, for example, falls within Young's seventh category; the importation of a top industrialist to advise on the management of the NHS (the Griffiths Report which led to the appointment of general managers) relates to his sixth; while the use of public funds to attract private sector investment into the inner cities (e.g. through Urban Development Grants) falls within his fifth category.

In this chapter the focus is largely on two forms of privatisation which, together, are commonly viewed as the main thrust of the policy in relation to local government and the health service. Most emphasis is on 'contracting-out', a policy designed to bring market pressures to bear on traditional public sector monopolies. Cleansing, catering and vehicle and building maintenance are common types of local or health authority service where public sector employees have not normally had to compete with private firms, and these are usually referred to collectively as support services. Some attention is also given to a second major form: that of altering the balance of service provision between the public and private sectors through policies such as the sale of council houses, disposal of land and encouragement of parallel service provision by the private sector (buses, schools, hospitals, old people's homes and so on). Even after focusing on just two forms of privatisation, it is still not possible to provide a comprehensive coverage of the empirical detail, due to the sheer scale of material. In addition, the shape of the second form is currently undergoing marked change as a result of legislation reforming housing tenancy and the structure and organisation of education.

Some major events: local government

Privatisation has been continually in the news in the 1980s. The major disposals like Telecom, Gas and the Airports have been seen by the media as front-page stories, with a mass of column inches every few months. But overall there have been many more column inches about council house sales and bus deregulation. Indeed, from 1979 to 1982 the sale of council houses alone contributed more money to public funds than did denationalisation (C. Evans 1985: 104). News events are frequent, and the flow of Government policy has been just as continuous (albeit in many different forms) as has been its policy on regular asset sales.

Apart from a pledge to sell council houses, the 1979 Conservative election manifesto made little reference to privatisation. It was, in fact, in the field of local government that the policy really got under way. The year 1980 saw three major pieces of legislation relating to privatisation in local government. Under the Local Government Planning and Land Act 1980 local authority direct labour departments were forced to compete against private builders for contracts over which they had normally had a monopoly. Furthermore, these departments were required to make a certain rate of return on their assets in their annual accounts. Failure to be 'profitable' could lead to a ministerial order of closure. Hence Lambeth Borough Council was, for example, ordered to close down its new building section in August 1987 due to repeated financial losses. The order banned the council from undertaking any further large-scale construction projects worth more than £1 million.

The Housing Act 1980 gave more than 5 million tenants the 'right to buy' their home from their local authority landlord, and gave the minister powers to offer both discounts and send in commissioners should a local authority be obstructive. In the case of Norwich, he did send in a commissioner, and the courts confirmed his default powers. Nationally, around 1 million council houses had been sold by the end of 1980, with discounts of 60 per cent being commonplace (the discounts were raised to keep the momentum of sales going after the first year or two). Arguably, it was the success of this policy which made privatisation attractive to the government (D.S. King 1987: 123).

Third, the Transport Act 1980 made it easier for new private operators to gain licences to compete with municipal and public sector buses. That they did not always succeed is clear from the case of Cardiff, where CK Coaches ceased operations after only two years due to intense pressure from the city and the county councils, and from the TGWU (C. Evans 1985: 100–4). However, the deregulation policy which underlay this Act was later developed much further, and in 1986 major changes in bus service provision took place (commonly termed 'deregulation'), thus ending the virtual monopoly in many areas of councils or of the National Bus Company.

Given these major legislative initiatives, it seems odd that ministers did little to enforce the contracting-out of local authority support services until June 1987. While Southend and, later, Wandsworth received a great deal of publicity because of their diligent pursuit of privatisation, the vast majority of local authorities either ignored exhortations from ministers to contract-out or drew back in the face of trade union opposition both locally and at TUC level (see e.g. T. Williams 1983; TUC 1984). Until 1984, when a Private Member's Bill showed ministers that large numbers of backbench Conservatives were demanding action, the Government was reluctant to legislate. Local government finance Bills and, later, the Bill abolishing the GLC and metropolitan counties were regularly consuming large amounts of parliamentary time and ministerial energy. Kate Ascher also believes that the likelihood of councils finding loopholes in any legislation was a further deterrent (Ascher 1987: 38–9). This was certainly the experience of Health Ministers, who were having difficulty in getting health authorities to comply with their instructions, as well as of Environment Ministers, who had had to do battle in the courts as well as the Commons over house sales, grant penalties and rate-capping.

Chope's Private Member's Bill (Christopher Chope, incidentally, had been Leader of Wandsworth Council, privatising pioneer, before entering Parliament in 1983) was the catalyst for action. A February 1985 Green Paper – in effect White rather than Green – promised legislation (DoE 1985, para. 7). Drafting difficulties and a lack of parliamentary time prevented legislation in 1986–7, to the annoyance of many Conservative backbenchers. The 1987 Local Government Bill was published in June, immediately after Mrs Thatcher's election victory. It seeks to enforce competition in relation to seven support services – collection of refuse, cleaning of buildings; other cleaning; catering for schools and welfare; other catering; maintenance of ground; repair and maintenance of vehicles. The minister is to have default powers, rather like the housing case discussed earlier, and he will also be able to add to the list of seven services. Universal competitive tendering seems, at last, to be imminent in local government.

Some major events: health service

The NHS has experienced more policy changes in relation to Young's seven categories of privatisation than it is possible to list in detail here. Prescription and dental charges have risen regularly, twice in both 1979 and 1980, from then on once each year. Optical services have been deregulated, and glasses can now be purchased from supermarkets and even garages, though eye tests can still only be performed by NHS contractors. Health authorities have been encouraged to sell surplus land, as well as any surplus residential accommodation for nurses and doctors, and to co-operate with the private sector. For example, in its 1985 Annual Report the DHSS expressed the view that 'it makes sense to use the spare capacity in the private sector to tackle the perennial problems of long waiting lists for non-urgent operations', and many health authorities did this in 1987 when they received one-off additional funds to reduce waiting lists in a Government decision during the run-up to the general election.

On the contracting-out of support services there was initially a good deal of scepticism among health authorities (Ascher 1987: 27–31). Three DHSS actions were designed, at least in part, to overcome this hurdle. The replacement of many regional and district health authority chairmen appointed in the late 1970s by the Labour Government ensured that authorities had a more sympathetic leadership, as did the vetting of the new general managers who were on short-term contracts. Circular HC (83) 8, issued in 1983, in effect instructed health authorities to seek tenders. It followed a series of draft circulars which had been ignored by many authorities. Now Regional Health Authorities were told that they must draw up a timetable for the tendering process, and ensure that every District Health Authority also drew up a timetable with completion by late 1986 as the target. Finally, ministers promised, as an incentive, that 'efficiency savings' which stemmed from contracting-out would be kept by the health authority. All in all, then, here was a classic policy mix of strategic appointments, carrots and sticks. Nevertheless, by November 1986 about one-third of tenders had still not been issued (Radical Statistics Health Group 1987: 123).

Constitutional status of local and health authorities

This very brief history of the development of privatisation policy has already revealed a difference in the approach adopted by the two main ministries, Environment and Health and Social Security, which relate to local government and to health authorities respectively. Environment has had to rely almost exclusively on legislation in its pursuit of privatisation, legislation which instructs local authorities to implement the policy and which contains strong default powers usable against any recalcitrants. In the case of bus deregulation the Department of Transport also used Acts of Parliament. Health Authorities, on the other hand, have been pressured into acceptance of privatisation through exhortation, changes in management systems, and Circulars: legislation has not been utilised, nor is it contemplated.

This contrasting approach reflects the differing constitutional status of local authorities and of health authorities, rather than any traditions of the ministries concerned or concern with constitutional principles. Indeed, both Environment and Health and Social Security have traditions of negotiation and consultation, rather than of instruction and coercion. In the 1960s the then Ministry of Health was described as offering a *laissez-faire* style of leadership to its local agencies (Griffith 1966: 515–28), and it was only in the 1970s that the merger to form a giant department began to change the style of management, partly because social security, a major aspect of the new department's work, is a rule-bound service which operates through a command hierarchy with limited autonomy given to local managers. Nevertheless, the tradition of cajoling health authorities, of promoting new policies and of operating through carrots coupled with potential sanctions (such as reduced budgetary allocations) continues to dominate. Major legislation on the NHS is normally avoided if an alternative approach can be found.

It is clear that the traditional preference of the Department of the Environment is also to avoid contentious legislation. The history of negotiation and discussion is a long one, with the associations of local authorities offering one of the clearest examples that there is of what is often described as 'consultative status'. The right of these associations to be consulted is even enshrined in many Acts of Parliament (e.g. the Secretary of State has to consult before determining the allocation of the Rate-Support Grant, the major grant paid to local authorities). In the case of town planning the norm is also to negotiate, this time with individual local authorities, before a structure plan or a significant proposed change of policy is approved: Griffith detected a *laissez-faire* approach here, too, in the 1960s. The use of coercive legislation, which inevitably means confrontation between the Department and local government, is largely a creature of the 1980s (see Leach and Stoker, Ch. 6 above), and it has been suggested that this is not an approach which finds much favour with senior civil servants (Wilks 1987). The new style of managing local authorities is one which has come from ministers anxious to implement controversial policies with some speed.

That Environment (and Transport) ministers have had to move away from tradition and increasingly utilise legislation, whereas Health ministers have not, reflects the different legal status and division of power between centre and periphery. Local authorities are, or local government is, elected locally. Those elected as councillors are accountable locally to the voters of the district, borough or county. They have to, literally, stand up and be counted every four years (this being the term of office for all councillors). More important, they owe no immediate loyalty or commitment to any Whitehall minister or department; indeed, they are very likely to view 'Whitehall' as potentially, and probably actually, obstructive. This is because councillors are likely to have ideas which they find unimplementable due, in part at least, to a lack of legal powers or of resources.

These remarks apply to all councillors. Party politics adds to their significance. The large urban councils in particular are mostly controlled by the Labour Party. Partisan issues – and privatisation is certainly one – find the existence of a local set of 'oppositions' which can be far more influential in affecting what actually happens to policy ideals than can Labour's parliamentary opposition. In addition, it is unlikely that all local councils controlled by the Conservatives will support wholeheartedly every detail of every Thatcher Government policy. Thus, for example, opposition to the compulsory sale of council houses came from many rural councils, controlled by the Conservatives. Such councils viewed the loss of village council houses as very serious, particularly in areas where house prices are high: the retiring farm labourer in his tied cottage would no longer be able to stay in his village if the council houses had been sold, nor would young families be able to be housed in the village of their family and upbringing. The 1987–8 legislation on housing, education, competitive tendering and the poll tax has again seen much Conservative unrest.

The implementation of privatisation therefore rested in the hands of elected councils, many of which were completely hostile to the policy whilst others had reservations about the details and the consequences even if they were broadly in favour of the principle. Successive Secretaries of State for the Environment understandably utilised and continue to utilise legislation, despite the inevitable consequences of such a strategy. Loopholes would be sought, feet would be dragged, and much energy would be needed in the face of an onslaught from large numbers of the 450 or so borough, district and county councils. Such are the costs of embarking on policies of confrontation rather than of consensus, costs which have been most apparent in the field of local government spending, where the discovery of loopholes has caused Local Government Finance Bills to be an annual event.

Regional and district health authorities, totalling just over 200, are very different bodies from elected councils. Crucially, they are appointed rather than elected. The Secretary of State appoints (and pays almost £10,000 a year) to the chairmen. He also appoints the remaining unpaid members of each Regional Health Authority, while other District members are appointed by the RHA, with the exception of 25 per cent, who are nominees of the local authorities in the area. At first sight, then, it is not difficult for government to ensure health authority support for its policies through judicious use of patronage.

In practice this presents an oversimple view of health authorities. In 1979 the Thatcher Government inherited authorities appointed by its predecessor. It also inherited a tradition under which preceding governments had always sought to at least give the impression of not using these powers of patronage to overtly pack appointed boards with 'card carrying party members'. Consequently, it took some years to rid health authorities of unsympathetic chairmen, and most still have something of a cross-section of members (not just because of council nominees). It is also too simple to assume that health authority chairmen and members will have overriding loyalty to national policy. Local people, they will reflect the traditions, needs and demands of their area and be subject to immediate local pressures. The use of direct labour to provide catering, cleaning and other support services is one such tradition; the expansion of the NHS another. Interestingly the former, the employment of direct labour, is actually a much more widespread tradition than is the case in local government. In the 1960s, for example, some sixty-four councils (out of 1,364 at that time, before the 1974 amalgamations) employed private contractors for their refuse collection (Ascher 1987: 217), and there are many other pre-1980s examples of the use of contractors after competitive tendering (see e.g. Minogue and O'Grady 1985: 35–7). In contrast, only one small London teaching hospital has a long tradition of using private contractors.

Because health authorities are appointed, they can also be collectively dismissed. Normally 'dismissal' is confined to the non-reappointment of a chairman or member at the expiry of his or her term of office. Collective dismissal has so far happened only once since the reorganisation of 1974: the then Labour Secretary of State dissolved the Lambeth, Southwark and Lewisham Area Health Authority when it refused to keep within its allocation of monies during the early years of financial restraint. Since 1985 there has been talk of further dissolutions as the local loyalty of some chairmen and members makes it hard for them to accept the need to close wards or hospitals in order to keep within budget. No government can assume complete loyalty from the beneficiaries of its patronage.

Nevertheless, on competitive tendering in particular, policy implementation is likely to be easier in the NHS because of the difference of constitutional status as between local government and health authorities. All manner of administrative pressures might need to be exerted semi-privately, but in the end, few, if any, health authorities are likely to be totally defiant. If they were, they could be dissolved. Hence implementation by Circular and by other informal means is feasible, thus saving parliamentary time and reducing the scope for bitter national public debate centring on the floor of the House of Commons. Relatively, health service privatisation is a private, closed process, whereas restructuring the role of local government is an open one. Though both health and local authorities are established by statute, this contrast implies and reflects a different 'constitutional status' for local government.

Implementing privatisation

It is now clear that local authorities are likely to range from 'enthusiastic supporter' to 'root and branch opponent' in their attitudes to the policy of privatisation, while health authorities are more likely to range only as far along any continuum as 'doubter, reluctant acquiescence'. In both cases there is certainly a variety of basic attitudes to be found, and patchy implementation can be anticipated.

It is this variety that government departments have to handle. In the case of local government the response has been to include default powers in Bills, with the hope that the threat of those powers being used will bring the recalcitrants to heel. In practice the tactics of opponents of privatisation have to centre on delay and a search for loopholes rather than on outright refusal to implement. Hence Norwich, the one case where a team of civil servants was sent in to sell council houses, based its unsuccessful appeal to the High Court on the allegation that government was expecting it to devote disproportionate resources to the provisions of the Housing Act 1980 (C. Evans 1985: 107). Its legal failure, and the subsequent presence of a single civil servant as 'commissioner' until 1985, meant only a small delay in getting sales under way. By 1983 some 5 per cent of Norwich's council houses had been sold, a proportion no lower than found in many other cities.

The privatisation of refuse collection and other support services offers a far more fascinating view of implementation, for here it has so far been an entirely voluntary exercise. Only those local authorities who actually wanted to privatise needed to proceed. Southend was the 1980s pioneer, but was far from unique in having a 'task and finish' system whereby, with better technology, bin-men were able to finish their day's work quickly and, with a rigid agreement, the council was unable to avoid paying them overtime to get the bins of new houses emptied. The winter of 1978–9 brought things to a head. It saw a series of strikes nationally which led to the downfall of the Labour Government in the May 1979 general election, and it gave Southend Council (and many others in a similar situation) an even stronger case to take on the unions which had refused several times to alter the 'task and finish' agreement. With public opinion apparently on its side, Southend was at last able to tackle the unions and, after obtaining five outside tenders plus one from the workforce, it employed Exclusive

Cleansing Services Ltd to collect refuse and clean the streets (C. Evans 1985: 98–100).

In the event, not many authorities followed Southend in actually privatising refuse collection or any other services. Wandsworth is probably the best known: it privatised fifteen activities after seeking tenders for as many as twenty-three, but at least seven of the fifteen could all be subsumed under the single heading 'cleaning' (Ascher 1987: 239). Thus between 1981 and 1986 some fifty-six tenders for refuse collection or street cleaning were issued by district councils, with twenty-nine being awarded to private contractors and twenty-seven to the in-house tenderers (D.S. King 1987: 125). In addition, sometimes the tendering process was not reached, but its mere threat led to union agreements on working practices being renegotiated. Thus the extent of privatisation as measured by the number of contracts awarded to the private sector (about 350 by mid-1987 according to PULSE, the Public and Local Service Efficiency Campaign, a pro-privatisation pressure group) does not necessarily reflect the full impact of the policy. According to PULSE, some 160 out of 450 local authorities have privatised at least one service or activity.

Inevitably implementation has been more marked in the health service, where the issuing of tenders for support services has now been expected of health authorities for five years. The earlier introduction, in 1982, of a review system has helped the Department to maintain pressure on individual health authorities. Under the review system each regional chairman meets about twice a year with the minister to consider the activities of the RHA during the period since the previous meeting. This results in an 'action plan' for the next six months, with progress towards tendering being inevitably one item in that plan. Within each region there are similar review meetings, this time between the regional chairman and individual district chairmen; again action plans result, and the privatisation momentum is sustained.

In the case of privatisation, DHSS monitoring was even more regular than this. Every three months RHAs had to send in details of progress towards competitive tendering in each of the districts. In addition, the 1983 Circular laid down a very clear target date of September 1986 for the completion of the process. However, despite this target, and despite the regular monitoring system, progress did not match the 1983 expectations. By September 1986 only 68 per cent of tenders had been issued, and only 43 per cent of support services had actually had contracts awarded (National Audit Office 1987: 1–2). Factors causing delay were seen by the Comptroller and Auditor-General to be 'underestimation by health authorities of the work involved in the tendering process, demands on management time, and authorities' concern about the impact of the initiative on industrial relations'. Certainly this last point is valid in explaining delay. It was tactically sensible for an authority to take its time before inviting tenders so that it could point out to its staff that it had had to be pushed somewhat unwillingly into the activity by its masters at region and in the department, and that it had been anxious to safeguard its employees' interests as far as it possibly could.

The impact of privatisation

If the speed and extent of implementation of privatisation is hard to measure (and the 350 contracts listed by PULSE include some oddities and trivia such as Salisbury's dog warden, Somerset's photographic processing and the sale of a single house in Enfield), then its actual impact is even more difficult to assess with any confidence or precision. Impact can be measured in at least three ways – the effects on people, on finance and on the quality of service. Material on the third, service quality, is patchy, largely anecdotal and always of doubtful validity because its source is often connected with extreme views for or against privatisation. How clean is Southend? Is Bromley's hospital food good? Are there fewer rats in Dover since Rentokil won the contract for pest control? Are the sheets now better laundered in Newcastle's hospitals? Such questions indicate the difficulty of measuring impact.

The workforce has been affected in several ways. Health authorities have spent £11.1 million in redundancy payments (National Audit Office 1987: 2), but we cannot assume that all recipients are unhappy at losing their job. Indeed, policies of voluntary redundancy have often produced a surplus of volunteers, whilst other contracts have seen former NHS staff being re-employed by the private contractors. On the other hand, it is also apparent that consequences of privatisation do often include fewer full-time jobs (because contractors prefer to employ part-timers, to save on national insurance), lower rates of pay (particularly when the bonus systems which have proliferated in the public sector are taken into account), and reduced holiday and sickness rights. In addition, part-timers may have less protection under Employment Acts, depending on their exact hours, particularly in the first five years of their employment.

The financial impact of privatisation is a little easier to measure, though caution is again necessary. The 'savings' announced by local or health authorities and by ministers may not include redundancy costs, or expenditure on management posts necessary to monitor the performance of contractors. The costs of drawing-up detailed tenders may or may not be estimated. Savings estimates may also assume no hiccups and will be based on estimates of what *might* have been the costs had there been no contract. Behind apparently neat figures will lie many assumptions.

That having been said, PULSE estimates that contracting-out has led to savings of £21.6 million per annum by local authorities in the case of the 200 contracts (out of 350) for which estimates are available. Clearly this is an underestimate, with 150 gaps and with many other savings made from changes in working practices caused by the very threat of privatisation, as we saw earlier. The Audit Commission has gone much further in identifying potential savings of up to £150 million per annum available to local authorities in just the three fields of housing maintenance, refuse collection and vehicle maintenance (Audit Commission 1987).

NHS financial savings reached £86 million per annum by the end of 1986, and the expected savings, when the competitive tendering exercise, launched in 1983, is finally completed, total £120–140 million. These figures reflect an average saving of some 20 per cent, with cleaning contracts at a higher level, but catering at only about 10 per cent because food and provisions are a significant part of the budget (National Audit Office 1987). The Audit Commission's estimate of above £500 million for local authorities appears to be based on a very similar percentage of potential savings.

These estimates of savings from privatisation do not just relate to contracts where private contractors have succeeded in replacing direct public sector provision of a service. Indeed, in the NHS, in-house teams have been increasingly effective in submitting low-cost tenders, and this, coupled with a certain lack of interest in NHS work, has led to the vast majority of contracts going to the present staff. Whereas in the first quarter of 1985 some 55 per cent of all tenders were awarded to the private sector, the proportion was a mere 8 per cent by autumn 1986 (National Audit Office 1987: 2). Thus the potential is there to match the levels of savings which private contractors can offer. though this usually means an in-house tender including reductions in staff numbers and staff costs. This ability to match the private sector has also been found in local government, in a survey of refuse collection cost savings (Domberger, Meadowcroft and Thompson 1986). The former director of the Audit Commission confirmed that the privatised refuse collection system in Southend was no more efficient than Sheffield's direct labour service.

Whether measured by money, by service quality or by human happiness, the impact of privatisation is significant. Its potential future impact is now also apparent, for the Local Government Bill 1987 will, when enacted, force every local authority to put seven services out to tender. Health service ministers are already talking publicly about the next stages of privatisation, covering services such as hospital portering, non-urgent ambulances, pathology laboratories and radiology. What began in the early 1980s as an exercise in bins, laundries and cleaning could develop in the early 1990s into a pattern of service provision scarcely yet even contemplatable. As one Conservative backbencher remarked during the second reading of the Local Government Bill 1987: 'He [the Secretary of State for the Environment] would like local authorities to meet once a year to award tenders then pack up and go home'. Teresa Gorman, MP for Billericay and active in the PULSE campaign, later tabled an unsuccessful amendment increasing the number of services covered by the Bill from seven to more than forty.

This is a view of local government far removed from the tradition of service provision or of what Minogue and O'Grady (1985: 35) describe as a 'welfare contract'. So, too, is the view of the NHS as a service using private radiologists, pathologists and possibly surgeons and hospitals. But these views are not the 1987 equivalent of science fiction. General practitioners and dentists are already self-employed people, holding a contract with a Family Practitioner Committee. Some local authorities already use neighbours to provide a service for them. Indeed, both these examples are long-standing. It is, therefore, at least possible that the local and health authorities and services of the future will be very different from those with which we are familiar. The constitutional consequences of privatisation, already significant, though little discussed, deserve long and careful consideration. Four such consequences are the prime concern of the remainder of this chapter: accountability and control; the role of the courts in the provision of local services; the impact on trade unions; and the nature of local agencies responsible for service provision. Each will be considered in turn.

Accountability and control

Public sector (and, ultimately, the general public's) control over the provision of basic components of the welfare state, such as housing, is clearly affected by several types of privatisation which were discussed earlier in the chapter. The selling-off of, currently 1 million, council houses reduces the stock available for letting to families in need of cheap rented accommodation. This is particularly true because councils have not been allowed to spend most of their income from sales on the building of replacement houses. Whilst sales have run at an average of close to 150,000 per annum, council new building has been reduced to well under 40,000. Control over bus services has been partly removed from local authorities, who now have to rely on the power of the purse through route subsidies to influence the level of services. Under current legislation, tenants will be able to choose a landlord, and schools will be able to 'opt out' of local authority control.

Contracting-out also changes the pattern of control. Direct control over managers, staff, equipment and service levels is replaced by indirect control. Wage rates and gradings are no longer determined by the local or health authority. Complaints about the quality of services cannot be handled immediately but must be referred to the contractor, with a request for an explanation. Newly appointed or elected authorities cannot change the pattern of service provision until contracts become due for renewal or cancellation, unless there is a clear breach of contract taking place or the contract can be renegotiated with the agreement of the contractor.

These and some other more detailed arguments have been rehearsed at length and frequently in health and local authorities up and down the country. They are, of course, part of the debate about the advantages and disadvantages of privatisation and they need to be placed alongside the case for the policy – the value of competition, the financial savings, efficiency and so on.

Important here is the impact of new forms of control on local government's accountability. The accountability of the workforce is altered in that workers relate to a new employer – the contractor. Any grievances they may have will no longer go through the public sector grievance procedures involving appeals committees of councillors (or health authority members). This applies particularly to pay and gradings, where there is no comparable industrial tribunal to which private sector workers can have recourse, or Whitley council system at which basic pay and conditions are jointly negotiated by management and unions. Councils can no longer redeploy or reorganise workers or services and can only change the level or quality of provision after negotiating new contracts. Demands from the electorate for change cannot be met directly.

Accountability is an issue in some activities or services more than in others. Where it is clear who is to receive a service, and what standard of service is to be expected, there is much less of a problem than where there is doubt about either distribution or performance (Minogue and O'Grady 1985: 43–4). Road-sweeping is an example – the beneficiaries and standards are not in great dispute and the issue is more one of control over the contractors than of accountability to the public. Early contracting-out has tended to be in areas like cleaning, but future developments are particularly likely to raise distributional or performance issues. If the private sector, or in-house contractors, were to be given discretion to decide who should, for example, receive meals-on-wheels or day-centre facilities, then the tradition of electoral accountability of councillors would be dramatically altered. While councillors might be blamed and discarded by the electorate, they would in practice be like health authority members who have only a minimal and a very indirect (through decisions on resource allocation) say as to who receives what treatment from their hospital doctors. What would develop would be a type of bargaining relationship between the council and its contractors, probably often undertaken in private despite recent legislation designed to open up more council activity to public scrutiny.

The changes must not, however, be exaggerated. The scale of local authority activities and the growth of professionalism and professional autonomy already means that councillors in practice delegate enormous amounts of discretion to officials. Officials in effect determine who receives what, subject to policy guidelines laid down by councillors in their committees. Some distributional guidelines could be incorporated in contracts, though the Bill outlaws many non-distributional clauses relating, for example, to pay and service conditions or to any equal opportunities policy. But a crucial difference would be that individual councillors would lose their right to direct access to line managers and the redress of grievances raised by constituents would become that much more difficult for councillors to handle. This ability to respond to local concerns, whether raised by individuals or by local groups, is central to the practice of councillor accountability and is under threat from privatisation policy.

The courts

Lawyers often seem to be among the main beneficiaries of inter-governmental conflict. The 1980s has seen an upsurge in the use of the courts to determine the distribution of power between central government and local authorities as individual councils have sought to challenge ministerial actions over council house sales, rate-capping, grant claw-back and many other issues (for a review, see R. Hogwood 1987: 61–4). Privatisation clearly falls within this category of issues where controversy is a central feature, and the Local Government Bill 1987 is certain to lead to legal action when it becomes law.

It is reasonable to also anticipate the courts becoming involved in disputes between local or health authorities and contractors. However specific and detailed the terms of a tendering document are, there will be room for differences of opinion about interpretation. In local government, in particular, relations between councils and contractors will inevitably be tense because many councils will have been forced to privatise. Recent past history offers little in the way of a guide because all the councils which have so far pursued a policy of competitive tendering have done so entirely voluntarily. But where other forms of privatisation or deregulation have been forced on councils, there is already, in the case of Norwich and council house sales, a history of legal conflict.

Courts can do more than merely adjudicate in disputes about what should be done or provided: they may also influence how it is done. The Norwich case is in fact a very good example of the courts influencing the methods of service provision. One of Norwich's methods of delaying council house sales was by refusing to use the District Valuer (a civil servant) to undertake house valuations. Norwich maintained that he was not the proper person to do this because he could later be called in by the prospective purchaser to do a revaluation – hence there was a role conflict. In the appeal courts the judges made it plain that Norwich should have used the District Valuer, thus in effect telling all councils that this was the correct way to sell their houses (C. Evans 1985: 107).

The public sector trades unions, bitterly opposed to privatisation, have sought legal rulings to further their campaign (see Ascher 1987: 123). Initially they succeeded in forcing Grand Metropolitan, contracted to undertake refuse collection in Wandsworth, to raise wages and cut hours because the council's Standing Orders specified that a 'fair wages clause' applied to all its activities. The council responded by amending its Standing Orders, and the Government later moved to outlaw the clause, thus also preventing health authorities from using it to maximise the chances of in-house tenders succeeding. Unions also sought, again with initial success, to prevent councils from unilaterally altering the conditions of service of staff. Finally, they threatened to test the legal status of the 1983 Circular, which instructed health authorities to privatise support services. In the event they drew back from this, probably because any victory would have almost certainly been short-lived.

Steadily, then, the courts are becoming involved in the privatisation policy. Whether they like it or not, their role cannot be confined to simple questions of 'who' is right. Judicial decisions influence what is provided, how it is provided, and to whom it is provided: the courts are becoming public policy makers.

The unions

It was natural for the public sector trades unions – NALGO, NUPE, GMBATU in particular – to spearhead the opposition to privatisation; after all, the policy posed a clear threat to their position as negotiators for better pay and conditions, and as negotiators with a high degree of access to policy-makers. Health and local authority staffs had more than doubled in the post-war period, unionisation (sometimes closed shops) had become the norm, and many of the classical features of corporatism clearly applied to public sector industrial relations.

Every type of privatisation posed a potential threat to this strong position in which the unions found themselves by the late 1970s. Selling off assets turned public sector employees into private sector workers or, in the case of council house sales, reduced the amount of work available as the new owner-occupiers made their own arrangements for repairs and maintenance. Deregulation included the abandonment of a fair wages clause. Contracting out caused further job losses or staff transfers from the public to the private sector.

When we add to this picture the dirty jobs strikes in the public sector during the winter of 1978–9, and the strikes of 1973 which played a significant part in the downfall of the Heath Government in February 1974, it becomes reasonably easy to construct a scenario within which a major objective of the Thatcher Government is to confront the unions, using as support the 'public's view that the breakdown of industrial authority had gone too far' (Ascher 1987: 100).

Ministers have been careful to avoid confirming the view of the unions and their defenders that privatisation is, to quote one of them, 'pure ideology and dogma, together with a concerted attack upon the public sector and public sector unions' (T. Williams 1983: 3). The stated aims continue to be cost-effectiveness and service efficiency, with changes forced upon industrial relations as officially a byproduct. Not that a concern to limit union power can be totally denied, for the 1980s has seen an unprecedented amount of labour legislation. The closed shop, secondary picketing and political funds have all been the subject of new laws, with the spin-off consequences of privatisation as merely an additional factor affecting the public service unions (Ascher 1987: 101).

Though not a formal institution of government, the public service unions had, in effect, become part of government. Nationally they are equal partners on the series of Whitley Councils which negotiate pay and conditions of service. Locally there is a network of joint consultative committees between employers (whether concils or health authorities) and employees, the latter being represented by the unions. Local agreements are commonplace and range widely from, perhaps, one on prcedures governing the introduction of new technology through to the type of 'task and finish' agreement which caused enormous frustration among the concillors of Southend (C. Evans 1985: 98). Individual union members have rights of representation at grievance and disciplinary hearings which go well beyond the legal minima. In short, consultation and negotiation characterise the public sector, with the unions rather than management frequently holding most of the cards.

The public sector unions remain large, influential organisations. Their structural position in the policy process has, however, been eroded. In the NHS alone, ancillary staff members (whole time equivalents) fell from 172,200 in 1981 to 132,000 in 1986, or by some 40,000 (Radical Statistics Health Group 1987: 53). The Whitley Councils found their autonomy reduced as the Government strengthened the management sides by reducing the numbers of regional members, sometimes with apparent loyalties to those health authorities sceptical of DHSS policies. Contracting-out, a policy with major potential consequences for the service, was introduced despite the 'normal' consultations on earlier draft Circulars revealing much criticism amongst health authorities. In local government the unions tasted defeat early in the 1980s when their support for Norwich and their hostility to Southend both failed to halt policy change (C. Evans 1985). Though they sometimes continued to obtain pay rises at levels above the wishes of ministers (because they negotiated with councillors as employers), further ominous signs came in 1986 when the Education Secretary imposed the pay awards to teachers and imposed new conditions of service. Such actions were unprecedented. They, as much as the privatisation activities, typify the new and subordinate constitutional status of public sector unions. The corporatist model has been radically overhauled; public sector industrial relations have been subjected to constitutional reform.

The future of local government agencies

In this chapter a series of constitutional developments associated with the privatisation policy have now been identified. Control of many services by councillors and health authority members has become indirect. Accountability is different, particularly in respect of the handling of individual or communal grievances. The courts are becoming increasingly involved in politics, and are having to arbitrate in disputes which affect how services should be provided, or the manner in which authorities distribute public services. Public sector unions, in contrast, are less involved in policy-making, and their influence has waned.

All these changes are a consequence not just of privatisation but also of a wider phenomenon: the development of a more assertive, more unitary style of government. The era of consensus politics has been replaced by one of confrontation politics. Command hierarchies increasingly seem more appropriate than models of devolution, delegation or decentralisation.

The existing system of local government and of regional and district health authorities, on the other hand, is based firmly on concepts of devolution and decentralisation. These concepts imply that sub-national agencies have a significant degree of discretion. The services they provide should fit the pattern of local needs, needs which will vary according to local circumstances. Geographic, demographic, socio-economic and political variables affect policy outcomes. In short, the existing system implies a variety of service provision, more notably in the case of local government than in the NHS where the very word 'national' implies some degree of central government involvement to ensure a reasonably homogeneous level of service provision. The local government system, based on direct elections to local representative bodies, invites variation from council to council. It can be argued that local government and, to a lesser extent, health authorities would be failing to perform properly if their activities and service outputs conformed to a common pattern.

As Leach and Stoker show (Ch. 6 above), block grant, targets, penalties and rate-capping have all threatened to reduce the autonomy of those councils which are sited towards one end of a continuum based on spending levels. Legislation affecting housing, transport and, shortly, competitive tendering reduces the discretion of every local authority, just as health authorities have in effect lost their choices over how best to provide 'support services'. In inner-city areas the creation of Urban Development Corporations and the use of central government subsidies (such as the Urban Development Grant) have been designed to introduce private sector investment; coupled with deregulation in Enterprise Zones, they have challenged the traditional primacy of local authorities as the agents to tackle urban deprivation (for a review of the use of subsidies to attract private investment into the inner cities, see S. Young 1985).

Three possible scenarios emerge from all these developments, developments which go beyond privatisation but which provide a setting within which privatisation must be placed. First, local and health authorities could stay much as they are now in constitutional terms, and adapt (or be adapted) to play a new role. Essentially they would buy in services from contractors, meeting periodically to determine the outcome of regular tendering processes, and to review complaints from both consumers and contractors. They would become regulatory bodies, employing directly a small number of officials to monitor the activities of contractors, to inspect some private sector facilities such as homes for the elderly, and to administer the tendering process. Small is here a relative term, for the vast bulk of the existing 4 million employees of local and health authorities would be working for contractors. The 650 local and health authorities might well need somewhere between 100,000 and 250,000 officers.

This development alone represents a major and a radical constitutional change. Traditionally citizens elect councillors to take direct responsibility for services; now the councillors (and health authority members) have only indirect control: the citizen-representative contract is thus very different, or would be if privatisation policies were expanded to cover a wider array of local government and NHS activities.

The second scenario also offers radical change, for it involves a major reform of the structure of devolved government. Unlike the reorganisations of 1974, and of 1965 in London, this next reform would usher in an era of very much *smaller* local authorities – in short, local government would become much more local.

Britain's local, and health, authorities are presently extremely large in comparison to those in other countries. This is because of their tradition of direct service provision, a tradition which has caused them to be large enough (in terms of population size and of financial resources) to individually deliver specialist services, and to provide for minority groups. The pre-1974 reform process was dominated by considerations of 'minimum size'. An education authority had to be large enough to provide special schools for deaf children, a full further education system,·a range of specialist advisers, and so on. The 1974 reforms were based on an (alleged) broad consensus of opinion that something like a population of 250,000 was needed as a minimum for an education authority; similar approaches led district councils to normally encompass at least 30,000 (see Wood 1976). Health authorities followed suit in being created to cover similar areas to those of education and social services authorities. This reflected the needs of direct service provision, for co-ordination could best be achieved if boundaries did not overlap.

Service provision by contractors removes most of those arguments which created large authorities. If authorities merely have a duty to 'secure the provision' of services, they can do this by joint tenders with neighbours or can themselves buy-in specialist provision as and when needed without creating a permanent establishment of staff, buildings and technology. (The phrase 'secure the provision of' services is not a new one but comes from the Education Act 1944.) The economies of scale approach being inapplicable, the structure of local government can be designed based on a local geography and community alone. Artificial amalgamations of towns which have little in common (Bootle and Southport, Wembley and Willesden, Brighton and Hastings, and many more) merely to create areas with large resources become unnecessary. Local government can become 'local', with anticipated advantages of greater public interest and of better feedback from consumers of services to those regulating the contracts awarded to the private sector. Paradoxically, by losing the direct provision of services local government is actually strengthened.

The third scenario runs in quite the opposite direction, by challenging the need for local government, or for health authorities, to exist at all. In the previous chapter Leach and Stoker charted the transformation of central–local relations, concluding that the centre has now amassed enormous powers and that for local government 'the future...is increasingly bleak' unless there is a wide-ranging review of its status. Privatisation accords with the views of those New Right theorists who see markets as self-regulating; whilst others believe that regulation can best be undertaken by bureaucracies and not by representative assemblies or local lay committees of appointees. Both schools of thought discount local and health authorities as being irrelevant at best and disruptive, sinister, anti-government influences at worst. The vociferous opposition to many government policies which has been a feature of many Labour controlled councils, some dubbed by ministers as the 'Loony Left', could in the end prove counter-productive. Local and health authorities, no longer direct service providers, could be abolished. Such would be the ultimate constitutional consequence of privatisation. Impossible? Only time will tell.

8

Trade Unions and the Constitution: the Impact of the New Conservatives

Keith Ewing

Introduction

In this chapter we move to consider the impact of the new conservatism on trade unions. To a large extent this is a question of labour law with the legal control of labour and its institutions having a direct impact on industrial relations and the position of the employee in the enterprise. But the relationship between trade unions and the constitution and consequently the boundaries between labour law and constitutional law are close. The starting-point of this chapter is to demonstrate how the state has intervened consistently (though there have been *ahistorical* tendencies – Thompson and Engleman 1975; Weekes *et al.* 1975) to underpin the power of organised labour, doing so in different ways at different times (see Kahn-Freund 1954, 1959, 1983; Wedderburn 1980, 1986). The policy has thus been to strengthen the power of autonomous, voluntary organisations which ultimately had the capacity to obstruct the path of government. On the other hand, however, there has been an attempt persistently to draw trade unions into the structure of government at various times of political and economic crisis in order to secure agreement and support for government policy which unions had the potential to frustrate. This is a phenomenon which reached a climax with the Social Contract in the 1970s, with the unions 'claiming the right to move nearer the core of government policy-making, even if the country's growing economic problems meant they did not always have their own way' (Elliott 1978: 34). The position since 1979 has, however, been one of constitutional retreat for the unions, and it is this development which is the principal concern of the chapter.

The liberal tradition

Post-war governments in Britain have inherited a system of labour law which was moulded in the traditions of late nineteenth-century liberalism. In the formative years, three strategies can be detected in the state's response to trade unionism. These may be identified as autonomy, encouragement and integration. Of these three, in the early period, the first was the most visible. Essentially, this took the form of strong legislative intervention to reverse decisions of the courts which either threatened the existence of trade unions or disabled them from taking effective economic measures to promote the interests of their members. This conflict between different institutions of the state reflected a deep-rooted dilemma of liberalism: on the one hand, the commitment of the judges to complete economic freedom; and on the other hand, the commitment to economic freedom for all and the awareness that the state must intervene if working people were to be free to compete, albeit not on equal terms, with capital (Hobhouse 1979). The commitment to autonomy also gave rise to another conflict, this time with constitutionalism. In providing a wide measure of autonomy to the unions, the legislature sought effectively to exclude the courts from regulating the activities of the unions. This took the form in 1871 of excluding the courts from adjudicating on any rule-book disputes within the unions. More controversially, it took the form in 1906 of legislation which protected the unions from employers by providing that a court could not entertain any action in tort against a trade union. Although such a measure was thought necessary to protect union funds, and although it remained possible to sue union officials for acting unlawfully, this provision nevertheless invited damaging rhetoric about the rule of law, rhetoric which was to haunt the unions for the following seventy-five years.

The second theme of the liberal tradition of British labour law was government intervention to encourage the growth of trade unionism, though this took a different form than the commitment to trade union autonomy. Partly as a result of industrial militancy, the period 1918–21 was one in which governments were very active in creating the institutional framework in which collective bargaining could be conducted or in which there would be some joint regulation of workplace relations. The most significant form of intervention in this direction was what might be termed a strategy of 'administrative regulation', the starting point for which was the Whitley Report (Whitley 1917: 3). The Committee recommended that in order to secure a permanent improvement of industrial relations, 'His Majesty's Government should propose without delay to the various associations of employees and employed, the formation of joint standing Industrial Councils [JICs] in the several industries in which they do not exist, composed of representatives of employers and employed'. It was anticipated that the JICs would deal with a wide-range of subjects. These included 'traditional collective bargaining' issues (Charles 1973: 103), including 'methods of fixing and adjusting earnings'; the settlement of disputes by 'the establishment of regular methods of negotiations for issues arising between employers and work people'; and security of employment, albeit 'without undue restriction upon change of occupation or employment' (Whitley 1917: 5). The Report also had broader social goals, with one of the projected areas of concern for JICs being the securing for workpeople 'of a greater share in responsibility for the determination and observance of the conditions under which their work is carried out' and by the observation later in the Report that 'what is wanted is that the workpeople should have a greater opportunity of participating in the discussion about the adjustment of these parts of industry by which they are most affected'. It was recognised, however, that the matters to be considered by the JICs would vary from industry to industry 'as different circumstances and conditions call for different treatment'.

These proposals were limited to 'the main industries of the country, in which there exist representative organisations on both sides'. In the 'well-organised' industries it was proposed that the JIC should operate on a three-tier basis: at works level, district level and national level. An important feature of the proposals is that employee participation in the JIC was to be by the trade unions. Whitley rejected 'the idea, sometimes put forward by particular groups of employers, that the constitution of Works Committees might provide a bulwark against the growth of Trade Unionism and render it unnecessary ... to recognise the Unions' (Cole 1973: 117). In the words of Fox:

> Success of the committees, declared the report, 'would be very seriously interfered with' if such an idea existed, and employee representatives on the committees were to be trade union members, duly elected. The whole scheme, indeed, rested upon full recognition of the unions at all levels.
>
> (Fox 1985: 294)

The Report thus proposed three major initiatives: to extend joint regulation into the workplace; to extend joint regulation into industries not yet covered; and to extend the range of issues which might be considered. In this it met an enthusiastic response from government in general and the Ministry of Labour in particular, which 'showed very considerable energy in the first stages' (Charles 1973: 202–3). Charles also notes that:

> few of the JICs were established spontaneously. With the exception of the two or three industries which were developing towards JICs independently of Whitley, even industries well disposed towards and able to form Councils needed the encouragement of official intervention and direction. Many ... were actually pressured into the formation of Councils.
>
> (Charles 1973: 124–5)

The effect of the ministry's intervention was the formation of twenty JICs in 1918, thirty-two in 1919, sixteen in 1920 and six in 1929 – seventy-four in all. If the seven JICs in government are excluded, this figure fell to sixty-two in 1923. It has been estimated that between 1919 and 1939 these sixty-two industries employed an average of some 2.05 million workers in each year (Charles 1973). Indeed, current workplace organisation in several industries can be traced back to the Whitley Report (Clegg 1979). So while for us there was 'No Wagner Act, no Weimar Constitution, no Front Populaire legislation' (Kahn-Freund 1943: 143) there was a functional equivalent.

A third tendency of the state in the formative years was towards corporatist integration of the unions in governmental decision-making, though this was not as strong as in other European states at the time (Maier 1975), or as persistent as the other two themes of the period. Nevertheless, it has been argued that the so-called 'Treasury Agreement' of 1915 (whereby union leaders agreed to relax existing trade practices to promote the war effort) (Pelling 1976) was the first of several antecedents to the Social Contract of the 1970s (Fox 1985: 291). Corporatist integration of this kind continued after the War, though perhaps not quite on the same scale (Middlemas 1979). One notable feature was the failure to construct any formal institutional framework – like the Weimar Economic Council – for such arrangements (Lewis and Clark 1981). An attempt was made to do so in 1919 when, on government initiative, the National Industrial Conference was established, consisting of representatives of capital and labour, 'convinced that its recommendations . . . would become law' (Charles 1973: 249). The initiative collapsed within two years, however, with some influential employers seriously alarmed by the over-generous concessions which were being proposed. These included the right of union membership, the 48-hour week, a legal minimum wage and improved social security benefits. In fact, the Conference may well have been a short-term government initiative to split the labour movement by encouraging the integration of the parliamentarians and the isolation of the Triple Alliance, which was prepared to be more flexible in its methods and was willing to countenance direct action to achieve its goals – even in the political arena (Martin 1980). But although the institutional framework collapsed, government continued to consult the unions, though after the economic slump of 1922 and the weakening of the Left, for the most part this may have been a relatively formal process. In other words, while the opinions of unions may have been canvassed, there is little evidence of any need for government to bargain with the unions to prevent the obstruction of its political goals (Martin 1980). Significantly, however, the collective bargaining arrangements established as a result of the Whitley Report tended to survive (MacDonald 1960: 22).

There were, however, other important developments, necessary for the corporatist initiative in the aftermath of the Second World War. So what we see in the period after the First World War is a strengthening of the institutional base of capital and labour to smooth the path for continuing corporatist integration. So far as labour is concerned:

> Bureaucratic consolidation affected also the TUC, which had functioned before the war as a talking shop and clearing house for political lobbying. War had brought big changes. The government involved TUC representatives in a wide range of consultative and collaborative machinery, with the result that additional staff were appointed, a committee structure was instituted and the old Parliamentary Committee was replaced in 1921 by the modern General Council.
>
> (Fox 1985: 305)

But the consolidation of the TUC involved more than bureaucratic rationalisation. The General Council had been established as the 'single central trade union authority' (Clegg 1985: 310). It alone spoke for organised labour, there being no question of shared sovereignty or competition with any rival organisation. Other possible contenders had disappeared (the Triple Alliance, broken in the wake of Black Friday) or were no longer in the running (the General Federation of Trade Unions). It is true, however, that this single representative body had been denied by its affiliates, the power 'To interfere with the autonomy of individual unions'- an important power in a corporatist context. But it is to be noted that here too an important advance was made in 1924 when:

> Affiliated unions were now formally obliged to keep the TUC informed about disputes. The General Council was empowered to initiate consultations with affected unions if a major stoppage seemed likely; and if its intervention was accepted by the unions, the Council was to give them such support as it considered necessary in the event of a stoppage.
>
> (Martin 1980: 192)

The corporatist climax

One of the most important features of the labour law in the period after the Second World War was the development and consolidation of the corporatist initiatives which have their origins in 1915. It is to be stressed that the reasons for what has been variously described as 'tripartism' (Grant and Marsh 1977), 'bargained corporatism' (Crouch 1979) and 'quasi-corporatism' (Beer 1956) was a post-war economic policy of all governments which embraced full employment as a central goal (Keynes 1961; for a full analysis, see Winkler 1975). From 1945 until 1979 this was accompanied by a continuing commitment to strong and autonomous organisations, and a continuing commitment, directly and indirectly, to encouraging the penetration of trade unions and trade unionism into the economic and political framework of the nation. The former policy was reflected in the repeal of the Trade Dispute and Trade Unions Act 1927, one of the measures exacted by the government by the way of reparations for the general strike. The latter was reflected by several strategies. One was nationalisation, important not for imposing a duty to bargain on the new corporations, but for extending the public sector which in itself would inevitably secure the influence of the unions in the industries in question. Public ownership is a form of intervention in industrial relations which has been greatly neglected by labour lawyers. A second strategy of encouragement and promotion was the extension of contract compliance provisions, albeit that their impact was equivocal (Bercusson 1978). From 1946 government contractors were under a duty not only to pay fair wages but also to recognise the freedom of workpeople to be members of trade unions. The third strategy of encouragement was by the use of legislation to strengthen the wages councils (Bayliss 1962), which had been set up (as trade boards) initially to eliminate sweating, but which changed significantly in purpose in 1918 to become a means of encouraging employers to set up collective bargaining machinery following the Whitley Report (Ewing 1986).

So far as corporatist developments are concerned, three initiatives are of major importance, the most important being the last, the Social Contract of the 1970s. This, however, has antecedents in the earlier developments. The first is what Beer (1965: 205) has called the Wage Restraint Bargain of 1948, a product of the need to restrain wage-push inflation, but in a manner which enjoyed the co-operation of the unions (Beer 1965: 203, 204). According to Beer (1965: 205), the bargain struck following negotiations (and 'negotiation' rather than 'consultation' is the correct term (Beer 1965: 204)) was 'remarkable as much for the way in which it was reached as for its content and results'. Thus:

> The principal negotiators were three – the Government, organized labour, and organized capital. The bargain was not itself embodied in any legislative instrument such as a statute or statutory order. Yet it achieved a regulation of an important aspect of the British economy that no such legislative instrument by itself could have done. Indeed, one may think of it as a kind of extra-governmental legislation. It was effective in the sense that the regulation of behaviour stipulated by it remained in force for the better part of three years and greatly assisted the Government in its efforts to maintain economic equilibrium.
>
> (Beer 1965: 205)

The bargain was reached following a Government proposal for restraint. The TUC reluctantly agreed in return for measures 'not only to stabilize but to reduce profits and prices' (Allen 1960: 286) and in return for the government's maintaining food subsidies. Beer (1965: 208) claims that the bargain was a success to the extent that it restrained the unions from exploiting to the full 'their powers of collective bargaining under conditions of full employment and labour shortage'. The bargain lasted until 1950 when it disintegrated in the face of devaluation, rising prices and the action of individual unions.

The second corporatist initiative is the 'most spectacular and commented upon institutional manifestation of tripartism', namely the National Economic Development Council (Richardson and Jordan 1979: 50). The NEDC was established by the Conservative government in 1962, the Chancellor, Selwyn Lloyd, declaring that 'the time has come to establish new and more effective machinery for the co-ordination of plans and forecasts for the main sectors of our economy' and that 'experience has shown the need for a closer link between government and industry in order to create a climate favourable to expansion and to make possible effective action to correct weaknesses in our economic structure' (quoted by Blank 1973: 171). The NEDC was designed to be a national planning body, composed of representatives of government, capital and labour (Dorfman 1974). But although the 'very existence of the NEDC ... is itself a declaration of faith that tripartite consultations are important and useful' (Grant and Marsh 1977: 140), it never met the expectations of the unions that it would 'be able to conclude binding agreements between major interest groups of a type which a traditional British parliament could not compass' (Shonfield 1965: 153). Thus the NEDC had no powers to direct economic policy, but acted merely as a sounding board and as a forum for the integration of union leaders with the thinking of employers and government (Crouch 1979). Grant and Marsh (1977: 141) concluded in similar terms, contending that while the NEDC has 'established a permanent niche for itself in the machinery of economic policy-making' and has 'provided the locale for much of the tripartite contact that has taken place', it has hardly evolved beyond 'a useful framework for the exchange of differing views'. But this reason for contact can in itself be important and useful, as during the Heath Government when relations between the Government and the TUC were strained. The existence of the NEDC meant that they at least continued to talk. And more importantly, although NEDC may have been a talking shop rather than a bargaining table, it did nevertheless help 'both sides of industry to become accustomed to tripartite discussions' (Grant and Marsh 1977: 141) and to that extent may have been an indispensable development in the emergence of the Social Contract of the 1970s.

This is in fact the third and most important corporatist initiative since the Second World War, the so-called Social Contract, being developed between Labour and the unions when the party was in Opposition, to be implemented on its election in 1974. Essentially it was an arrangement between government and the TUC designed again to deal with economic crisis. For its part the Government proposed to repeal the aberrant Industrial Relations Act 1971 and also statutory wage controls, thereby restoring free collective bargaining. As part of this first stage the Government would also introduce an independent Conciliation and Arbitration Service, 'to facilitate the quick solution of disputes' (TUC 1974: 288), and establish a Royal Commission on the Distribution of Income and Wealth. In the second stage there would be an Employment Protection Act 'to extend the legal rights of workers and unions'. According to the TUC:

> Among the positive gains for workpeople there should be provisions for improved job security, particularly guaranteed work arrangements and facilities for retraining; adequate negotiating machinery at all appropriate levels to deal quickly and effectively with specific situations as well as with principal pay negotiations; and adequate flows of information and systems of communication.
>
> (TUC 1974: 289)

In fact, the Employment Protection Act 1975 was wide-ranging, giving unions the right to recognition, union officials the right to information, time off and consultation on redundancies; and employees generally improved rights not to be unfairly dismissed and to time off to look for new employment in the event of redundancy (Bercusson 1976; Wedderburn 1978). The third stage in this package was to be the publication of a White Paper on Industrial Democracy. This was done in 1978 following the establishment of the Bullock Committee and the publication of its report in 1977 (Bullock 1977), though the Government's proposals on this issue, which were much weaker than Bullock's (Hepple and Fredman 1986), were never implemented. Nevertheless, what we see in 1974 and 1975 is a continuity of the commitment first to strong autonomous organisation (secured by repealing the Industrial Relations Act 1971 and restoring in TULRA much of the Trade Disputes Act 1906), and second, to encouraging the legitimate role of trade unions in the workplace, secured this time by direct statutory intervention in contrast to the bureaucratic intervention of the period 1918–21.

In return for these benefits, the TUC agreed to exercise restraint on wages. Thus the General Council asked union negotiators to 'take account of the general economic and industrial situation and of the economic and social policies being pursued by the Government' (TUC 1974: 289). Specifically the General Council made a number of recommendations to union negotiators: 'a central negotiating objective in the coming period will...be to ensure that real incomes are maintained'; 'this will entail claiming compensation for the rise in the cost of living since the last settlement'; and 'priority should be given to negotiating agreements which will have beneficial effects on unit costs and efficiency' (TUC 1974: 290). Significantly, the General Council would 'keep the developing situation under review', and expected 'unions in difficulties in conforming to the spirit of this policy to inform the General Council of the circumstances and to seek their advice'. The TUC was thus prepared to go to considerable lengths to increase its 'influence on economic affairs' (Elliott 1978: 34). In the end, however, the Social Contract failed to live up to expectations despite its enormous scope 'for securing the unions' political and social goals' (Crouch 1979: 96). Thus it has been explained that 'in practice the Social Contract operated in a very different way from what had been envisaged, because neither side was able or willing to deliver fully what had been promised' (P. Davies 1986). Davies continues by asserting that:

> the government not only failed to fulfil its promises, it also kept some promises that were at odds with the assumptions of the social contract. In particular, at the urging of the International Monetary Fund, it began to implement monetarist policies, which were to be so much further developed by the Conservative government of Mrs Thatcher elected in 1979, and to allow the level of unemployment to rise. The TUC perhaps did more on its side. It delivered adherence to a very tight incomes policy in 1976–8, but was unable to secure grass-roots support for wage restraint thereafter.
>
> (P. Davies 1986)

This contrasts with the views of one minister who participated in the Social Contract who was later to complain that the only give and take in the contract was that the Government gave and the unions took (quoted in Hennessy 1986: 83). This, however, seems a rather jaundiced view.

Labour in the new constitution

Since coming to power in 1979 the Thatcher Government has turned its back on these key features of labour and constitutional law. Indeed, the attack on the unions has been a principal feature of the Government's legislative programme. Earlier in this volume, Gamble (Ch. 2) warned of the dangers of dwelling on the influence of ideology as a factor explaining the development of government policy. It is important, nevertheless, to point out that the approach has been highly programmed by a distinctive economic philosophy, with political factors dictating the manner of its introduction. The key to understanding this programme is to be found in the work of Hayek, who has become as influential on governments of the 1980s as Keynes had been in the post-war period (Green 1987). According to Hayek, trade unions had great powers of coercion over employers, a power derived from their 'primary power of coercing fellow workers'. This power enabled a union to 'exercise almost unlimited pressure on [an] employer and ... particularly where a great amount of capital has been invested in specialised equipment, such a union can practically expropriate the owner and command nearly the whole return of his enterprise' (Hayek 1960: 264–70). Although Hayek doubts whether unions in practice raise real wages of workers, he is nevertheless concerned:

> If unions have in fact achieved much less by their wage policy than is generally believed, their activities in this field are nevertheless economically very harmful and politically exceedingly dangerous. They are using their power in a manner which tends to make the market system ineffective and which, at the same time, gives them a control of the direction of economic activity that would be dangerous in the hands of government but is intolerable if exercised

by a particular group. They do so through their influence on the relative wages of different groups of workers and through their constant upward pressure on the level of money wages, with its inevitable inflationary consequences.
(Hayek 1960: 272; see also Hayek 1944: 153)

Gamble has shown how the monetarist policies of the Government required the withdrawal of the state from economic management, but also intervention by the state to reduce the perceived economic power of labour. As we have seen, Hayek too saw the position of the unions as being crucial. He was to argue, however, that the solution of this particular problem lay essentially in the rediscovery of constitutional principle, particularly the rule of law. Thus unions had acquired 'exceptional privileges', and although this was true of unions in most Western jurisdictions, 'The acquisition of privilege by the unions has nowhere been as spectacular as in Britain' (Hayek 1960: 267–8). Here Hayek was referring particularly to the 'Trade Dispute [*sic*] Act of 1906', which conferred 'upon a trade union a freedom from civil liability for the commission of even the most heinous wrong by the union or its servant, and in short confers upon every trade union a privilege and protection not possessed by any other person or body of persons, whether corporate or unincorporate' (Dicey 1904: xlvi). Hayek condemned 'the picket line as an instrument of intimidation': 'even so-called "peaceful" picketing in numbers is severely coercive', permitting 'a kind of organized pressure upon individuals which in a free society no private agency should be permitted to exercise' (Hayek 1960: 274–5). Also singled out for criticism as the chief factor next to picketing 'which enables unions to coerce individual workers' was the closed shop and related practices. These, says Hayek, 'constitute contracts in restraint of trade, and only their exemption from the ordinary rules of law has made them legitimate objects of the "organizational activities" of the unions' (Hayek 1960: 275).

Although picketing and the closed shop thus appeared to be the principal targets of Hayek's concern, there were others. Thus, '[w]e must also regard as inadmissible methods of coercion all secondary strikes and boycotts which are used not as an instrument of wage bargaining but solely as a means of forcing other workers to fall in with union policies' (Hayek 1960: 275). So far as prescription is concerned, Hayek did, however, concede that 'legal prohibition of unions would not be justifiable', partly because in 'a free society much that is undesirable has to be tolerated' (Hayek 1960: 275). Indeed, he accepted that there was a need for only minor changes in law in order to produce far-reaching and decisive changes. Thus, 'We are... experiencing a pronounced decline of the rule of law in the field of labor. Yet all that is really needed to remedy the situation is a return to the principles of the rule of law and to their consistent application by legislative and executive authorities' (Hayek 1960: 283–4). What this required in turn was the 'mere withdrawal of the special privileges either explicitly granted to the union or arrogated by them with the toleration of the courts' (Hayek 1960: 278). Specifically, he proposed that 'all picketing in numbers should be prohibited'. Secondly, 'the unions should not be permitted to keep non-members out of employment'. This means that closed-shop contracts should be treated as contracts in restraint of trade and denied the protection of the law – they should be treated in the same way as contracts prohibiting union membership. For some inexplicable reason, the invalidation of all such contracts would, 'by removing the chief objects of secondary strikes and boycotts, make these and similar forms of pressure largely ineffective'. Hayek would also make unlawful the extension of collective agreements to employees who have not voluntarily given the union the power to contract on their behalf.

Hayek's claims and assertions are astonishing for their simplicity. Trade unions are too powerful, giving rise to economic difficulty. That trade union power is a product of state intervention which violates the first principle of the constitution – the rule of law. And by the rule of law we mean the rule of law as devised by *Dicey*. So not only is there a direct link between constitutional law and economic policy, but there is also a direct line linking the writings of Dicey with the labour law of the Thatcher government. Yet Hayek's work in this area is not only astonishing for its simplicity. It is even more astonishing that bold assertions of truth, statements of unshakeable logic, can be made on the basis of what appears to be a very fragile grasp of the legal regime which he condemns. It is trite yet true that labour law is not the same throughout the world, and Hayek has a tendency to write about a legal system which is based on parts of several. It is never clear whether and to what extent he is dealing with Britain, the United States or the Western world, with the result that much of what he writes is irrelevant from a British perspective. But to the extent that he does appear to be writing about British law, he appears remarkably misinformed. Take his principal target, picketing. It simply is not the case, as Hayek implied, that picketing in numbers was permitted. Picketing was permitted for the purpose only of peacefully communicating information, or peacefully persuading workers to work or abstain from working. Large numbers would betray a presence for some additional purpose, as was later to be confirmed by the courts. In fact, a year after the publication of *The Constitution of Liberty* a decision of the Divisional Court highlighted the fragile nature of the freedom to picket in English law. The extent to which picketing is permitted and by whom was ultimately entirely a matter of police discretion – a state of affairs giving rise to real problems about the rule of law rather than the quixotic ones identified by Hayek and the disciples.

But the confusion was not confined to this issue. Take his second target – the closed shop and related practices. Here the concern was to make such contracts in restraint of trade and unenforceable. (This in itself gives rise to interesting questions of principle. As we have already seen, Hayek felt constrained to tolerate the existence of trade unions. Yet if trade unions are to be tolerated, is it consistent with the rule of law to deny their contracts any legal effect?) The reality is, however, that such contracts were already regarded as being in restraint of trade by English common law. And although the Trade Union Act 1871 provided that the purposes of trade unions were not unenforceable merely because they were in restraint of trade, the same Act also enacted that agreements between trade unions and employers' associations (including collective agreements about union security) were unenforceable. It was in any event subsequently established that collective agreements were unenforceable at common law, independently of the restraint of trade doctrine and regardless of the statute. It is true that the closed-shop agreement, although unenforceable between the 'contracting' parties, could nevertheless have normative effect in the relationship between employer and employee to the extent that the employee could be under a contractual duty to be a union member and could be dismissed for non-membership. But it is crucial to note that a union could not require an employer to enter into such an agreement; that the union could not enforce the agreement against the employer if he or she failed to implement it; and indeed, that there is little an employee could do if a fellow employee was hired in breach of the agreement or he or she themselves were dismissed in breach of the agreement. For despite any such agreement, the employer had the power to hire and fire for any reason whatever provided that proper notice was given, the notice period at common law not being very long where manual workers were concerned.

A third area of confusion is perhaps the most important, partly because the misconceptions are widely held. The Trade Disputes Act 1906, section 4, was an unfortunate measure, which was widely criticised (Webb and Webb 1919; Schumpeter 1974) though its practical importance is not to be exaggerated. The crucial provision of the 1906 Act for excluding the courts from industrial conflict was section 3, which gave a limited immunity from liability for the commission of specific torts. Although both of these measures are taken together (see Hanson 1984), it is hard to see how section 3 can seriously be seen as inconsistent with the rule of law. The claim merely illustrates the Humpty Dumpty qualities of the doctrine: the rule of law is a doctrine pregnant with ambiguity which means whatever its author would like. Although of great rhetorical value in the political debate, such assertions are meaningless. In fact it can be strenuously contended that section 3 is consistent with the rule of law in the sense that it removes tortious liability which in practice applies only to trade unions. In other words, the conferring of privilege is an illusion; the section was designed to remove unequal treatment and to place trade unions on the same footing as everyone else. To contend otherwise is to misunderstand the interventionist qualities of the common law and to ignore the reality that Parliament must sometimes intervene to remove laws of special application developed by the judges or to prevent violations of the rule of law by courts distorting legal principles in their partial application to disfavoured parties.

It is indeed to be asked how restoring tort liability would be consistent with the rule of law. Quite apart from the fact that the torts in question tend to apply in practice to trade unions, the individual torts were applied differently according to who were the parties to the dispute. So for conspiracy, if the defendants were a trading cartel of capitalists, the judges would turn a blind eye. But if the defendants were individual workers, they would be met by the full force of the legal system (Elias and Ewing 1982). Despite Dicey's claim that these developments were 'thoroughly sound' (Dicey 1904: 530), this is hardly consistent with his teaching about the equal application of the law. In truth, arguments about the 1906 Act based upon the rule of law barely disguise a desire to return to a position of detailed legal intervention, the principles of intervention being developed by the judiciary rather than the legislature, a notion which must at least raise questions about its political legitimacy.

Constitutional change has affected industrial relations in two ways. First has been the influence of constitutional principle – particularly the rule of law, as developed by Dicey and Hayek. The second has been institutional change and reform designed to have an institutional impact at the constitutional level. Thus we see the dismantling of the corporatist arrangements of the 1970s and an attempt to break the long-term political influence of the unions by challenging the role of the Labour Party as a potential party of government. Although the legislation has been wide-ranging, leaving little of the inheritance from the 1970s untouched, the central pillar of concern was the Trade Union and Labour Relations Act 1974, sections 13, 14 and 15, measures contained originally in the Trade Disputes Act 1906, sections 1, 2, 3 and 4. The changes to these measures have been introduced over a four-year period (in the Employment Act 1980, Employment Act 1982 and Trade Union Act 1984), and the account here does not necessarily follow the chronological order of their introduction. (Detailed comment is to be found in Kahn *et al.* 1983; Lewis and Simpson 1981; Davies and Freedland 1984.) The first point to note, however, is that the section-13 immunities, described as 'extraordinary privileges' (Hanson 1984: 70) have been greatly curtailed. In Hayek's terms, perhaps, the rule of law is still violated, though not to the extent that it was before 1984, though it is accepted by his disciples that 'very considerable inroads' have been made 'into the grossly excessive trade union immunities' (Hanson 1984: 75). The restrictions have taken several forms. First, the definition of a trade dispute has been narrowed, so that the permitted purposes of industrial action have been limited, an initiative highlighted by *Mercury Communications* v. *Scott-Garner* [1984] ICR 74 (see Ewing and Rees 1984), demonstrating that 'politically-motivated strikes no longer enjoy immunity' (Hanson 1984: 74). Indeed, if 'the Secretary of State had not changed the definition of a trade dispute [*sic*] ... the politically-motivated strike would have been lawful, and a major part of the Government's privatisation and competition policy might have been frustrated by trade union opposition' (Hanson 1984: 74).

But limiting the purpose of permitted action is not the only qualification of section 13 which has been introduced. Also important is the fact that the Government has limited the freedom to take secondary action, a restriction which proved initially very important in the shipping industry, with the shipping unions finding themselves powerless to police international safety standards and to impose sanctions on those owners who flagrantly violated their obligations. More important, however, was the requirement introduced in 1984 that the operation of the section 13 immunities in some cases depends upon a ballot being held to approve or endorse the action (Hutton 1984). The secret ballot must take the form of the marking of a ballot paper, a majority of those voting must vote in favour of industrial action, and the ballot paper must include a question (however framed) asking those voting whether they are willing to take part in action which may involve them in committing breaches of their employment contracts. This has proved to be a very important device for restraining industrial action, and has been the means of stopping strikes in the Post Office, on the London underground and in the civil service, the Government for the first time seeking an injunction to prevent a strike by its own staff (Hutton 1985). It is to be pointed out that not only will an injunction be available to restrain a strike for any minor breach of the sometimes difficult ballot requirements, a ballot will not authorise a strike which is otherwise unlawful, because, say, it is not in furtherance of a trade dispute or because it is unlawful secondary action (Ewing and Napier 1986). And of great importance is the fact that the repeal of section 14 meant that a remedy will be available against the union as an entity (thereby exposing its funds) as well as against individual officials. In 1982 the great target was finally struck in an Act which had been sponsored by Mr Tebbit. It is to be noted, however, that the repeal of section 14 did not expose the unions to unlimited liability in tort, the Government carefully introducing a concept of limited liability in damages, the amount of the damages depending on the size of the union, and the union being liable at all only if the act was committed by a 'responsible' person.

The repeal of section 14 of TULRA has been described as a 'most radical provision' (Hanson 1984: 74). Without the repeal of section 13 as well, however, its impact would have been rather limited given the rather expansive interpretation which the courts (perhaps cynically) were willing to place on that measure (Simpson 1980). In other words, if there was no liability, there would be no defendant to sue. The substantial modification of section 13 increased the likelihood of litigation by extending the legal power of employers and consequently increased the likelihood that trade unions would appear as defendants. In practice this has happened, important work by S. Evans (1985, 1987) demonstrating a readiness on the part of employers to exploit their new powers and to exercise these powers against unions as well as their officials, as they were required to do before 1982. An important feature of the fact that trade unions may now be sued in tort is not simply the fact that union funds may now be liable in damages.

This is, of course, important despite limited liability, particularly where there may be multiple plaintiffs suing on unprotected torts. Thus, it has been pointed out that in *Duport Steel* v. *Sirs* [1980] ICR 161, there were fifteen plaintiffs and that if all of them succeeded, and if each was entitled to the maximum permitted damages, the loss to the union would be £3.75 million in addition to costs, in relation to which there is no ceiling (Ewing 1982). But of greater importance than liability in damages are the consequences of a failure to comply with an injunction. This, perhaps unanticipated consequence of repeal, has been devastatingly important. An order may now be made against a union which, if it fails to comply, will be in contempt of court for which it may be subject to an unlimited fine, and if the contempt continues, its funds may be sequestrated (seized) by the court until it purges the contempt (Kidner 1986). Several unions have now been fined for contempt, and the assets of some have been sequestrated, including the NGA and SOGAT. The funds of the NUM were also sequestrated, though not as a result of the repeal of section 14. The NUM was a victim of its refusal to comply with a court order that it should act in accordance with the terms of its own rule-book (Ewing 1985). In other words, this was an action arising in contract rather than tort.

As already pointed out, industrial relations have been affected by two important constitutional developments. The first was the influence of constitutional principle, and the second was institutional reform. The most notable institutional reform has been the dismantling of the corporatist structure of the 1970s. That this major constitutional change has taken place without any legal changes is another reflection of the fluid and dynamic nature of the British system of government. Yet so far as tripartism or bargained corporatism is concerned, it has simply ceased to exist. Thus one sympathetic account of the first Thatcher Government points out that:

> the first six months witnessed a fundamental change in relations between Mrs Thatcher's government and the trade unions compared to that of previous post-war governments. The attempted close relations between governments and unions that had dominated the post-war period of consensus Keynesianism was simply jettisoned. The idea that the unions had a role to play in formulating government policy – the essence of the corporatist approach – was repudiated.
>
> (Holmes 1985: 34; see also Bruce-Gardyne 1984: 170–1).

Holmes also observed that:

> This change of attitude was arguably more fundamental a change than that proposed in the 1979 Conservative manifesto to amend trade union law. The significance of the end of the corporatists' approach cannot be overstressed in understanding both economic policy sources and the nature of contemporary Conservatism under Mrs Thatcher's first administration.
>
> (Holmes 1985: 34)

Thus trade union leaders are no longer actively consulted on major economic questions. It is true that the NEDC still exists, but this has little influence and has been downgraded. It is true also that union leaders may make representations to ministers, including the Prime Minister, on issues such as labour law reform and the ban on unions from the Government Communications Headquarters (GCHQ). But increasingly these are matters of form and courtesy which lead to little change in government thinking. Indeed, such is the lack of influence of the TUC in the corridors of power that on one important occasion it refused to make representations in the belief that it would not receive a fair hearing from government, preferring instead to use the House of Commons Select Committee on Employment as a platform for its views.

This rejection of corporatism has been possible as a result of a government programme which has eschewed a formal incomes policy: one of the principal reasons for bargaining with the unions has thus disappeared. In the view of Holmes:

> Central to the government's new non-corporatist approach was the discarding of incomes policy as a policy tool. The institutionalised and cumbersome bureaucratic nature of successive incomes policies had greatly increased trade union power and prestige. The unions had fed upon the entrails of incomes policy for several decades.
>
> (Holmes 1985: 35)

It is also the case, however, that the abandonment of corporatism and the rejection of an incomes policy has taken place in (and perhaps has been lubricated by) an economy in deep recession as a result of which the economic power of the unions was in sharp decline, to an extent unprecedented since the Second World War. High unemployment has been associated with the collapse of the manufacturing base and of industries in which trade unions traditionally have been strong. And while it is true that employment may be rising, this is tending to take place not in areas of union strength, but in the service sector, high-technology areas and tourism, areas where unions have been unable to penetrate to any significant extent. Added to this is the fact that many of the new workers are engaged on temporary, short-term or casual arrangements (Deakin 1986; Leighton 1986), forms of employment which have traditionally been resistant to unionisation. So constitutional change (the revocation of corporatism) is a product of economic change (the decline in the power and the fortunes of one of the two principal producer groups). Government has not of course been passive in the face of the economic decline of labour, having intervened by legislation in a manner unhelpful to the problems faced by the unions. Thus the penetration of trade unionism into new areas is not helped by privatisation (see Ch. 7 in this volume and Ascher 1987) and the elimination of contract compliance requirements; by the repeal of the duty of employers to recognise trade unions, a duty contained in section 11 of the Employment Protection Act 1975; by the elimination of the closed shop (see Hanson *et al.* 1982) and by rendering unlawful industrial action designed to ensure that an employer deals only with a union plant. Similarly, the process of marginalisation of the labour force is encouraged by, taking young people out of wages council protection and by increasing from six months to one year and then to two years the period of service which must be completed before employees are eligible to claim for unfair dismissal.

But although economic conditions have permitted an important institutional change in the structure of British government, it is not the only change of institutional significance. Also important is the Trade Union Act 1984, which seemed designed to weaken the political influence of the unions by weakening the capacity of the Labour Party to compete for power. The Labour Party was created by the unions to represent their interests in Parliament, and it is funded mainly by the unions, with most of its annual income coming from this source, the unions providing an even higher proportion of the Party's income for election expenditure (Ewing 1987). Trade union political activity had been governed by the Trade Union Act 1913, which required unions wishing to adopt political objects to hold a ballot of their members. If the members approved, the union could then establish a political fund, from which political expenditure (as defined) had to be met, and to which members of the union had the right not to contribute and not to be discriminated against for choosing to exercise this right. Although no evidence was presented to establish that these measures were ineffective to protect individual dissidents in trade unions, the Government moved nevertheless in the Trade Union Act 1984 to impose further restrictions on trade union political expenditure. The most important of these was an obligation that trade unions should ballot their members every ten years for approval to continue to operate their political funds, the first ballots to be held by 31 March 1986. No doubt the hope and indeed the expectation was that trade union members would vote not to continue political objects, to the obvious detriment of the Labour Party. Thus the Prime Minister is on record as saying that she would be immensely pleased if 'the trade unions were not a part of the Labour Party' (quoted in Ewing 1984). Similarly, one well-informed source has written that the purpose of the legislation was 'the political one of quickening the decline of the Labour Party, and perhaps also assisting the realignment of the left' (quoted in Ewing 1984). Indeed, the Government had every reason to believe that the ballot requirement would bite deep: less than one-half of British trade unionists voted Labour in 1983 and in some unions only a slight majority of members (or even a minority) paid the political levy. Yet remarkably the political fund ballots were a great success: all unions with funds which conducted ballots voted to retain them, and a few others (including the civil service unions) voted to set one up for the first time. But although the 1984 Act backfired on the Government first time round, it is to be borne in mind that the ballots will have to be repeated in 1995–6. If

Labour should lose the next general election it remains to be seen whether trade unionists will so enthusiastically endorse the continuation of funds which are used mainly to sustain the Party.

Conclusion

So far as trade unions are concerned, two important constitutional developments have occurred under the Conservative Governments of Mrs Thatcher. The first has been the revival of constitutional fundamentalism, particularly the vacuous 'rule of law'. Constitutional doctrine has thus become an intellectual justification for limiting the economic power of organised labour. The second has been institutional change in the sense that the formal structure of the constitution has been modified to exclude trade unions from participation in the decision-making process. The corporatist decline is not, however, absolute, for the fact remains that some of the tripartite agencies of the 1970s, such as ACAS and the Health and Safety Commission, still operate. It is, however, the case that these institutions are being marginalised and that the decline of corporatism is steady and continuous. There has, in addition, been a third and final contribution of constitutionalism to the decline of the labour movement. This is simply the absence of any formal constitutional restraint on the ability of government to push back the frontiers. This is evident particularly in the way in which the administration removed the right of workers at GCHQ to remain members of the civil service unions and in the way in which questionable police practices were encouraged and condoned during the miners' strike (Miller and Fine 1985; Wallington 1985). Here the unions fell victim to the flexible and open-ended nature of the constitution. Just as their influence grew without any formal change to the structure of the Westminster system, so they could be excluded in much the same way. And just as the government could extend the freedom of the unions by bureaucratic or statutory means, so it can as easily limit that freedom by its unregulated control of the legislature. It is tempting to argue that this experience highlights the need for restraints on the power of government. For organised labour, however, it is likely that salvation will be found only with either the election of a sympathetic government, or economic revival with full employment, or a combination of both. Recent experience from jurisdictions such as Canada suggest that institutional reforms, such as a Bill of Rights, will at best give a veneer of legitimacy to government attacks on trade unions, and at worst will be an additional source of weakness giving further ammunition to those concerned to undermine organised labour.

9

Law, Order and the State

Paul Wiles

This essay will examine the way in which the Conservative Government, since 1979, has used law to maintain order. Essentially, it is about how modern Britain is policed both by its police and penal system. However, it is a central theme of the essay that policing cannot be understood in isolation from other events. By this I do not mean the trite claim that policing must be understood in an historical context – although that is perfectly correct. I am more concerned with the way in which policing, and the use of police power, articulates with the government's broader claim to legality. The use of police power can always be used as an acid test of the lawfulness of any government. Indeed, the nature of policing is frequently used as an indicator of whether a government is legitimate and constrained by the rule of law, or arbitrary and oppressive. In the case of Mrs Thatcher's Government this indicator has been pushed to the fore by that Government's own actions. Disputes over economic policy, and the attendant conflict with the trade unions; the struggle between central and local government and the crisis of the inner cities and the attempt to create a new moral normality in Britain, have all produced problems for policing. An examination of how policing has fared under this Government will give us some clue, therefore, as to the nature of legality in contemporary Britain.

Before proceeding to examine policing *per se* we must say something about law and legality and how this was presented as a political problem by the incoming Government.

Law and the legality of government

Law holds out the promise of a society based on human interactions and exchanges which are peaceful, just and fair. Law is the antithesis of the uses of power to serve sectional interests. This is not merely an ideal of law; it is what law *is*. If law does not pay attention to the needs of justice and fairness, then it is not law but power – that is, the ability of one group to enforce its will regardless of the interests or desires of others. If what claims to be law turns out on examination to be nothing but power, then there is no law: the claim is a sham. When political institutions claim to rule in other than sectional interests then they are making a claim to legality. To use Weberian concepts, with which sociologists may be more familiar, they claim to be exercising legitimate authority. This claim to legality, and the test of whether it is truly lawful, is what separates legitimate political governance from oppression. However, the test of lawfulness cannot be simply that a claim to legality is made (the mere existence of a statute or court judgment is not in itself enough even if prima facie indicative), or that the claim is generally accepted (the democratic resonances of this test must not blind us to the fact that democracy may well be a tested means of trying to achieve a fair and just society, but not the thing itself). Similarly, Max Weber's (1969) flirting with an empirical and pragmatic concept of 'legitimacy' – that people accept an action as legitimate – will not do either. Instead, claims to legality and legitimacy are to be tested against a universal concept of law.

I state this meaning of law simply as a stipulative definition, not because I think that the matter cannot be demonstrated by argument (see e.g. Beyleveld and Brownsword 1986) but, since this is not an essay in jurisprudence, I want this meaning as the basis for examining more mundane, practical matters. In the mundane world, even if all people of goodwill accept this meaning of law, there are still profound difficulties in determining whether the polity is acting lawfully – or if you like, whether the drift of political decision is towards a more lawful and therefore more just and fair society. The Government of Britain which came to power in 1979, headed by Mrs Thatcher, indicated its desire to be a radical Government. It is generally accepted, I think, that it has indeed been radical. Radicalism means change and change raises the question of whether both the means and the outcome are more, or less, lawful. In the case of Mrs Thatcher's Government, the question is particularly apposite.

In the campaign which led up to the 1979 general election the Conservative Party stressed two themes: the decline of law and order and the need to shift the balance of power between groups in society, especially those representing employees and employers. These two themes were elided together in a populist appeal which must, in large measure, take the credit for the subsequent election victory. The reason for this popular support was to be found in the events preceding the election, when the Callaghan Government's attempt to impose a public sector wages policy had created a conflict between national and local trade union leaders, between public employees and their employers and between trade unionists and the police. The 'Winter of Discontent', as this period became known, was a symbol which encompassed all the failures and growing bankruptcy of post-war British politics into a simple ideological message. Part of the power and popular appeal of that message was its claim to have identified a break-down in law which needed correcting. Law in this context meant both the ability to maintain civil order and a lawful framework for decision-making. The first of these is broadly a matter of policing and has been much discussed by the Thatcher Government under the banner of 'law and order'. The second is broadly a matter of constitutionality and as such has been much less discussed. Indeed, at least in the early period of government, commentators were left to infer a constitutional doctrine (of a minimalist state) from the Government's economic philosophy: both being derivable from classical liberal ideals of *laissez-faire*. (Classic texts for such a linkage were provided in the works of Frederick Hayek, especially since they were approvingly quoted by Mrs Thatcher. See, in particular, Hayek 1979b and the discussion in Ch. 1 of the present volume.) The fact that these two strands of thinking did not always harmonise led some commentators to point to what they perceived as a contradiction in the Government's policies.

The purpose of this brief essay is to examine and assess the policing aspects of Mrs Thatcher's Government's approach to legality. However, this will only make sense if this is done within the framework of how the legality of governance in general was conceived by the Government. How these two aspects were interwoven can be illustrated by examining the Government's treatment of the legality of trade union activities and how this in turn affected the policing of trade disputes. It is a particularly suitable place to begin our examination because, as already indicated, the policing of trade unionism was a major element in the Conservative Party's appeal during the 1979 general election.

The new Conservative government and the trade unions

The post-war history of Britain had been dominated by the attempt to halt economic decline by involving representatives of employers and employees in the business of government and economic planning – what was known as 'tripartism' or more broadly 'corporatism'. However, the Winter of Discontent, the resort by the Labour Government to the International Monetary Fund and the imposition of deflationary policies at their insistence, appeared to signal the failure of this attempt. At any rate, the Conservative Party capitalised on this apparent failure in its election propaganda and argued that tripartism was the cause of the problem, not the solution, because it handed over power which properly belonged to the state to the trade unions. In this analysis, curtailing the trade unions was seen as the essential prerequisite of economic recovery. The trade unions were, therefore, going to have to be changed. Part of the power of trade unions lay in their role within tripartism; that could be removed simply by the new Government ceasing to operate the mechanisms of tripartism. The other aspect of trade union power lay in their use of the tactics of conflict during industrial disputes; that was much more difficult for the Government to affect directly, and any attempt to do so carried with it the danger of confrontation on the streets and an enormous policing problem. The previous attempt by a Conservative Government, under Edward Heath, to affect such a change had ended in confrontation and failure. Popular mythology said that trade union opposition had brought down the Heath Government and, even if not strictly accurate, the Conservatives needed no reminding of the dangers of the task they were about to embark upon; indeed, it was out of that previous failure that Mrs Thatcher had emerged as party leader.

Within the new Conservative Government, which came to power in 1979, there was no consensus on how the trade unions should be tackled. One faction (later to become known as 'wet') wished to persuade the trade unions to change via a modified version of tripartism. Another faction (later to become known as 'dry') wanted to curtail trade union power by state action. This latter group was headed by the Prime Minister herself and, as we now know, was in the end to become the dominant voice in the Government. However, at the time of the election victory that domination did not exist and Mrs Thatcher was obliged to appoint an arch wet, Jim Prior, to the position of Secretary of State for Employment. Some aspects of how that domination was achieved, such as the ruthless use of Prime Ministerial patronage, need not detain us in this essay, even though they raise crucial questions for constitutional lawyers. From our point of view what is important is that curtailing the trade unions, by the use of state power, was a case that had to be argued even within the Conservative Party. This was not only because of the factional dispute within the Conservative Government but also because, notwithstanding the Winter of Discontent, the trade unions were still seen as legitimate institutions with a fair degree of popular support. In other words, there was an ideological struggle which had to be waged so that trade union power could be successfully reduced. Moves against the trade unions could be, and were, defined by the labour movement as the use of state power to serve the partial interests of capital against labour. If such moves could not be presented in a different way, then there would be no claim to legitimacy: the use of law to change the trade unions would be seen as illegitimate, the legality of government undermined and the policing of trade union activities rendered problematic.

The arguments which Mrs Thatcher's Government offered to justify the curtailment of trade union power, therefore, are worth examining. This is not to indulge in some species of legal idealism – that the construction of an argument which claims legitimacy for legal change is itself sufficient. Instead, such claims can be examined as to their validity and consistency in relation to the concept of law. We can also examine whether such claims are accepted by various groups in society. In the context of the present essay we are especially interested in whether the police accepted these claims as a justified basis for changing the policing of industrial disputes. Ideological struggles are critical to the legality, or otherwise, of change, but this does not mean that such struggles are won or lost purely as a matter of propaganda (or in its modern guise the use of advertising agencies), important though such means may be. Rather, what is at issue is whether a particular interpretation of events fits the objective experience of different groups and can be allied to ideas of legality, justice and fairness. The arguments which the Thatcher Government offered to justify the use of law to curtail trade union power were an essential element, therefore, of the success or failure of that attempt.

Shifting the balance of power

Mrs Thatcher's Government won its first election at least in part because there was support for the notion that labour, especially in the form of trade unions, had gained too much power relative to employers. It was argued that this represented an historical shift of power, from capital to labour, which had distorted the cost of labour and so been a major factor in the decline of the British economy. For a Government which believed in the rightness of the judgements of the market, such a shift could not have occurred naturally. Instead, it was the outcome of the post-war attempt to create a corporatist state through the instrument of tripartism: government had used its ability to make law to grant powers to trade unions which the market would have denied them. Reducing the power of trade unions, therefore, was not to pursue the vested interests of capital but rather to restore the natural balance of power. To use law to achieve this purpose was not to subvert legality: law had previously been used improperly to grant privileges and immunities from normal legal constraints to trade unions. Trade unions had used the power, granted to them by the state under tripartism, to themselves subvert legality. They had granted themselves power in law which no other groups in society possessed. They had then used this power to defend the use of tactics during industrial disputes which, if they had been used by any other groups, would have been declared unlawful under the criminal law. The police had not prosecuted the criminal law in such cases with the result that policing had become partial and unfair.

Such, in essence, was the Conservative Government's case. Although such an argument was not always put forward by Mrs Thatcher's first Employment Secretary, Jim Prior, it was presented most forcefully by her second, Norman Tebbit, and has become the general Government position. It has been articulated on numerous occasions in more or less detail, for example in the Green Paper *Trade Union Immunities* (1981 Cmnd 8128), which preceded the 1982 Act. This argument was used to justify a series of reforms of industrial law which constrained the use of picketing as a tactic, severely curtailed the use of secondary action, created more stringent conditions for the existence of closed shop agreements, enforced the use of ballots before strike action and limited the use of union internal disciplinary procedures against members who refused to participate in industrial disputes. Such changes were enforced by civil remedies and as unions such as the miners and print workers were to discover, the power to sequestrate their funds was a powerful sanction to gain their compliance. More broadly there was an attempt (largely unsuccessful at the time of writing) to reduce the political role of the trade unions by trying to undermine the existence of political funds. Such legislation was a radical attempt to curtail trade union power. The result has been that trade union power certainly has been curtailed, although how far this is a result of the legislation and how far a consequence of more fundamental shifts in the economy, is difficult to judge (for an attempt to assess the impact of the first in this series of legislative changes – the Employment Act 1980 – see Kahn *et al.* 1983). The legitimacy of such radical changes depends on the acceptability of the justification for them which the Government put forward. On a political level, as already indicated, the labour movement attacked the changes as a partial use of state power. Whilst the evidence is difficult to quantify, the continued electoral success of the Conservative Party does suggest that this challenge to the legitimacy of the changes has not found widespread popular support, even allowing for the fact that the present Government did not receive support from a straightforward majority of those voting. Nevertheless, we can critically examine the legitimacy claims for these changes on a number of grounds and then examine the practical consequences of these criticisms for policing.

One thing which has to be said about the Government's case for trade union reform is that it was historically inaccurate: the trade unions were not granted general legal immunities but rather immunities from constraints which had largely been developed uniquely to curtail their activities (for a more detailed examination of this see Kahn *et al.* 1983: 31–8, and Ch. 8 in the present volume). The trade unions may well have gained in power under tripartism, although it ought to be noted that this was at the expense of an increasing centralisation which was itself often the cause of disputes within the trade union movement. However, the way in which the Government argued its case tended to shift attention away from the straightforward issue of what the proper balance of power between employers and employees ought to be, and what were the proper forms of organising that power. Instead, attention was shifted onto the claimed dubious legality of the increase of trade union power and of their actions. Trade unions were thus presented not simply as having too much power but both having achieved that power by dubiously lawful means and then using it to threaten lawful authority. In this way trade unions were shifted from a central role in the business of government under tripartism, to a marginal position from which their attempts to be involved in decision-making were presented as a subversion of legitimate government. The dispute tactics which trade unions had traditionally used now took on a more sinister role as undermining civil order and lawful government and hence were criminalised at the ideological level.

Problems for legality and policing

This approach to the trade unions, and the argument offered to justify the approach, achieved a measure of popular support; indeed, the case was presented in such a way as to create populist support for the Government's actions. Nevertheless, the use of populist ideology carried with it the danger of undermining the legitimacy, and therefore ultimate lawfulness, of the shift in the balance of power which the Government hoped to achieve. Furthermore, the approach was to produce quite specific difficulties for policing.

The first problem with the Government's approach was that if there was a case that tripartism had given unwarranted power to trade unions, then that ought to have led to a debate about what a proper balance was and how it was going to be achieved. The Government's use of law suggested that they were not prepared simply to allow employees and employers to fight the matter through outside a legal framework. Although the Government's references to the idea of employers and employees operating in a free market sometimes seemed to suggest the opposite, no government can allow such conflicts to occur without any legal constraint otherwise they abrogate the business of government. The Government's search for support through populist slogans masked a proper debate which should have taken place about alternative forms of representing employers and employees, of dispute settlement and of the legal framework within which this could operate. To this day the Government has not addressed this issue and instead has focused entirely on curtailing existing trade union activity – so creating a debate in which only highly partisan voices can play any part. It is difficult to tell from recent industrial legislation, and the justification offered for that legislation, what role is envisaged for trade unions in the future. There has certainly been no attempt to create a legal structure of rights, obligations and constraints, or a procedural framework for industrial disputes. Whilst one would not expect Mrs Thatcher's Government to support an elaborate procedural framework for industrial disputes, her claimed adherence to the philosophy of a minimalist state ought to have led to a legal statement of rights and duties. The economic facts of recession and unemployment have produced a new discipline in workplace bargaining, and legislation has no doubt curtailed the activities of trade unions and their use of some dispute tactics. Whether this new discipline would survive in a different economic climate is doubtful. At any rate the Government has done little to create a framework for industrial disputes which can claim legitimacy by appealing to fundamental concepts of lawfulness, and is accepted as such by those involved in disputes.

One result of relying upon populist slogans, rather than reasoned debate, has been to obfuscate the true nature of the matters involved by focusing on the highly charged issue of criminality. Although the legislative changes were almost entirely of a civil law nature, the ideological justification for them frequently referenced the claimed criminality of some trade union activity. I have argued elsewhere that this obfuscation meant that it was often popularly believed that more had been altered in terms of the policing of industrial disputes than the actual legal changes demanded (for further analysis of this, see Kahn *et al.* 1983, Ch. 5). For example, a suggestion in a code of practice attached to the Employment Act 1980 led many to believe that it was now a criminal offence to have more than six pickets, and that the police had a lawful duty to impose such a constraint.

More specifically, the Government's industrial legislation has created some real difficulties for the police. At the beginning of the Government's first term of office senior police officers, through the Association of Chief Police Officers, argued that existing law was quite adequate to deal with any criminal offences committed during industrial disputes. They were especially concerned that new legislation should not curtail their discretion in the policing of industrial disputes. The reason for this was that the police in Britain had carefully cultivated a claim to neutrality in industrial disputes which crucially depended on them possessing enough discretion to negotiate with the parties concerned as to how a particular dispute was to be policed. The police argued that law was still being enforced, but the use of law had to depend on judgements as to how civil order was to be maintained. The ability of police officers to use their discretion in this way in turn depended on at least some general acceptance that the law was broadly fair, so that the police's claim to be impartially upholding the rule of law might be accepted. Of course, these claims to neutrality and impartiality were never entirely, or always, accepted and trade unionists sometimes had a healthy scepticism about police actions. However, in the post-war period this scepticism had only really reached damaging proportions, from the police's point of view, during certain *cause célèbres* in industrial disputes. The police feared that the legislating activity of the Government might be seen as highly partial by many trade unionists. Lobbying by the police did prevent a too rigid framework for the policing of industrial disputes being created and in particular helped prevent the significant use of criminal law in this area. In this sense the police have maintained their discretion to police industrial disputes in a flexible manner to maintain civil order. However, the way in which the Government argued its case for legislation, and some of the legislation itself, was seen as highly partial by at least part of the trade union movement. Although the police successfully resisted new criminal offences being created within industrial legislation, this perceived partiality of legislation has damaged the police's ability to successfully legitimate their actions as maintaining the rule of law.

The perceived partiality of industrial legislation has had a broadly damaging effect on policing. The Government wished to alter the balance of power between employers and employees by the use of law. However, as already discussed, they did not wish to do so by creating a new legal framework of rights and duties. Instead, law was used to curtail certain tactics which trade unions had previously used during industrial conflicts – most commonly by making such tactics liable to civil claims by employers. The result, as intended, has been to make some tactics too costly compared to any advantage which a trade union might gain from that use. This shift in the costs and benefits of dispute tactics does not directly involve the police, being a matter of civil law. However, in industries where traditional tactics have been particularly affected, this has created major confrontations between trade unions and employers. Such confrontations raise issues of civil order in which the police inevitably become involved. We have had a series of such confrontations under the new industrial legislation, of which the most dramatic have involved the miners and the print unions.

There can be no objection, in principle, to the idea that the police have a duty to maintain civil order, but in the present context serious problems have arisen. The way in which parties to a dispute pursue matters can make it more or less likely that confrontations which challenge civil order will be engendered. A cynical employer, for example, would be able to act in such a way as to narrow the choice of trade union tactics to those more likely to create such confrontations and then, by presenting the issue as one of civil order, effectively hijack police power to his advantage in the dispute. Allegations have been made that this has occurred under the new legislation, for example during the print workers' dispute at Wapping. Whether such allegations are justified or not there is something seriously wrong with a legislative framework which can grant plausibility to such complaints. If police power is used to maintain civil order in the public interest, then the actions of the police may be open to criticism according to whether the 'public interest' is legitimately conceived, but that criticism will be much more damaging if police action is seen as pursuing a private interest. The police themselves have been concerned that their duty to maintain civil order has forced them to act in situations where their legitimacy and impartiality have been open to question.

During the policing of recent industrial confrontations genuine issues of the legality of public and private actions have arisen; for example, during the miners' strike the right of the police to prevent miners' pickets moving around the country was such an issue. Unfortunately, such issues have tended to be decided in relation to the exigencies of a particular political crisis about how an industrial dispute was to be settled. The result has been far-reaching judgements (e.g. *Moss* v *McLachlan* [1985] IRLR 77) about public and private rights with little in the way of political debate, or general consideration of our legal framework of such rights. In part the responsibility for this failure can be traced to the nature of our legal tradition for which all recent governments must take responsibility. English law, compared with law in most other developed nations, has a woefully undeveloped structure of public law. Public issues are frequently treated as private matters, and there is little in the way of general constitutional principles which can be appealed to in settling such issues. As already indicated, the present Government must take responsibility for failing to provide a similar set of principles for industrial law, although in view of the immediately preceding point it must be admitted that to have done so would have been radically innovative in the English legal tradition. More significantly, the way in which the Government proceeded in the industrial sphere, by extending civil law remedies whilst at the same time ideologically presenting trade union actions as a threat to legality, meant that the public interest and the public law framework was repressed during such confrontations, which were in effect, privatised as matters of concern only for the parties involved or as individual criminal acts.

The overall effects of the Thatcher Governments' industrial relations policy and legislation on policing, therefore, has been complex and contradictory. Industrial legislation *per se* made no difference to the policing of industrial disputes: the police's own desire not to be involved in industrial disputes was respected. Yet the Government's justification for this legislation focused attention on the claimed unlawfulness and illegitimacy of some trade union action and at the ideological level specifically raised the issue of criminalising trade union actions. The Government's policy was to prevent the kind of confrontations which had occurred under the Callaghan Government, but at least in the short term, the Government's industrial relations policy sharpened confrontations between labour and capital either indirectly by creating a new climate of industrial relations, or directly by influencing the negotiating positions of public concerns. The Government wished to bring trade union activity within a new framework of lawfulness and at times did so by appealing to general principles of lawful authority, for example in demanding more democratic ballots within trade unions. Generally, however, an appeal to general principles of lawfulness was not made: no general framework of rights and duties was created and legislation had the stated purpose of changing the balance of power between employers and employees, which without such a framework had the danger of being perceived as the antithesis of lawfulness – the use of state power to serve sectional interests.

The Government's action left the police in a curious position. On the one hand, since the industrial legislation was a civil matter, it could be claimed that the policing of industrial disputes had not changed, and formally that was correct. Ideologically, Government discussions raised expectations that the police were now able to respond to industrial disputes in a new way, and for many involved in such disputes, including some police officers, there was great confusion about what the new legal position was. In other words, the police were expected to police industrial disputes differently because it was believed they had new legal powers to do so, even though in fact they had no new legal powers through industrial legislation. The Government increased the pressure on the police by themselves adopting a tough negotiating stance with their own employees and those in public concerns. The nature of the industries involved inevitably produced dispute tactics which created policing problems; for example, the nature of civil service employment in many local offices, combined with split unionism and non-membership, means that secondary picketing (as defined by the new legislation) is an obvious tactic during a major civil service dispute. The consequence of this position was that the police's traditional claim to impartiality during industrial disputes was undermined. They were all too easily seen as a tactical weapon of the employers. This perception was further reinforced, especially in the public sector, when the police were uniquely exempted from the undeclared public sector wages policy. Finally, the police's claim to objectivity, as the upholders of the rule of law, was undermined because the law in question was seen by many trade unionists as partial.

The effects of government policy and legislation, in the industrial sphere, on policing highlights some of the contradictions which have been created for the police. However, these have been but part of a more deep-seated set of problems for policing in modern Britain. As already discussed, part of Mrs Thatcher's appeal in 1979 was the claim to be the party of law and order, and against the chaos of the Winter of Discontent, such an appeal produced widespread popular resonances. But the populist appeal of the politics of law and order resonated not just with industrial disputes but also with rising crime generally, a crisis of the penal system and growing worries about civil order, especially in the inner cities. Each of these have produced their own problems for policing under the present administration, and it is all of them taken together which are determining the shape of policing for the future.

The crime problem

With one or two slight hiccups the level of crime in Britain has been rising steadily since the last war. Upon taking office, Mrs Thatcher's Government claimed that it would reverse this trend. So far it has failed to achieve this goal, but the approaches it adopted to the problem are none the less worth examining.

The first thing which marked out the Government's approach to the problem of rising crime was the belief that it was not inevitable. They simply did not accept that rising crime was an inevitable price of social change. Furthermore, they did not accept that the level of crime was a consequence of broader social forces. Instead, crime was to be understood purely as a result of individual wrong-doing. It was the same philosophy of radical individualism which marked the Government's economic policies, applied now to the problems of crime and deviance. From within such a position the problem of rising crime could be tackled in three ways: by changing the moral balance in society so that fewer people chose to commit crime; by deterring people from choosing to commit crime, and by making it more difficult to commit crime.

Changing the moral balance was clearly a longer-term objective. In the short run all that could be done was to reassert individual responsibility. The Prime Minister did so, for example, by stating that blaming unemployment for crime was insulting to those unemployed people who chose not to commit crimes, and also by expounding the ideal of the family as a morally responsible unit. More generally, support for deviant values came in for fierce criticism from within the Conservative Party, and attempts are being made, in the Local Government Bill, to prevent local authorities granting financial support to organisations representing deviant life-styles. In the longer term Mrs Thatcher's first Secretary of State for Education, Sir Keith Joseph, made it clear that education was ultimately the means of shifting the moral balance. The consequences of this for education have so far been rather thin. There has been an obsessive interest in sex education, and especially in discussions of sexual deviance, but this has had much more to do with the assertion of heterosexual normality than with crime reduction. Other than that there has been the odd rather blunt device; for example, the Education Act 1986 requires the governing bodies of schools to explain, in their Annual Report to parents, what contact their school has had with the local police. None of this amounts to a clear policy of moral re-education. The Government has not even tried to discover systematically what is actually taught in schools during compulsory religious instruction lessons. There does not seem to have been any attempt to define what moral shifts were required to reduce crime and no attempt to work these into an education policy.

The two other elements of the Government's crime reduction strategy – deterring people from committing crime and making it more difficult to commit crime – were concepts which the administration seemed far happier with. The idea of making it more difficult for people to commit crime meant that crime reduction strategies could be shifted away from examining the social causes of crime and their possible amelioration, to the much simpler notion of reducing opportunities for crime. The result was that crime reduction policies were developed on the basis of a simplistic opportunity model of human behaviour, and became obsessed with physical security measures. Such an approach had the advantages of being easy to translate into policy prescriptions and of shifting the responsibility for crime reduction away from the macro social policies of government to the security precautions of individuals and communities. At a seminar on crime reduction, chaired by the Prime Minister herself at Downing Street, the main focus was on better physical security and whether this could be encouraged by differential insurance premiums. The idea of deterrence was dear to the heart of the Thatcherite wing of the Conservative Party; it followed naturally from their concept of society as made up of individuals making choices on the basis of a calculation of probable costs and benefits. The belief in deterrence by this faction was maintained irrespective of any evidence to the contrary because it flowed from the ontology built in to their basic political philosophy. Two attempts have been made under Mrs Thatcher's premiership to reintroduce capital punishment as the ultimate deterrent. In spite of the Prime Minister's support, both attempts have been defeated by a combination of Opposition members of Parliament and other factions within the Conservative Party. However, the Government has continued to subscribe to the idea of deterrence even to the point of reintroducing a sentence for young offenders – the short sharp shock – which was known not to have deterrent value.

The police in various ways have become involved in these crime reduction policies. The police were seen as offering the best deterrence against crime both in the straightforward preventative sense but also in that the probability of being caught is an important general deterrent. To enhance these possible effects, funding for the police has increased relative to other public services. The police have also been encouraged to contribute more specifically by becoming more involved in anti-crime education in schools, and by helping to foster the setting up of neighbourhood watch schemes.

In spite of these crime reduction policies, crime has not been reduced in any significant way. At the end of its second term of office, when the Government fought a general election, its record on crime reduction was somewhat embarrassing. Nevertheless, the Government fought the election campaign with the same law and order policy. It was able to do so only by concentrating on the relevance of its policies to deal with any future civil disorder and so was able to play on popular fears of such a possibility. It also mobilised popular support for the victims of crime behind its policies, and just before the election announced new funding for victim support schemes. In spite of the election victory, it was clear that the crime reduction policies of the Government were not working, and since the election it has become known that considerable rethinking of those policies is under way. Ironically, it seems as if this rethinking will involve bringing back into crime reduction the social causes of crime, but to save the embarrassment which such a theoretical turn around may produce, this is being presented as based purely pragmatically on French experience.

The prison problem

One consequence of the Government's crime policies has been that the prison overcrowding problem, which it inherited, has steadily got worse.

This has happened not only because crime has continued to increase but also because the Government's philosophy of crime reduction has encouraged the idea that prison is a deterrence against crime. A major decline, during the 1970s, in the belief that crime could be reduced by suitable treatment of offenders left penal measures to be justified as either 'just deserts' or as deterrence (for one examination of this process, see Hudson 1987). This shift was mirrored in the Conservative Government's stress on individual criminal responsibility. As a result, the search for the development of alternatives to imprisonment was robbed of much of its impetus. Mrs Thatcher's Government has faced a mounting crisis in the prisons, only occasionally signalled in public view by the outbreak of prison riots. By the Government's third term of office the problem had begun to engulf the police because of the number of remand prisoners being held in police cells.

Home Office policy has become dominated by attempts to reduce the prison population. Any initiative, no matter how minor – be it channelling legal advice to remand prisoners or seeking sentence tariff reduction by mediation schemes – is latched on to if it might reduce the prison population. Unfortunately, the answer lies elsewhere. First, what is needed is a penal policy which is part of an overall policy of law and justice. I will return to this aspect shortly. Second, as part of that overall policy, certain constitutional arrangements need to be re-examined. The fact that one ministry of state (the Lord Chancellor's Department) is responsible for courts whilst another ministry (the Home Office) is responsible for dealing with court disposals, creates obvious difficulties about co-ordination. More fundamentally, the Government has failed to find a way of influencing the overall level of sentencing, without interfering in the autonomy of the judiciary. Yet models for such an attempt do exist – for example, the recently created Sentencing Commission in Canada. Unless changes of this order are made, then in all likelihood the prison population will continue to grow. Unless a major prison-building programme is rapidly implemented, the consequences will almost certainly be continuing disturbances in the prisons.

The civil order problem

As already discussed, Mrs Thatcher's Government came to power after, and partly as the result of, a series of industrial disputes during the Winter of Discontent. The notoriety of that period, and what made an impact on the general election, was not just the industrial disputes *per se* but the form the disputes took, which appeared to threaten the basis of civil order. Mrs Thatcher's law and order policy was above all else a promise to deal resolutely with any future threats to civil order. That promise has been tested during her premiership, which has seen major industrial disputes, from the steel workers to the miners and inner-city riots starting in Bristol and then spreading to many major towns in Britain.

The most serious of these events was the series of inner-city riots, in a number of British towns in 1981, which culminated in riots in Brixton during April of that year. These events were undoubtedly a threat to civil order: the police had great difficulty in controlling the situation and army units were on standby to come to their aid. The ability of the Government to live up to its promise to maintain civil order was questioned, but even more important the legitimacy of the Government's approach to the problem of civil order was placed in doubt. Just two days after the Brixton rioting had ceased, the Home Secretary set up a public inquiry under Lord Scarman to examine the disorders and make whatever recommendations he felt appropriate. The choice of Lord Scarman was shrewd. He had already conducted other inquiries into public disorder and was known to be one of the very few senior judges who favoured reform of English law to include a Bill of Rights and freedom of information. In spite of his judicial seniority, Scarman had the common touch and the way in which he conducted the inquiry was itself an immediate calming influence. Lord Scarman's report was a nice balance between examining the policing aspects of the disorders but also the underlying social causes. Scarman identified weaknesses in day-to-day policing of Brixton, particularly with regard to racial prejudice and harassment, but on the other hand thought that the police response to the riot had been proper, but lacked sufficient preparedness to respond quickly and vigorously enough. As regards the underlying social causes, Lord Scarman analysed the problems of inner-city areas with regard to employment and housing, and pointed out how these problems were magnified for ethnic minorities. The policy recommendations about these social problems were hardly radical: Lord Scarman, for example, shied away from the idea of positive discrimination, even though it had been widely used in the United States and accepted by the American courts. Nevertheless, Scarman clearly pointed out that the problem of maintaining civil order could not be limited to questions of policing. As he put it, 'Any attempt to resolve the circumstances from which the disorders of this year sprang cannot be limited to recommendations about policing but must embrace the wider social context in which policing is carried out' (Scarman 1981, para. 8.43). As far as policing itself was concerned, Lord Scarman offered two principles of policing in a free society against which reforms ought to be judged: these were 'consent and balance' and 'independence and accountability' (Scarman 1981, para. 8.19).

Lord Scarman's report, in other words, was at pains to try and ensure that the development of government policy with regard to civil order paid due attention to the social conditions which could generate disorder and to the way in which policing generally, and the policing of public disorder in particular, could be conducted within a lawful framework. The Government's response to the social conditions which Lord Scarman identified has been minimal, and it was not until Mrs Thatcher's third term of office that the problems of inner-city areas were given any prominence on the political agenda. On the policing side the Government took Lord Scarman's advice and set up consultative committees, but their attempt to create an independent police complaints system has not yet met with widespread approval and they virtually ignored his advice on the lack of need for new legislation in passing the Public Order Act. What was taken up much more vigorously was Scarman's criticisms of the police's ability to respond quickly and vigorously. Even before Brixton, after the riot in the St Paul's area of Bristol, the ability of one police force to come to the aid of another had been shown to be seriously deficient, and plans already existed to use the universal system of Police Support Units as the basis for a system of rapid deployment of police from one force area to another. After Brixton this system was reinforced by the creation of a national centre to co-ordinate requests for mutual aid. The riots in 1981 also showed up serious deficiencies in the equipment available to police for use during riots, and the next few years saw a rapid build up of new equipment from mesh-protected transit vans to flameproof overalls and short attacking shields. Where local Police Authorities objected to such developments they were overruled by direct supply from the Home Office (see *R* v. *Secretary of State for the Home Department ex parte Northumbria Police Authority* [1987] 2 WLR 998). The problem with these new developments was they created a technological and organisational fix. The new equipment could only be sensibly used if the police operated on a tight command structure, and mutual reinforcement necessitated that all police could operate within the same command structure. The result was at its most marked in the policing of public order, but technological innovations in other areas of policing were also pushing in the same direction. By the time of the miners' strike, in 1984, most of these new developments were displayed and anxieties began to be expressed about the direction in which policing was developing.

Policing and law

It is not difficult to see that the business of policing under Mrs Thatcher's Government has been pushed in a number of contradictory directions. The development of militaristic elements in modern policing has been most often noted, especially by the political left. But this must be set against the attempts to develop community policing, consultative committees and other such measures. One can, of course, dissolve this apparent contradiction by claiming that the second set are simply a sham, and one can point to the inadequacies of things such as the consultative committees to support such a view. Although such a solution has the advantage of great simplicity, I do not find it very helpful for a number of reasons. To begin with, it assumes a monolithic concept of the state with a clear will and purpose: the 'Thatcherism' of popular debate often comes near to this with its suggestion that the state has become subject to the will of a single person. Mrs Thatcher's style of premiership, and her willingness to support legal and administrative means by the use of personal patronage, does lend credence to such a view. However, this ignores the fact that although Mrs Thatcher has ruthlessly sought domination in her party and Government, she still leads a faction – albeit a powerful one. Contradictory forces have been at work during the Thatcher premiership, and although these are often hidden, they are visible often enough to warn against too monolithic a view of government will and purpose. Government itself, of course, is not the totality of the state, and in spite of Mrs Thatcher's attempt to impose her will across the state, this has been by no means completely successful. This is hardly surprising since elements of the state may have different interests. In the present context, if we regard the police as an element of the state, then the peculiar history of the British police has given it interests which do not necessarily accord with those of a particular party government. Portraying the police as willing dupes of 'Thatcherism' just won't do: the evidence is there, if you look for it, of examples of the police resisting government instruction, as I previously cited in the case of introducing new criminal offences into industrial legislation. One can *create* a single theme for the Thatcher Government's approach to questions of policing and law and sometimes such a creation helps clarify a possible trend (such as the idea of the 'strong state' pushing towards a more militarised police). However, one must remember that the theme has been created out of analysis – imposed on reality retrospectively. The reality itself is much more murky, the themes often contradictory and unclear, and pragmatically shifting with events outside of their immediate sphere. The overall approach of the Thatcher Government to law and policing is the result of these contradictions and shifts.

Not only is the state not monolithic but as long as government attempts to claim legitimacy and does so at least in part through law, then that also constrains their actions. This is not idealism, but rather to point out that claims to legitimacy through law are conditional: they may, or may not be accepted. Furthermore, as I pointed out in the introduction to this essay, that conditionality in the end depends on whether they *are* lawful. The alternative is that government abandons the search for legitimacy through law and resorts instead either to fascist-style populism or simple dictatorship by force without any legitimacy. Mrs Thatcher has used populism to try and gain legitimacy and sometimes, as in the case of industrial legislation discussed earlier, this has come close to at least obscuring if not subverting legality, but overall we are still clearly dealing with a government that seeks lawful legitimation. The link between legitimacy and law is often obscured and sometimes undermined by the nature of constitutionality and law in Britain. We do not have a clear statement of general legal principles, laid down in a constitutional document, against which claims to legality can be tested in the first instance. The doctrine of the supremacy of Parliament does mean that government, and especially one with a large parliamentary majority, can place what it will onto the statute book. Nevertheless, whether such law making will in the end legitimate government depends on whether it is accepted as fair and just or resisted as unfair, partial and unjust. Claims to legality which are generally not accepted as fulfilling the criteria of lawfulness will in the end fail to legitimate government action and create a crisis about the legitimacy of that government. It was this that Lord Scarman was pointing to when he insisted that policing in a free society must pay attention to the principles of 'consent and balance' and 'independence and accountability'.

With these constraints in mind let us examine how Mrs Thatcher's Government has attended to the problems of policing in modern Britain.

Maintaining order

All governments have a duty to maintain civil order; claims to pursue 'law and order' appeal to this duty. However, government action can enhance or exacerbate civil order. As has often been pointed out, 'law and order' is different from 'law or order'; in other words, the two terms are not necessarily synonymous. An order created by the use of force is not the same thing as a lawful order. In Britain, we have attempted, in recent history, to signal this distinction by keeping a clear division between the police and the military. The police are responsible for maintaining civil order under the rule of law and the military will only be used if civil order has collapsed. Indeed, once the military has been called to the 'aid of the civil power' then the legal constraints on their actions are rather unclear.

Mrs Thatcher's Government has not always paid sufficient attention to this distinction. It has allowed a gradual militarisation of the police which is in danger of eroding the police–military distinction. This is not only a matter of style or of weaponry, important though these are, but the encouragement of a unit-command type of operation which has enabled the police to overwhelm disorder by superior organisation of force. The recently enacted Public Order Act has further facilitated this type of operation. The police are now more able to deal swiftly with disorder, but there is a danger that they come to rely on this capacity rather than defusing conflicts, and that this type of operation spreads beyond those incidents in which civil order is seriously endangered.

The need to use such tactics is much more likely to have to be resorted to if police impartiality in disputes is not accepted. The police themselves have not dealt adequately with complaints of partiality, which incidents such as the Brixton riot highlighted, and they still need to convince the black communities that racism is not a feature of their operations. Government itself has not helped the police by failing to deal resolutely with the social causes of such suspicions. The police have been left to contain the frustrations, especially in inner-city areas, which are the consequence of broader government policies – a role which they have often bitterly resented. Finally, government has served the police ill by not thoroughly overhauling the procedures for complaints against the police. The police themselves may not accept the case, but their impartiality and hence the safety of their mode of operating would be better supported by a totally independent complaints procedure at all levels.

Industrial conflict

I have already discussed how the new industrial legislation aimed to change the balance of power between capital and labour and was seen therefore by many trade unionists as partial. This created problems for the policing of industrial disputes in its turn. The police may have successfully resisted the creation of new criminal offences within industrial legislation, but ironically the end result of this has been to hasten the criminalisation of some industrial dispute tactics by pushing them into the realm of civil disorder. Both ideologically, and now in terms of policing, industrial disputes have been defined as having a high potential for joining riots as threats to civil order. Some industrial tactics, such as large-scale mass picketing, may threaten civil order, but the new policing now has a much more effective counter-force to use against them. The style of policing industrial disputes has shifted and any large-scale industrial dispute is likely to trigger the new arrangements for dealing with possible civil disorder. This change can be seen in the contrast between the policing of the steel strike, at the beginning of Mrs Thatcher's term of office, and that of the miners' strike just four years later. Undoubtedly the miners' tactics were more ferocious, but so was the police response. The police may feel that they will never again have to retreat, as they did at Saltley in 1972, but we have all paid a price for this in terms of lingering bitterness and hostility to the police. There is the danger of escalation in the present position and of an eventual backlash. Without a lawful framework for settling industrial disputes, the alternative is likely to be outbreaks of overt conflict which easily escalate into civil disorder.

Reducing crime

The Government seems to be moving towards an acceptance of the idea that reducing the crime rate will involve responding to the social causes of that rate. This is going to be difficult for an administration which has refused to explore the relationships between that rate and factors such as unemployment. Simply accepting the lack of macro-correlation between unemployment rates and crime rates (even if true) just will not do. The culture of unemployment may affect employed and unemployed alike in high-unemployment areas. Furthermore, the low level of unemployment benefits, and the intrusive way in which benefits are administered, have encouraged the deviance of evading the regulations and developed a huge black economy. An under-class has been created in Britain, whose only chance of sharing in the life-style aspirations of the rest lies in minor

breaches of social security regulations and dealing in the black economy –
activities which may hover on being criminal but from which the rest
benefit by the supply of cheap labour.

The saddest thing about crime in Britain is that a significant proportion of
it is highly localised both geographically and socially. Some crime is
predatory across social and geographical boundaries, and some areas, such
as city centres, are high-risk areas, but much crime is contained within
localised residential areas. Areas which have high offender rates also often
have high offence rates: areas with a lot of criminals also have a lot of
victims (see Bottoms and Wiles 1986). In such areas the categories of
'criminal' and 'victim' are not necessarily fixed attributes: many 'criminals'
have also been 'victims'. The general point is that the nature of crime rates
varies significantly between different communities. Policing designed to
reduce crime will have to pay attention therefore, to such detailed
differences. Crime prevention policies will have to be developed at local level
in response to the needs of individual communities. The obvious way to do
this would be by local authorities and police forces together developing
policies which will need a blend of policing and other strategies aimed at
housing, employment, education and so on. Unfortunately, Mrs Thatcher's
Government's antagonism to local government and their refusal to
contemplate any means by which local authorities could be involved in
developing policing policies have made such an approach impossible. Under
Mrs Thatcher the drift of government in general, and policing in particular,
has been towards centralisation not localisation. A solution to the crime
problem will need local development and although this may be attempted by
devices which by-pass local authorities – such as are being used for inner-
city developments – this will probably lead to muddle and inefficiencies.

Policing and law under Mrs Thatcher

Mrs Thatcher's Government has faced a number of problems about policing
and law ranging from a rapidly rising prison population to industrial
conflict, rising crime and inner-city riots. To each of these problems they
have responded vigorously. By so doing they have fulfilled one duty of
government not to avoid social problems, and they have reaped the electoral
advantage of being seen to act resolutely. However, another duty of
government is not just to act resolutely but to do so with justice and
fairness. Vigour and resoluteness alone do not create legitimate
governance – that only comes from creating a lawful framework for solving
problems. Mrs Thatcher's Government has too often seen policing and law
as simply a means to enforcing order rather than creating lawfulness.
Enforced order is a fragile social state; it is too easy a prey to reaction and to
ignoring the underlying causes of disorder. If 'Thatcherism' is open to a
criticism, it is that it has lacked a social vision which could respond to the
need for fairness and justice. Our legal system lies stagnant and

undeveloped in its principles to adjudicate the justice of public decision-making; we seem to have no penal philosophy to guide sentencing and the purposes of alternative disposals; we have not developed a general frame-work for resolving industrial disputes; we have no coherent and integrated policies for responding to inner-city decay and racial exclusion; we do not yet have a policy which is likely to reduce crime, and our police are left to cope with the consequences of broader social problems whilst they drift towards a more repressive style unconstrained by the necessary, even if difficult, framework of new procedures for local accountability and complaints mechanisms. Mrs Thatcher has succeeded in creating a social order, but its basis may prove fragile in the long run. Market mechanisms may produce efficiency, and it can be argued that they produce a form of justice in allocation and supply, but a philosophy is also needed for how justice is to be provided in instances where the market has failed or in areas outwith the market. In the end, social order needs an overall philosophy of justice.

10

Conclusion

Cosmo Graham and Tony Prosser

The Conservative Party won the 1979 election on the basis of what was claimed to be a radical programme to stem Britain's decline, economic and otherwise. They did not, however, have a detailed plan for accomplishing this. Policies have been adopted, modified or abandoned in accordance with changing circumstances. Even in the core field of economic policy successive Conservative Governments' approaches to controlling the growth of the money supply have fluctuated (see Riddell 1983, Ch. 4; Thain 1984). Nevertheless, the sense of creating a new society, of rejuvenating Britain, has remained a central element of Conservative rhetoric. Commentators have referred to this as Thatcherism's 'hegemonic project' (Hall 1985) or, more cautiously, 'political argument hegemony' (Bulpitt 1986). Much of this rhetoric, such as 'rolling back the frontiers of the state', creating a 'popular capitalism', creating an 'enterprise culture', can be seen in constitutional terms. These notions involve redrawing the boundaries between the public and private spheres and changing the principles on which public bodies should act.

It would be inaccurate to see this as simply a return to an idealised nineteenth-century minimal state. As Gamble (1985, and Ch. 2 in the present volume) has argued, creating a free economy does not imply a weak state: a strong state is required to create and maintain the appropriate conditions. Taking this a step further, Harden (Ch. 3 in the present volume) maintains that, if the state is going to pursue these policies through being a player in the market-place, then corporatist forms of intervention provide certain advantages. So simple disengagement has not been an option for the Conservatives. Indeed, although they attempted a quango cull early on in the first administration (Hood 1981), they have since created and used quangos as enthusiastically as any post Second World War government; to list only a few examples, see the Urban Development Corporations, Joint Boards, the MSC and the Securities and Investments Board. A more useful approach is to say that the forms of state intervention have undergone major changes.

The weakness of our constitutional safeguards has allowed the Conservatives to undertake these changes with relative ease. Furthermore, the Conservatives have not been forced to articulate a consistent rationale for their changes, and instead have been allowed to talk about 'democracy' and the 'rule of law' in abstract ways in particular contexts. Compare this with the struggles over nationalisation in France after 1981 and deregulation in the United States under Reagan against the privatisation of nationalised industries in Britain (Harden and Lewis 1983; Delion and Durupty 1982, Ch. 4).

We have seen in the preceding essays that the Conservatives have not taken a coherent institutional approach to the constitution, and internal inconsistencies in their own approach can be identified. For example, they have accepted freedom of information in local government but have steadfastly resisted any attempt to extend this to quasi-government or central government. They have insisted on provision for 'democratic' ballots for trade unions, building societies and schools opting out of the state system; however, the procedures and majorities needed in each case vary dramatically. Finally, although trade unions have been forced to ballot on political funds, company donations have not been touched, even though there are equally valid arguments about the lack of shareholder control (Ewing 1987).

The 1987 general election manifesto (Conservative Central Office 1987) showed no change in this approach. There were several commitments of the utmost constitutional importance; for example to allow schools to opt out of local authority control, to limit further the powers of trades unions, to privatise water and electricity, and to limit even more the powers of local authorities through requiring further privatisation, establishing new Urban Development Corporations, and most importantly of all, replacing domestic rating with a 'Community Charge' or 'poll tax'. Yet no reference is made to any coherent rationale linking these plans, still less to any coherent overhaul of the mechanisms of government.

Undoubtedly some Conservative policies, such as council house sales, the privatisation of nationalised industries, are, in part, aimed at creating a 'natural' constituency for the party. However, one must not forget that the Conservatives have also responded to real problems, for example over the unpopularity of nationalised industries. This is, in part, no doubt why they have retained a remarkably loyal core of support from the electorate (around 40 per cent) which, combined with the quirks of our electoral system, has resulted in an equally remarkable longevity. This has created a great dilemma for those political groupings opposed to the Conservatives. Wholesale criticism of the Conservatives, without any alternatives, is unconvincing, but any alternative must not be seen simply as a return to the pre-1979 era. How they have responded at a constitutional level we shall discuss shortly, but some further discussion of the Conservatives and civil liberties is required now.

Civil liberties

Although a rhetorical concern with 'rolling back the frontiers of the state' and providing an inviolable private sphere might seem to imply a concern with civil liberties, generally Conservative thought has been hostile or, at best, indifferent to civil liberties, although there are honourable exceptions, for example, the Human Rights Bill sponsored by Edward Gardner. A strain in traditional Conservatism, which insists on the importance of 'authority', while 'New Right' thinking on civil liberties, at its most extreme, denies the existence of such liberties or, at best, is ambivalent or inconsistent (Belsey 1986). Such attitudes (not peculiar to Conservative Governments; for the Attlee Government's appalling attitude to the European Convention on Human Rights, see Lester 1984: 49–55) have meant that civil liberties issues have been tackled in a piecemeal and unprincipled fashion, although technological and organisational changes have rendered existing protections inadequate in many areas (Wallington 1984). The Government has acted only when forced to by international obligations and, even then, has only done the minimum required. This can be illustrated by looking at data protection.

Protection of privacy first arose as an issue in Britain in the 1960s. Concern was expressed at the combination of the amount of information the government possessed on individuals in order to carry out its activities and the potential of new computer technology which could manipulate that information in unforeseen ways. (Generally, see Campbell and Connor 1986). This problem was not unique to Britain, and a number of other liberal democracies have also had to deal with it (see Mellors and Pollitt 1984).

Where Britain differed from the rest was that, although there were numerous piecemeal inquiries into various aspects of privacy, nothing was done until developments outside the country forced a change. The key event was the creation of the European Convention on Trans-Border Data Flows, which laid down minimum standards of protection for data. The sanction was that its signatories would undertake not to transfer data to those countries which did not provide equivalent protection. The threat of being excluded from the European data market brought forth the Data Protection Act 1984, which can fairly be described as a minimalist measure (see Austin 1984).

It is minimalist not only because the Data Protection Registrar (DPR) is understaffed but also because the DPR has few effective powers to obtain information and undertake investigations into compliance. There is also a wide-ranging exemption for information pertaining to national security and somewhat narrower exemptions for police, tax, health and social work records. Controversially, manual files are totally excluded from the Act. The fate of an all-party group in the House of Commons to secure equivalent protection for manual files is instructive. Although the Government agreed in principle, they were not prepared to accept the width of the original Bill (HC Debs Vol. 110 cols. 1211–17, 20 February 1987) and only agreed to extend coverage to local authority housing and social work records. The Act covers only *access* to records, without any rights to, for example, correction of inaccurate records, and the scope of the protection will depend entirely on regulations which the Minister is under no obligation to make (Access to Personal Files Act 1987, s.3). However, the Government promised to use its best endeavours to make regulations by the end of 1988 unless the consultation process disclosed difficult problems (Standing Committee C cols. 58–9, 1 April 1987). Whether anything at all, let alone a progressive measure, will emerge must be doubtful.

More recently a darker side to the Conservatives has emerged in civil liberties matters, taking the form of an increasing intolerance of certain groups in society. The best illustration is the clause in the Local Government Bill banning local authorities from 'promoting homosexuality'. The contributions from the Government side make it clear that, at best, they see homosexuals as second-class citizens:

> I do not believe that it is any part of a local authority's duty . . . to encourage youngsters to believe that [homosexuality] is on an equal footing with a heterosexual way of life.
>
> (Standing Committee A col. 1209, 8 December 1987)

Even such minimal tolerance is beyond some Government supporters (see 124 HC Debs cols. 993, 1000, 1006, 15 December 1987). Such an approach was also evident in Mrs Thatcher's attitude to the 'hippy convoys': 'I am only too delighted to do anything I can to make life difficult for such things as hippy convoys' (HC Debs vol. 98 col. 1083, 5 June 1986). So although a commercial free market is desirable, a free market in life-styles is another matter. Indeed, adoption of certain life-styles should be positively discouraged by the state. In the absence of any entrenched protections for individual rights, the implications of such views are highly disturbing.

So the same lack of coherent constitutional thought that was evident in collective decision-making processes can be seen in the area of civil liberties. We now need to address the alternatives on offer. An inevitable limitation is that much of our discussion is based on the manifestos for the 1987 general election. Our interest is not in the detail of these documents but in the general approach they take to matters constitutional.

The Labour Party and 'market socialism'

The results of the 1987 election showed that the most effective political challenge to the Thatcherite Conservative Party is likely to come from the Labour Party, and we will examine their proposals first. Unlike the 'longest suicide note in history', produced for the 1983 election, in 1987 the Labour Party manifesto was brief and concise (Labour Party 1987). It did include important constitutional proposals. These included (most importantly of all) the replacement of section 2 of the Official Secrets Act by freedom of information legislation, Parliamentary scrutiny of the security services, new ombudsmen for education and police complaints, state aid for political parties, the ending of privatisation in the NHS and the restoration of an elected authority for London together with greater autonomy and fewer financial penalties for local authorities. An elected Scottish Assembly was to be established, together with a new Wales Economic Planning Council, and the Government would 'consult widely' about the most effective regional structure of government and administration for England and Wales.

Although, at the time of writing, the Labour Party has just embarked on a wide-ranging review of all its policies, we feel the broad thrust of the issues facing the Opposition parties will remain, although the details may alter. Indeed, Bryan Gould has been quoted as saying that after the review, 'we might end up with 95 per cent of our present policies. There is no implication that we will change fundamentally' (*The New Statesman*, 6 November 1987).

Social ownership

Inevitably in such a brief manifesto there are no details of new institutional design or suggestion of wider constitutional principles – for these we must look elsewhere. A key document is the collection of Statements by the Party's National Executive Committee to the 1986 Annual Conference (Labour Party 1986). There is little in this or in similar documents about general constitutional issues, for example of civil liberties, and such issues have been left largely to splinter groups such as the Labour Campaign for Criminal Justice. However, there is extensive discussion of the issue of public, or social, ownership of industry. This is of absolutely crucial importance for the Party, partly because most versions of socialism have hitherto contained central reference to public ownership, partly because of the Party's implementation of nationalisation when in power, but most importantly because of the popular identification of the Labour Party with nationalisation: 'In the public mind ... Social ownership – indeed Socialism itself – has become identified with the remote and bureaucratic state corporation' (Hattersley 1987a: 159). As we suggested in our discussion of privatisation above, the failure to develop effective and legitimate arrangements for nationalisation by previous Labour Governments has been a source of part of the appeal of privatisation. The 'Social Ownership' proposals put forward by the National Executive Committee represent a partial attempt to come to terms with this.

The background is dissatisfaction with the arrangements so far adopted for nationalisation, and in particular the model of the public corporation at arm's length from government, associated with Herbert Morrison. Instead, the proposal is that there should be a plurality of different types of institution. A key text is a quotation from Sydney Webb commenting on Clause 4 Part IV of the Party's Constitution which he had drafted:

> This declaration of the Labour Party leaves it open to choose from time to time whatever forms of common ownership - from co-operative store to the nationalised railway - and whatever form of popular administration and control of industry - from national guilds to ministries of employment and municipal management - may *in particular cases* be appropriate.
>
> (Quoted in Hattersley 1987b: 12)

In practice, the new social ownership would seem to mean two things (the following discussion is taken largely from Labour Party 1986: 1–12). First the public utilities would remain in public ownership because of their monopoly status, because of the need to satisfy rights to equal service irrespective of the cost of supply, and because of their strategic role as regards the rest of the economy. There would be further public ownership, or at least a strategic stake retained by government, in oil, aerospace, steel and shipbuilding and in much of the defence industry. However, even in relation to large-scale state enterprises, there is criticism of the Morrisonian model as 'outdated, leaving behind it a legacy of unresponsive monoliths' (Labour Party 1986: 2). The defects of this model are to be overcome by a wider representation of interests on industry boards, a more open and participative process of corporate planning, the development of more sophisticated performance indicators and of fuller economic and social audit by the Monopolies and Mergers Commission, and clearly defined contractual payments from government for the cost of the pursuit of wider social objectives. The industries would also be allowed to diversify and be freed from the constraints of external financing limits.

Apart from in the public utilities and other basic industries, a plurality of different forms of public ownership would be encouraged. One means of developing this would be through a holding company, to be called British Enterprise, taking strategic stakes in particular industries. This would be supplemented by the work of local and regional enterprise boards and by a British Investment Bank as a source of investment capital. In addition, legal measures would be taken to encourage the development of co-operative enterprises and to encourage democratic employee shareholding schemes.

Other aspects of industrial policy would also attempt to restore the legitimacy of public ownership. Thus provision would be made throughout industry to increase employees' rights to information, consultation and representation. A new National Consumer Agency would represent nationalised industry consumers instead of the fragmented consumer councils currently existing, and would for example be able to investigate proposed price increases and monitor performance. Consumer advice agencies and their management committees would represent consumers at a local level, and grievances would ultimately be dealt with by an ombudsman for each of the industries.

These proposals are by no means free from ambiguity; for example, the degree to which they would resolve the problems of the Morrisonian model as regards even the basic utilities is unclear. Probably *the* major difficulty with the Morrisonian form of nationalisation was the unreality of assuming that a strategic industry could ever operate at 'arm's length' from government. The result of this was that the inevitable government intervention took place *ad hoc* and in secret; as a result the industries had no consistent objectives and, even more seriously, accountability was reduced to vanishing point. Who could be held accountable if it was not clear if a policy was the responsibility of the board or the Minister? The Deputy Leader of the Labour Party has stated that in the key area of pricing policy, 'The rule ... should not be that the government should not interfere, but that when it does it should interfere openly and honestly' (Hattersley 1987b: 183–4). However, the important point is not the intention of members of a government but the institutional machinery to *compel* openness. This is strikingly lacking in the social ownership proposals. This omission is particularly to be regretted in view of the fact that ten years earlier the National Economic Development Office had made proposals for quite sophisticated new structures for the industries to achieve precisely such openness (NEDO 1976). The proposed freedom of information legislation will of course help in this, but one finds an unwillingness to think beyond it into new political structures which can give expression to an open and accountable democracy.

Nevertheless, there is a willingness in the Labour Party to think more imaginatively about the forms of public ownership. This is one reflection of a much larger process occurring both within and without the Labour Party with the aim of rethinking the basic justifications for, and tenets of, socialism. This has even found its way to practising politicians; two leading members of the Party have published relatively sophisticated attempts to justify and clarify the philosophical bases of socialist principles (Gould 1985; Hattersley 1987b). The wider debate has two themes of the greatest importance: the reassessment of the role of markets and, more haltingly, the realisation of the importance of the constitutional issue of how to design public institutions that can engage in planning democratically and legitimately.

Market socialism

The brief discussion possible here will involve violent oversimplification of a rich literature, but some important key points can be extracted from it (see in particular Nove 1983; Hodgson 1984; Forbes 1986). The first is that, whilst criticising the unreality of perfect markets underlying much neo-classical economics, there is equal dissatisfaction with the idea of centralised planning associated with much socialist theory and practice. To quote Nove:

> Authors of pedestrian textbooks can confine their analysis to a 'world' of perfect competition, perfect markets and perfect knowledge, in which the initial axioms and definitions eliminate all the problems of real life. Socialists, understandably, have little patience with such models. They, in their turn, cannot substitute for them an equally unreal model of their own, in which all-knowing 'democratic' planners provide all that is needed for the good of society, and in which the (predictable) difficulties which these planners will face are assumed not to exist ... perfect competition and perfect computation are alike in being perfect (and equal in their unreality).
>
> (Nove 1983: 8)

To a large extent the critique of planning is based on experience of East European regimes; as a result the system of centralised planning through the issue of binding instructions from the planning office is rejected for two reasons. First, it is argued that such planning is associated with political despotism (Nove 1983: 77–8). The second problem is that total centralised planning is impossible for informational reasons: quite simply, it is impossible for a planning authority to acquire sufficient information to co-ordinate the economy effectively. Thus Nove quotes a 'doubtless sarcastic' Soviet author as remarking that 'Mathematicians have calculated that in order to draft an accurate and fully integrated plan for material supply to the Ukraine for one year requires the labour of the entire world's population for 10 million years' (Nove 1983: 33). These limitations on planning have of course been notably reinforced by the changes in the Soviet Union under the Gorbachev regime, notably the move from annual planning to long-term and strategic five- and fifteen-year guidelines (*Guardian*, 30 June 1987).

Despite their acknowledgement of the limitations of planning, market socialists do not advocate unfettered markets throughout the economy. Rather the key question is how the inevitable combination between markets and planning is to develop. One answer to this has been given as follows:

> The lesson of Soviet-type and British-type economies, therefore, is that economic planning should cover no more and no less than macro-variables such as employment, aggregate income, investment share and its broad allocation, public consumption and criteria of income distribution, the balance of international payments flows for trade and capital; while markets should cover no more and no less than the structure of output (by sectors and enterprises) and relative prices; with policy instruments, instead of direct orders, being used to make markets fit with the plans.
>
> (Nuti 1986: 374; cf. Hattersley 1987b: 212–13)

The implication is that major areas for planning will remain, but that it will be impossible to operate these simply through an authoritarian centralised authority issuing orders to economic actors. The new thought on market socialism has also highlighted the need to determine how to plan effectively and legitimately.

The stress in the new writing is that it is important to retain pluralism in the planning process so as to enable learning to take place. It has been neatly summarised:

> no individual or party can be justly certain that any particular political strategy or economic programme is the best, or even adequate: all are possibly false and governed by a degree of uncertainty. This fact confounds the closed and secretive type of government which is found in most advanced capitalist democracies.... Closed, secretive government ... exacerbates the problem of uncertainty and incomplete information by failing to create open and informed debate.
>
> (Hodgson 1984: 161-2)

This means that planning should be subjected to a continual process of correction through political participation:

> In brief, the argument is as follows: any politico-economic strategy for the transition to socialism, and any economic plan within socialism itself, is based on inadequate information, suffers partial distortions, and embodies faults of a more or less serious nature. This ever present potential for failure means that alternative plans and strategies must be given scope for political expression.
>
> (Hodgson 1984: 162; see also Hodgson 1984: 31-2 and Ch. 10)

One element for attaining this is to develop a mix of different types of socially owned institutions so that one can learn from experience which is the most appropriate for particular purposes (see Nove 1983: 200). The other is to develop regulatory techniques which will institutionalise the process of learning. This would involve a revolutionary change in British political and constitutional culture; there are signs that the importance of such change is at last being recognised in socialist thought.

Socialism and constitutional design

Despite an honourable record of concern over issues of civil liberties, socialists have shown remarkably little interest in the design of institutions and constitutions. This may have been partly due to a naïve faith in the withering away of law and its replacement by administration with the achievement of socialism (see O'Hagan 1984). It has certainly also been influenced by a desire to leave socialist governments as free as possible from inconvenient constraints when in power. There are signs that this is changing, partly under the influence of the shifts in attitude away from centralisation referred to above. For example, Paul Hirst has written that a central problem facing socialist thought is the need for:

> political theorizing to convert socialism into a specific and practical political doctrine – changing it from an anti-capitalist economic theory and a set of values and political sentiments into an account of a new and superior constitution, of political institutions that permit both democratic account-ability and efficient government.
>
> (Hirst 1986: 1)

Indeed, one of the strains of thought within the market socialism debate suggests a role for the state remarkably similar to that of the currently-influential theories of 'reflexive law': 'the market socialist government sets up the framework of laws and institutions that enable different forms of economic organisation spontaneously to evolve in an advantageous way' (Winter 1986: 16; for 'reflexive law' see Teubner 1983).

The implications of such a concern with new institutional and constitutional design do, of course, lead far beyond current Labour Party policy. This has been recognised by some writers, notably Michael Rustin. Thus he has advocated proportional representation, initially as a lever to force more radical policies from the Alliance in the event of coalition in a hung Parliament, but also as a desirable goal in itself, reflecting changes in the social bases of Labour support. This is to be combined with a process of radical decentralisation of power to localities, regions and constituent nations of the United Kingdom and a strengthening of the ability of the local state apparatus to undertake economic intervention. There would also be state funding of political parties, increased resources for elected members at all levels of government for research and policy development, and fixed-term Parliaments to diminish Prime Ministerial power (Rustin 1986: 52–5; cf. the Alliance proposals discussed below).

Electoral reform has had some appeal to others on the Left, though not in the form of single transferable vote advocated by the Alliance (Scargill 1986; Cook 1987). To a large extent this reflects the serious problems of Labour's declining electoral base, in turn due to social and class factors which are likely to prove irreversible (see Jacques and Mulhearn 1981). Such concern with constitutional issues is at least a start, and as we have suggested above, there is a growing body of theoretical work on the meaning of 'feasible socialism', representing the greatest diversity of socialist thought since early in this century. We also know what particular institutions to be introduced by a Labour Government would be likely to look like in terms of their detailed operation.

What is lacking, however, is the development of specifically socialist thought linking general theoretical principles and the design of particular institutions – constitutional thought in the sense referred to in this book. As we have suggested, some socialist writers are now asking the right questions about the need for constitutional and institutional design.

Similarly, in much of the writing referred to above there is stress on the need for political institutions which are open, participative and accountable (e.g. Hirst 1986: 38, 86, 102). This would represent a revolutionary change in British government; however, apart from the proposed freedom of information legislation, there is little indication that the Labour Party has come to terms with the need to develop the institutions to make it possible. Thus the Leader of the Labour Party has written of the need to engage in participative forms of planning, but seems only to be able to suggest reinforcing the role of the National Economic Development Office and of the 'Little Neddies' as the vehicles for this (Kinnock 1986: 106–10).

A similar lack of interest in constitutional principle can be found in Labour Party attitudes to a Bill of Rights. This is best exemplified in the failure of the Human Rights Bill introduced by a Conservative backbencher to incorporate the European Convention on Human Rights in British law so making it enforceable in domestic courts and obviating the need to bring lengthy and expensive actions in Strasbourg. Such an unentrenched form of constitutional protection would hardly have represented constitutional revolution, but nevertheless if used effectively it could have had an important educative role in developing the notion of the citizen as a bearer of rights rather than as a subject of paternalist government. Perhaps even more importantly, it would have permitted much more extended rights-based argument in everyday cases in the lower courts on such issues as police powers and public order (see Gifford 1987). The Labour Party, however, seemed generally to be caught between two contradictory attitudes explaining lack of support for the Bill. On the one hand, it was argued that the Bill did not go far enough and would be meaningless without more fundamental social and economic reform. To quote an academic commentator:

> Only when the major economic, financial and commercial forces have been wrested from the government by political means will it be time to consider whether a new constitutional settlement, including a bill of rights, might be the appropriate way to ensure a truly open system of government. To go down that route now would worsen not improve the present crisis as it would hold out false hopes of betterment for the people and in fact achieve nothing of moment at all.
>
> (McAuslan 1986)

On the other hand, arguments were deployed against the Bill that were frankly constitutionally reactionary; for example, we were treated to the sight of opposition by a Labour spokesman on the grounds that the Bill would harm the separation of powers and politicise judges as if anyone could still believe that British government was characterised by separation of powers and that our judges were not already up to their necks in politics (Mr Brown at 109 HC Debs col. 1276, 6 February 1987). At the end of Second Reading only seventeen Labour members voted for the Bill; it fell due to a failure (by six votes) to achieve the necessary support of 100 MPs. As a supporter put it:

> we rushed to kill the bill instead of leaving that embarrassment to a government which was going to do it anyway. Our speakers were forced to parrot Tory myths about Parliament protecting rights, and judges being embarrassed by politics, even though rights proffer one of the few available weapons to resist the Thatcher counter-revolution. The Gardner Rights bill was defeated last Friday because fewer Labour MPs supported it than any other party. Nor is this just passing incompetence. Our attitude to rights is part of a syndrome. We say we will advance freedom only by methods growing rusty.
>
> (Mitchell 1987)

(For the horrifying attitudes of members of the Attlee Government to the European Convention, see Lester 1984: 49–55.) This is aside from the most radical reason for supporting such a Bill. To quote another commentator:

> Here, at last, the underlying point of a Bill of Rights begins to appear. The thin end of a gigantic wedge is being inserted. I don't know how much the Bill would do for bullied British subjects. But one thing is certain: it is absolutely alien to the practices and theory of the British State and, if it survived, would begin to subvert, split and topple them one after another. And that is why – on balance – I am for it.
>
> (Ascherson 1987)

This constitutional conservatism in the Labour Party would not matter so much if the Party had a developed alternative strategy for the protection of rights and the creation of a more effectively accountable form of government. However, the evidence is that the Party does not: one is left with the impression that it would retain ineffective Parliamentary protections operating very much as they do now, and whilst campaigning on particular civil libertarian issues, would not attempt any fundamental thought on potentially more effective mechanisms for ensuring the protection of civil rights. Ironically, the most innovative forms of Labour experimentation in new forms of economic intervention have occurred in the field of municipal socialism (see e.g. Blunkett and Jackson 1987; Mackintosh and Wainwright 1987). However, these are now exceedingly vulnerable since the 1987 election given the lack of any means of protecting the autonomy of elected local government against the increasing centralisation of the state.

However, the Labour Party was not the only opposition to the Conservative Party in 1987; it would seem, at least superficially, that the Alliance was prepared to give much greater prominence to constitutional rethinking. We will now consider their policies and related thought.

The Alliance: a better yesterday?

The unique contribution of the Liberal and Social Democratic parties to political debate in Britain is their insistence on constitutional reform being a necessary precondition for solving society's ills, in particular that of relative economic decline (Liberal/SDP Alliance 1983: 5, 36). Their ideas therefore deserve serious consideration even though, at the time of writing, there is no immediate possibility of their entering into government. Indeed, at present the future of the Alliance itself is in considerable doubt, given the refusal of David Owen and his supporters to join a merged party and the violent arguments over the policies to be adopted by a merged party. Despite these differences, we will treat the Alliance as one entity for the purposes of this chapter, unless otherwise specified, because the major points of conflict appear to be defence policy, attitudes and personalities, although there is also some dispute over the 'social market' (see Andrews 1985). The need for constitutional reform remains, for the present, as common ground between the various protagonists, and has been considered in a relatively systematic way, unlike the Labour Party.

According to the Alliance the problems of British politics are mainly caused by two phenomena: adversarial politics and increasing centralism. Adversarial politics is seen at its most institutionalised in the daily confrontations in the House of Commons, but it also reflects deeper, class divisions in British society (S. Williams 1982: 132–3). Institutionalising such divisions within the political process encourages the adoption of 'ideological' politics, a trend on the increase in recent years. The result is an endemic short-termism in the British policy-making process; one party is elected and puts its solutions to work, then when it loses office its successor undoes all these previous policies. So there is little stability and continuity in policies, and this particularly affects the government's management of the economy (Holme 1987: 88–90; Liberal/SDP Alliance 1987: 1; Holme and Muggridge 1987a: 1–3). Centralism simply means that there has been an increasing tendency to bring more public powers and functions under the aegis of central government. This discourages diversity and policy innovation, contributes to governmental overload threatening further the rationality of policy-making and, when combined with adversary politics and a lack of checks, has serious implications for citizens' rights (Holme 1987: 54–5, 88; Liberal/SDP Alliance 1983: 8).

So the institutional structure of the British constitution prevents rational policy-making. Therefore, a precondition for solving the ills of society is institutional reform. Four proposals are central to the Alliance programme: proportional representation, freedom of information, decentralisation and the incorporation of the European Convention on Human Rights into British law. We will concentrate on the first two, but putting freedom of information into the wider context of reform of the Parliamentary and governing processes. This means passing over the Alliance proposals for decentralisation (Liberal/SDP Alliance 1983: 17–27; Liberal/SDP Alliance 1987: 3–4; SDP, no date [c]) and strengthening individual rights through the incorporation of the European Convention, a proposed Human Rights Commission, access to personal information and a reform of administrative law, to mention only some ideas (Liberal/SDP Alliance 1983: 28–35; SDP 1983; SDP no date [a]). Although these are important issues, our major concern is the effect the Alliance proposals will have on public decision-making processes.

The overall aim is to close the gap between the words and the deeds of the constitution and return to 'Parliamentarism' (Marquand 1982: 80). The Alliance interpretation of the constitution, especially as regards collective decision-making processes, looks to the nineteenth-century myth of a Parliament which made laws and called governments to account (Marquand 1982: 74, 81; Liberal/SDP Alliance 1983: 6–7). An example is David Owen, who objects to the growing 'corporatism' on the grounds that committee decision-making produces a consensus which erodes decisive democratically elected and responsible decision-making (Owen 1981: 39, 55). We will argue that this is an unrealistic objective. Parliamentary scrutiny of government action can be made more effective, and this is a worthwhile reform in itself, but to expect Parliament to govern a complex welfare state is to hanker after a chimera. Furthermore, by pinning their hopes on Parliament, the Alliance ignores the real foci of decision-making, the complex networks of bargaining that exist between government departments, semi-autonomous agencies, pressure groups and the private sector. We shall argue that, although Alliance proposals assume the necessity for such networking, they provide no coherent set of proposals for institutional design which will open up such deliberations to a wider public. As a result, although their constitutional reforms would bring a different set of actors into key positions, the fundamental problems would remain.

Before dealing with the details of the proposed reforms, one more comment on the Alliance analysis is needed. A critique of adversary politics can, as Gamble and Walkland (1984: 24–8) have pointed out, have at least three variants. The first is that the adversary system in Britain has been the cause of significant and frequent reversals in economic policy. The second is that the political market causes each party to bid for support from the electors, thus creating a spiral of rising expectations. The third variant, identified with Ashford (1981), is that adversary politics is a symptom of a deeper-seated constitutional weakness. British government is seen as too centralised and secretive. Adversary politics produces conflict on a few issues but other areas remain relatively neglected. In high-profile areas policy analysis is difficult to conduct because of the conflict, while in low-profile areas policy is not analysed because Britain lacks mechanisms outside the adversarial conflict:

There is no official voice outside Parliament that provides a continuing critique of how well government is working.... Within government,... untangling...policy problems continues to rest almost entirely with the cabinet and higher civil servants. Perhaps the greatest loss is that learning from past errors and experience depends on a remarkably small number of persons who in fact have very little time, and very little incentive, to make the critiques and evaluations of policy effectiveness that are more pronounced in most other democratic political systems.

(Ashford 1981: 16)

The Alliance analysis is mainly variant one, with occasional references to the second. Gamble and Walkland (1984) and Ashford (1981) have argued that this is not an accurate characterisation of British politics. In some areas, such as nationalisation and trade union reform it is reasonably accurate, but not in others, for example foreign economic policy, stabilisation policy (see Gamble and Walkland 1984: 29–34, Ch. 3). If variant one is the favoured explanation, then proportional representation and coalition politics become central parts of the platform. However, the message of the Ashford thesis is rather different. It is that the policy process has to be opened up to competing views and analysis; in so far as electoral reform accomplishes this it is a positive gain, but it is not enough on its own.

Proportional representation

It is well known that the Alliance favours the introduction of proportional representation (PR) into the electoral system, preferably using multi-member constituencies and the single transferable vote. The strongest argument used is an implicit rights argument, that everyone should be treated equally, and this implies that all votes should have an equal value (Holme 1987: 94; Liberal/SDP Alliance 1986: 7–8). Under the present first-past-the-post system, it is argued, large numbers of voters are denied any representation for their views. More interesting, for present purposes, are the expected effects.

The first result would be the replacement of adversarial politics by the politics of negotiation and consensus, as it is extremely unlikely that any one party would have obtained an overall majority in Parliament (or any equivalent, e.g. local government). This would change dramatically the nature of the governing process. The manifesto would no longer be, in any sense, a binding pledge to the electorate but would set out the parties' main priorities and subsidiary goals, which would then be negotiated over (Holme 1987: 121–3). This process would, it is suggested, in itself, contribute to open government (Owen 1982: 245) because, if there was a formal coalition agreement this would put the parties' agreement into the public sphere (Holme and Muggridge 1987b: 7).

The second result envisaged is that power would be returned to Parliament (and this provides a context for the proposed Parliamentary reforms). Backbench MPs would be less able to opt out of their legislative responsibility by simply following the party line, and they could get involved in the preparation of legislation (Holme 1987: 99, 130). Finally, PR would encourage better policy-making within British government. The process of negotiation would aid the search for long-term strategies and, by creating a consensus, ensure that they survived beyond the term of one Parliament (see Holme and Muggridge 1987a: 4, and 1987b: 4, 7; Holme 1987: 124–5; Owen 1987: 12).

These beliefs can be criticised at a number of levels. It is not clear why the negotiation of a coalition agreement is more open to the *public* than the creation of a party manifesto. Nor is it clear why negotiated politics should encourage a strategic approach to government; short-term bargaining seems, *a priori*, just as likely. However, the most important weakness in the arguments for PR is that they assume relations between politicians are all-important. This in turn assumes a sharp distinction between politics and administration, policy and implementation. Politicians create the policies and civil servants put them into practice. However, in the real world of British government, politicians' and civil servants' political functions are inextricably intertwined (see Harden and Lewis 1986: 137–43). If this is accepted, it becomes just as important to open up the civil servants' views to the public and competing analysis. Freedom of information, even excluding civil servants' advice to ministers, would be a necessary first step.

Freedom of information and reform of government

The Alliance has always given a Freedom of Information Act a central place in their list of desirable changes, and this would be a crucial constitutional reform. (Yet eight of their MPs failed to support the Sheperd Protection of Official Information Bill.) Their argument is that in a genuine democracy the people must have more than just the ability to cast a vote: they must be able to scrutinise the workings of government (Liberal/SDP Alliance 1986: 5). This is clearly right: implicit in the very notion of a *choice* between candidates is the notion that you must be able to exercise this choice on rational grounds. Without information on how your representatives have carried out their promises, the notion of choice becomes illusory (see Harden and Lewis 1986: 41–2).

For the Alliance, freedom of information is mainly important because it would aid Parliament in its work. Although there are mentions of a wider role for freedom of information, such as improving government's learning curve (Holme 1987: 116, 134) and improving the process of consultation with interest groups (Holme and Muggridge 1987a: 5, and 1987b: 4), the underlying premise is that 'Freedom of Information, however useful to the private citizen, depends for its public utility on a parliamentary system capable of using the information wisely and effectively' (Holme and Muggridge 1987a: 5). This means, not merely that Parliament would be able

to scrutinise executive action more effectively, although this is acknowledged to be an important gain, but also that Parliament will become an equal
partner in the policy-making process (Holme 1987: 131; cf. also Owen 1982:
248).

This becomes clearer if freedom of information is set against the context
of other proposals. For example, the Alliance has proposed that specialised
select committees should take on more of a pre-legislative role, that more
use should be made of the special standing committee procedure by which
such a committee can call evidence and witnesses before commencing to
examine a bill, that time for debate, either in committee or in the House of
Commons, should be available for *all* statutory instruments, draft European
Community regulations and directives and that there should be more time
for Private Members' Bills (Liberal/SDP Alliance 1983: 12). Underlying such
proposals is a barely concealed nostalgia for a 'real' Parliament, but they
would be ineffective without consequent changes in the executive.

Hence it is proposed to strengthen ministers' analytical capabilities by
providing them with a Ministerial Policy Unit, to reconstitute the Central
Policy Review Staff and to ensure that Cabinet is truly the centre for
strategic and collective decision-making (see, respectively, Holme and
Muggridge 1987c: 6, and 1987b: 6; Holme 1987: 118, 125-9). These
recommendations assume that ministerial responsibility is a central
constitutional convention. However, the doctrine is:

> mythical in two senses. It does not describe the actual world in which ministers
> and civil servants are 'inextricably mixed up with each other' but nor, in
> modern conditions, does it describe a possible world. It does, however,
> function as a powerful ideological consideration. Attempts at reform must be
> consistent with preservation of the myth and thus must not challenge the
> distinction between policy and administration. This of course guarantees that
> the reforms could not succeed in the real world.
>
> (Harden and Lewis 1986: 143)

Industrial policy

If such proposals will not arguably increase the rationality of government
decision-making, there is also another defect. That is that they do not
encompass the realm of 'extended government', the complex network of
institutions and bargaining which exists between government and other
actors and characterises the British policy-making process (see Harden and
Lewis 1986, Ch. 6). The Alliance solution seems to rest mainly on
strengthening the powers of legislatures and creating new ones (Regional
Assemblies) (though cf. SDP 1983) and thus, we have argued, rests on
untenable views regarding the role of legislatures and politicians. If the
Alliance's industrial strategy is dissected, it can be seen to rest on, partly,
creating new institutions and processes and partly on utilising existing ones
in different ways. What is striking is that the constitutional implications are

not addressed. In particular, the Alliance's lack of concern over designing institutions to ensure openness matches that of the Labour Party. Freedom of information is of course a prerequisite of openness but, as experience in the United States has shown (Dresner 1980), a Freedom of Information Act is only the beginning, it needs to be buttressed by other institutions.

These points can be illustrated by examining the Alliance's proposals for nationalised industries. Alliance thinking indicates that, if in government, they would be likely to retain some nationalised industries, as the question of ownership is seen as something of a distraction from the real issues. How then would they solve the problems faced by the nationalised industries? The SDP would begin by distinguishing monopoly industries from those in a competitive environment (SDP, no date [b]: 27). As regards the latter, competitive pressures would ensure efficiency and therefore no government controls would be needed. Such companies should be reconstituted as Companies Act companies, with the government possibly holding a residual shareholding. The assumption that there is a pure private sector is startlingly naïve, especially in a document which recognises that public purchasing power should be used for industrial policy purposes and that governments may have to stave off bankruptcy in certain industries.

As for the monopolistic nationalised industries, the SDP proposes to set up an Efficiency Audit Commission for Nationalised Industries (SDP, no date [b]: 28–9) which will be able to scrutinise all the activities of the industries as well as their relations with government. As for relations with government, the main thrust of the policy is to try and insulate the industries from political interference in their day-to-day running (see also Liberal Party, no date: 3; Rodgers 1982: 162). This is to be done partly by setting up a system of supervisory boards and partly by a self-denying ordinance (SDP no date [b]: 29–30). This is simply unrealistic. To quote the same document (p. 7), talking about the private sector, 'government cannot operate a "hands-off" policy because government is itself a major purchaser and producer of goods and services, and has responsibility for the legal, social, fiscal, trade and economic framework within which industry operates'. If institutions are set up assuming non-intervention as the norm, this then encourages secretive, *ad hoc* interventions, as illustrated by the history of nationalised industries.

So we have seen that, although in certain areas, especially individual rights, the Alliance's constitutional views are more progressive than the Labour Party's, neither has come to terms with the constitutional problems of governing a modern welfare state. The Conservative Party, it has been argued throughout the book, has little interest in constitutional issues. What, then, does the future hold? It is to this we now turn.

Looking through a glass darkly

Certainly while the Conservative Party in its present incarnation retains power there is no chance of any principled constitutional reform. Changes will continue to happen, not only through the implementation of Conservative policies, but also in response to external pressures. Here the most significant pressures are likely to come from Europe, especially the European Court of Human Rights, although the influence of the EEC should not be forgotten. Important as these institutions may be, they are only designed as a long-stop; they cannot substitute for proper domestic procedures and information. Domestically, the crucial reform is freedom of information, the *sine qua non* of a liberal democracy. The all-party Freedom of Information Campaign, having won the arguments, will continue to battle away, and may even score isolated successes. However, at the moment the chances of gaining the general principle are nil.

This is illustrated by the response to Richard Sheperd's Protection of Official Information Bill. This Tory Private Member's Bill was a liberalising measure, but in an unprecedented move, a three-line whip was imposed on Conservative MPs in order to ensure its defeat, albeit only by thirty-odd votes. The Government failed to produce any arguments against the Bill in public, simply asserting that it was not a fit subject for a backbencher, and promising a White Paper in the summer of 1988.

This should be seen in the context of an atmosphere increasingly hostile to the unauthorised disclosure of information. One recent incident was the police and Special Branch raids, in early 1987, on the offices of BBC Scotland and *The New Statesman* in the aftermath of the cancelled *Secret Society* programme on the Zircon spy satellite. It is worth recalling that the programme dealt with issues of Parliamentary accountability rather than national security. Given the catch-all nature of section 2 of the Official Secrets Act some criminal offence would appear to have been committed. However, it has been announced that the maker of the programmes, Duncan Campbell, will not be prosecuted (123 HC Debs col. 483, 1 December 1987 [written answer]). In the light of this outcome, the raids look purely punitive.

No doubt, after the Ponting trial, the Government is unwilling to put section 2 to a jury. Instead, it has turned to the civil law on confidential information, most notably in the case of *Spycatcher* and Peter Wright who, as an Australian resident, could not be prosecuted under the criminal law. The Government seems determined to obtain a decision imposing a life-long duty of confidentiality on members of the security services to which there will be *no* exceptions. In particular, they are not prepared to accept that the need to expose wrong-doing can override the obligation of confidence, nor that widespread publication of the information outside Britain ends the need for secrecy in Britain.

In this quest to stifle discussion, the English courts have at times been most helpful to the Government. For example, in *A-G* v. *Newspaper Publishing* (1987) 3 WLR 942, the Court of Appeal ruled that anyone having notice of injunctions restraining the publication of confidential information, whether named in the injunction or not, could be liable for contempt of court, if they published the material. However, on the substantive issue, it is unclear whether the courts will ultimately back the Government. The question of whether to lift the interim injunction after the publication of *Spycatcher* in the United States produced extraordinary divisions in the House of Lords (*A-G* v. *Guardian* [1987] 1 WLR 1248), with the Government winning by three to two. At the trial proper (*Guardian*, 22 December 1987) the Government lost the first round with the trial judge suggesting that the ban sought could not be achieved this side of the Iron Curtain and this decision was upheld by the Court of Appeal (*The Times*, 11 February 1988). The ruling of the House of Lords is awaited.

In order to support this case the Government seems to feel obliged to prevent *any* public discussion of security matters through use of the civil law. This is most clearly shown by the injunction obtained against the BBC radio programme *My Country Right or Wrong*. This was, apparently, just a general discussion of the accountability of the security services, which had been cleared by the D Notice Committee. Nevertheless, an injunction was obtained to prevent its being broadcast. The terms of the original injunction were drawn so widely that they prevented even Peter Wright's *name*, or the names of Burgess, Philby and Maclean, from being broadcast. This ban also, due to the decision in *A-G* v. *Newspaper Publishing*, extended to third parties with notice of the injunction. Similar proceedings have also been taken against Duncan Campbell and Anthony Cavendish, author of *Inside Intelligence*, although the terms of the injunctions have gradually been narrowed.

These developments are worrying because the legal basis of the Government's actions – breach of confidence – can potentially apply to *any* government employee. The interpretation given by the courts to this rather vague doctrine has given the Government a powerful weapon to prevent disclosure of embarrassing information. A government committed to 'conviction' politics cannot, of necessity, tolerate dissent publicly expressed. It will, therefore, be prepared to use such a weapon.

Looking beyond the Conservative Party the most likely prospect for constitutional reform would seem to be a Labour–Alliance coalition. However, there is a long way to go before that becomes a viable proposition, let alone the question of whether such a coalition could win an election. Furthermore, it cannot be automatically assumed that constitutional reforms would flow from such a coalition. The Lib–Lab pact of 1978–9 did not produce reform of the Official Secrets Act even though it was on the agenda at the time. Perhaps the greatest spur would be a determination on the part of non-Conservative politicians to create a set of arrangements which were not so easy to capture and manipulate. Such arrangements always have their attractions while in power. In effect, Britain faces a cruel irony. At a time when constitutional reform is most needed, it is least likely to occur.

References

Accounting Standards Committee (1981) *Setting Accounting Standards.* London, ASC.
  (1983) Review of the standard setting process. *Accountancy,* July, 115–20.

Allen, V. L. (1960) *Trade Unions and Government.* London, Longmans.

Andrews, L. (1985) *Liberalism versus the Social Market Economy.* Hebden Bridge, Hebden
  Royd.

Arthurs, H. (1985) *Without the Law · Administrative Justice and Legal Pluralism in Nineteenth
  Century England.* Toronto, University of Toronto Press.

Ascher, K. (1987) *The Politics of Privatisation: Contracting Out Public Services.* London,
  Macmillan.

Ascherson, N. (1986) The Abolition of the GLC and the Mets. *Observer,* 30 March.
  (1987) The Real Case for A Bill of Rights. *Observer,* 1 February.

Ashford, D. (1981) *Policy and Politics in Britain.* Oxford, Basil Blackwell.

Audit Commission (1984) *The Impact on Local Authorities' Economy: Efficiency and Effectiveness of the Block Grant System.* London, HMSO.
  (1987) *Competitiveness and Contracting-Out of Local Authorities' Services.* Occasional Paper
  3. London, HMSO.

Austin, R. (1984) The Data Protection Act 1984. *Public Law,* 618–34.

Baldwin, R. (1985) *Regulating the Airlines.* Oxford, Clarendon Press.

Ball Committee (1978) *Report of the Committee on Policy Optimisation,* Command Paper
  7148. London, HMSO.

Barker, A. (ed.) (1982) *Quangos in Britain.* London, Macmillan.

Barry, N. (1979) *Hayek's Social and Economic Philosophy.* London, Macmillan.

Bayliss, F. J. (1962) *British Wages Councils.* Oxford, Basil Blackwell.

Beer, S. H. (1956) Pressure Groups and Parties in Britain. *American Political Science
  Review,* 50, 1–23.
  (1965) *Modern British Politics.* London, Faber & Faber.

Beesley, M. and Littlechild, S. 1983. Privatisation: Principles, Problems and Priorities. *Lloyds Bank Review*, 149, 1–20.

Belsey, A. (1986) The New Right, Social Order and Civil Liberties, in R. Levitas (ed.) *The Ideology of the New Right*. Oxford, Basil Blackwell.

Bercusson, B. (1976) *The Employment Protection Act 1975*. London, Sweet & Maxwell. (1978) *Fair Wages Resolutions*. London, Mansell.

Berrill, K. (1986) Regulation in a Changing City: Bureaucrats and Practitioners. *Midland Bank Review*, summer, 14–19.

Beyleveld, D. and Brownsword, R. (1986) *Law as a Moral Judgement*. London, Sweet & Maxwell.

Bienkowski, M., Allen, K. and Walker, R. (1986) *Government Support for British Business*. Glasgow, Centre for the Study of Public Policy, University of Strathclyde.

Birch, A. (1984) Theories of Political Crisis. *British Journal of Political Science*, 14, 135–60.

Birkinshaw, P., Harden, I. J. and Lewis, N. (1987) *Corporatism and Accountability: The Democratic Dilemma*. Report to ESRC. Unpublished.

Blank, S. (1973) *Industry and Government in Britain: The Federation of British Industries in Politics 1945–65*. Farnborough, Saxon House.

Blom-Cooper, L. (1982) The New Face of Judicial Review. *Public Law*, 250–61.

Blunkett, D. and Jackson, K. (1987) *Democracy in Crisis: The Town Halls Respond*. London, Hogarth Press.

Bosanquet, N. (1981) Sir Keith's Reading List. *Political Quarterly*, 52, 324–41. (1983) *After the New Right*. London, Heinemann.

Bottoms, A. E. and Wiles, P. (1986) Housing Tenure and Residential Community Crime Careers in Britain, in A. J. Reiss and M. Tonry (eds.) *Communities and Crime*. Chicago, Chicago University Press.

Breyer, S. and Stewart, R. (1985) *Administrative Law and Regulatory Policy*, 2nd edn. New York, Little Brown & Co.

Brindley, T., Rydin, Y. and Stoker, G. (1988) *Rethinking Planning*. London, Unwin Hyman.

Brown, L. N. and Garner, J. (1983) *French Administrative Law*, 3rd edn. London, Butterworths.

Bruce-Gardyne, J. (1984) *Mrs Thatcher's First Administration*. London, Macmillan.

Buchanan, J. (1978) *The Economics of Politics*. London, Institute of Economic Affairs.

Buckland, R. (1987) The Costs and Returns of the Privatization of Nationalized Industries. *Public Administration*, 65, 241–57.

Bullock, Lord (1977) Committee of Inquiry on Industrial Democracy. *Report*. Command Paper 6706, London, HMSO.

Bulpitt, J. (1986) The Discipline of the New Democracy: Mrs Thatcher's Domestic Statecraft. *Political Studies*, 34, 19–39.

Business Law Review (1987) Judicial Review of the Panel on Takeovers and Mergers. February, pp. 29 and 57.

Cabinet Office/Treasury (1985) *Non-Departmental Public Bodies: A Guide for Departments*. London, HMSO.

Cabinet Office (1986) *Public Bodies 1986*. London, HMSO.

Calamari, J. (1982) The Aftermath of *Gonzalez* and *Horne* on the Administrative Debarment and Suspension of Government Contractors. *New England Law Review*, 17, 1137–74.

Campbell, D. and Connor, S. (1986) *On the Record: Surveillance, Computers and Privacy*. London, Michael Joseph.

Cawson, A. (1982) *Corporatism and Welfare: Social Policy and State Intervention in Britain*. London, Heinemann.

Cawson, A. and Saunders, P. (1983) Corporatism, Competitive Politics and Class Struggle, in R. King (ed.) *Capital and Politics*. London, Routledge & Kegan Paul.

Charles,.R. (1973) *The Development of Industrial Relations in Britain 1911–1939*. London, Hutchinson.

Clegg, H. A. (1979) *The Changing System of Industrial Relations in Britain*. Oxford, Basil Blackwell.

(1985) *A History of British Trade Unions since 1889*, Volume II, 1919–1933. Oxford, Clarendon Press.

Cocks, R. (1983) *Foundations of the Modern Bar*. London, Sweet & Maxwell.

Cole, G. D. H. (1973) *Workshop Organisation*, 2nd edn, with an introduction by A. I. Marsh. London, Hutchinson.

Conservative Central Office (1987) *The Next Moves Forward*. London, Conservative Central Office.

Cook, R. (1987) Labour Needs Electoral Reform. *New Statesman*, 17 April, p. 16.

Coopers & Lybrand (1984) *Streamlining the Cities: An Analysis of the Costs involved in the Government's Proposals*. London, Coopers & Lybrand.

Crouch, C. (1979) *The Politics of Industrial Relations*. Glasgow, Fontana.

Daintith, T. (1985) The Executive Power Today: Bargaining and Economic Control, in J. Jowell and D. Oliver (eds.) *The Changing Constitution*. Oxford, Clarendon Press.

Daintith, T. and Willoughby, G. D. M. (1984) *United Kingdom Oil and Gas Law*, 2nd edn. London, Sweet & Maxwell.

Davies, H. W. E., Edwards, D. and Rawley, A. R. (1986) *The Relationship Between Development Plans, Development Control and Appeals*. University of Reading.

Davies, P. (1986) Labour Law and Corporatism in Britain in the 1980s. Unpublished.

Davies, P. and Freedland, M. (1984) *Labour Law Text and Materials*, 2nd edn. London, Weidenfeld & Nicolson.

Deakin, S. (1986) Labour Law and the Developing Employment Relationship in the UK. *Cambridge Journal of Economics*, 10, 225–46.

Delion, A. and Durupty, M. (1982) *Les Nationalisations de 1982*. Paris, Economica.

Delmas-Marsalet, J. (1969) Le Contrôle juridictionnel des interventions économiques de L'État. *Études et documents du Conseil D'État*, 22, 133–60.

Department of Energy (1986) *Authorisation Granted and Directions Given by the Secretary of State for Energy to the British Gas Corporation under the Gas Act 1986*. London, HMSO.

Department of the Environment (1985) *Competition in the Provision of Local Authority Services*. London, HMSO.

(1987) *The National Rivers Authority: The Government's Proposals for a Public Regulatory Body in a Privatised Water Industry*. London, HMSO.

Department of Trade & Industry (1984) *Licence Granted by the Secretary of State for Trade and Industry to British Telecommunications under Section 7 of the Telecommunications Act 1984*. London, HMSO.

(1985) *Financial Services in the United Kingdom*. Command Paper 9432. London, HMSO.

Dicey, A. V. (1904) The Combination Laws as illustrating the Relation between Law and Opinion in England during the Nineteenth Century. *Harvard Law Review*, 17, 511–32.

Domberger, S., Meadowcroft, S. and Thompson, D. (1986) Competitive Tendering and Efficiency: The Case of Refuse Collection. *Fiscal Studies*, 7, 69–87.

Dorfman, G. A. (1974) *Wage Politics in Britain, 1945–67*. London, Charles Knight.

Douglas, I. and Lord, S. (1986) *Local Government Finance: A Practical Guide*. London, Local Government Information Unit.

Dresner, S. (1980) *Open Government: Lessons from America*. London, Outer Circle Policy Unit.

Drewry, G. (1983) National Audit Act: Half a Loaf? *Public Law*, 531–7.

Dunleavy, P. (1982) Quasi-governmental Sector Professionalism: Some Implications for Public Policy-Making in Britain, in A. Barker (ed.) *Quangos in Britain*. London. Macmillan.

Dyson, K. (1980) *The State Tradition in Western Europe*. Oxford, Martin Robertson.

Elias, P. and Ewing, K. (1982) Economic Tests and Labour Law: Old Principles and New Liabilities. *Cambridge Law Journal*, 41, 321–58.

Electricity Consumers' Council (1987) *Coal and the Interest of the Electricity Consumer*. Privatisation Discussion Paper 3. London, ECC.

Elliott, J. (1978) *Conflict or Cooperation? The Growth of Industrial Democracy*. London, Kogan Page.

Evans, C. (1985) Privatisation of Local Services. *Local Government Studies*, 6, 97–110.

Evans, S. (1985) The Use of Injunctions in Industrial Disputes. *British Journal of Industrial Relations*, 23, 133–7.

(1987) The Use of Injunctions in Industrial Disputes May 1984 to August 1987. *British Journal of Industrial Relations*, 25, 419–35.

Ewing, K. D. (1982) Industrial Action: Another Step in the 'Right' Direction. *Industrial Law Journal*, 11, 209–26.

(1984) *The Conservatives, Trade Unions and Political Funding*. Fabian Tract 492. London, Fabian Society.

(1985) The Strike, the Courts and the Rule-Books. *Industrial Law Journal*, 14, 160–75.

(1986) Labour Law in the 1920s: The British Experience. Unpublished.

(1987) *The Funding of Political Parties in Britain*. Cambridge, Cambridge University Press.

Ewing, K. D. and Napier, B. W. (1986) The Wapping Dispute and Labour Law. *Cambridge Law Journal*, 45, 285–304.

Ewing, K. D. and Rees, W. M. (1984) Meaning of Trade Dispute. *Industrial Law Journal*, 13, 60–2.

Fairburn, J. A. (1985) British Merger Policy. *Fiscal Studies*, 6(1), 70–81.

Forbes, I. (ed.) (1986) *Market Socialism: Whose Choice?* Fabian Tract 116. London, Fabian Society.

Forrester, A., Lansley, S. and Pauley, R. (1985) *Beyond Our Ken*. London, Fourth Estate.

Fox, A. (1985) *History and Heritage: The Social Origins of the British Industrial Relations System*. London, Allen & Unwin.

Friedman, M. (1977) *Inflation and Unemployment*. London, Institute of Economic Affairs.

Gamble, A. (1979) The Free Economy and the Strong State. *Socialist Register 1979*, 1–25.

(1985) Smashing the State: Thatcher's Radical Crusade. *Marxism Today*, June, 21–6.

Gamble, A. and Walkland, S. (1984) *The British Party System and Economic Policy 1945–83*.

Oxford, Clarendon Press.

Ganz, G. (1972) Allocation of Decision-Making Functions. *Public Law*, 215–31, 299–308.

Gifford, T. (1987) Human Rights under the Law. *New Statesman*, 6 February, p. 11.

Gilder, G. (1982) *Wealth and Poverty*. London, Buchan & Enright.

Gist, P. and Meadowcroft, S. (1986) Regulating for Competition: The Newly Liberalised Market for Private Branch Exchanges. *Fiscal Studies*, 7(3), 41–66.

Goldthorpe, J. H. (ed.) (1984) *Order and Conflict in Contemporary Capitalism*. Oxford, Clarendon Press.

Goodison, Sir N. (1985) The Stock Exchange at the Turning Point. *Stock Exchange Quarterly*, March, pp. 7–11.

Gould, B. (1985) *Socialism and Freedom*. London, Macmillan.

Gower, L. C. B. (1982) *Review of Investor Protection: A Discussion Document*. London, HMSO.

(1984) *Review of Investor Protection: Report: Part I*. Command Paper 9125. London, HMSO.

(1985) *Review of Investor Protection: Report: Part II*. London, HMSO.

Graham, C. and Prosser, T. (1987) Privatising Nationalised Industries: Constitutional Issues and New Legal Techniques. *Modern Law Review*, 50, 16–51.

Grant, M. (1986) The Role of the Courts in Central–Local Relations, in M. Goldsmith (ed.) *New Research in Central–Local Relations*. Aldershot, Gower.

Grant, W. (1982) *The Political Economy of Industrial Policy*. London, Butterworths.

(1983) *Chambers of Commerce in the UK System of Business Interest Representation*. Working Paper No. 32. Department of Politics, University of Warwick.

(ed.) (1985) *The Political Economy of Corporatism*. London, Macmillan.

Grant, W. and Marsh, D. (1977) *The Confederation of British Industry*. London, Hodder & Stoughton.

Grant, W. and Nath, S. (1984) *The Politics of Economic Policy-Making*. Oxford, Basil Blackwell.

Gray, J. (1986) *Hayek on Liberty*, 2nd edn. Oxford, Basil Blackwell.

Green, D. G. (1987) *The New Right*. Brighton, Wheatsheaf.

Griffith, J. A. G. (1966) *Central Departments and Local Authorities*. London, Allen & Unwin.

Gyford, J. and James, M. (1983) *National Parties and Local Politics*. London, Allen & Unwin.

Habermas, J. (1976) *Legitimation Crisis*. London, Heinemann.

(1985) Law as Medium and Law as Institution, in G. Teubner (ed.) *Dilemmas of Law in the Welfare State*. Berlin and New York, Walter de Gruyter.

Hailsham, Lord (1978) *The Dilemma of Democracy*. London, Collins.

Hall, S. (1985) Authoritarian Populism: A Reply to Jessop *et al. New Left Review*, 151, 115–24.

Hall, S. and Jacques, M. (1983) *The Politics of Thatcherism*. London, Lawrence & Wishart.

Hammond, M., Helm, D. and Thompson, D. (1985) British Gas: Options for Privatisation. *Fiscal Studies*, 6(4), 1–20.

Hanson, C. G. (1984) From Taff Vale to Tebbit, in F. A. Hayek (ed.) *1980s Unemployment and the Unions*. 2nd edn. London, Institute of Economic Affairs.

Hanson, C. G., Jackson, S. and Miller, D. (1982) *The Closed Shop: A Comparative Study in Public Policy and Trade Union Security in Britain, the USA and West Germany*. Aldershot, Gower.

Harden, I. J. (1987) A Constitution for Quangos? *Public Law*, 27–35.

Harden, I. and Lewis, N. (1983) Privatisation, De-regulation and Constitutionality: Some Anglo-American Comparisons. *Northern Ireland Legal Quarterly*, 34, 207–29.

(1986) *The Noble Lie: The British Constitution and the Rule of Law*. London, Hutchinson.

Harlow, C. and Rawlings, R. (1984) *Law and Administration*. London, Weidenfeld & Nicolson.

Hattersley, R. (1987a) *Economic Priorities for a Labour Government*. London, Macmillan.

(1987b) *Choose Freedom*. London, Penguin.

Hayek, F. A. (1944) *The Road to Serfdom*. London, Routledge & Kegan Paul.

(1960) *The Constitution of Liberty*. London, Routledge & Kegan Paul.

(1972) *A Tiger by the Tail*. London, Institute of Economic Affairs.

(1973) *Rules and Order*. London, Routledge & Kegan Paul.

(1979a) *The Political Order of a Free People*. London, Routledge & Kegan Paul.

(1979b) *Law, Legislation and Liberty*. London, Routledge & Kegan Paul.

Helm, D. (1987) RPI Minus X and the Newly Privatised Industries: A Deceptively Simple Regulatory Rule. *Public Money*, 7, 47–51.

Hennessy, P. (1986) *Cabinet*. Oxford, Basil Blackwell.

Henney, A. (1986) *Regulating Public and Privatised Monopolies: A Radical Approach*. Newbury, Public Finance Foundation.

Hepple, B. A. and Fredman, S. (1986) *Labour Law and Industrial Relations in Great Britain*. Deventer, Klimver.

Hills, J. (1986) *Deregulating Telecoms: Competition and Control in the United States, Japan and Britain*. London, Frances Pinter.

Hirst, P. (1986) *Law, Socialism and Democracy*. London, Allen & Unwin.

Hobhouse, L. T. (1979) *Liberalism*. New York, Oxford University Press.

Hodgson, G. (1984) *The Democratic Economy*. London, Penguin.

Hogwood, B. (1979) *Government and Shipbuilding*. Farnborough, Saxon House.

Hogwood, R. W. (1987) Shaping Policy Through the Courts. *Public Policy and Administration*, 2, 56–67.

Holme, R. (1987) *The People's Kingdom*. London, Bodley Head.

Holme, R. and Muggridge, H. (eds.) (1987a) *Parliament Today*. London, Constitutional Reform Centre.

(eds.) (1987b) *Cabinet Government Today*. London, Constitutional Reform Centre.

(eds.) (1987c) *Whitehall Today*. London, Constitutional Reform Centre.

Holmes, M. (1982) *Political Pressure and Economic Policy*. London, Butterworths.

(1985) *The First Thatcher Government 1979–1983*. Brighton, Wheatsheaf.

Hood, C. (1980) The Politics of Quangocide. *Policy and Politics*, 8(3), 247–65.

(1981) Axeperson, Spare that Quango . . . , in C. C. Hood and M. Wright (eds.) *Big Government in Hard Times*. Oxford, Martin Robertson.

House of Lords Select Committee on Science and Technology (1985) *Interim Report on the 1985 Local Government Bill: Scientific and Technical Services*. London, HMSO.

Hudson, B. (1987) *Justice through Punishment*. London, Macmillan.

Hutton, J. (1984) Solving the Strike Problem: Part II of the Trade Union Act 1984. *Industrial Law Journal*, 13, 212–26.

(1985) Ballots before Industrial Action. *Industrial Law Journal*, 14, 255–62.

Institute of Chartered Accountants in England and Wales (1987) *Annual Survey of Published Accounts*. London, ICAEW.

Ingham, G. (1985) *Capitalism Divided: The City and Industry in British Social Development*. London, Macmillan.

Jacques, M. and Mulhearn, F. (eds.) (1981) *The Forward March of Labour Halted?* London,

New Left Books in association with *Marxism Today.*

Jessop, B. (1982) *The Capitalist State.* Oxford, Martin Robertson.

Jessop, B., Bonnett, K., Bromley, S. and Ling, T. (1984) Authoritarian Populism, Two Nations and Thatcherism. *New Left Review*, 147, 32–60.

Johnson, N. (1977) *In Search of the Constitution.* Oxford, Pergamon.

(1980) Constitutional Reform: Some Dilemmas for a Conservative Philosophy, in Z. Layton-Henry (ed.) *Conservative Party Politics.* London, Macmillan.

Jones, G. and Stewart, J. D. (1985) *The Case for Local Government,* 2nd edn. London, Allen & Unwin.

Jones, L. (1984) The Changing UK Securities Market: A Stock Exchange View. *The Company Lawyer,* 2, 97–100.

Joseph, K. (1979) *Solving the Trade Union Problem is the Key to Economic Recovery.* London, Conservative Central Office.

Kahn-Freund, O. (1943) Collective Agreements under War Legislation. *Modern Law Review,* 6, 112–43.

(1954) Legal Framework, in A. Flanders and H. A. Clegg (eds.) *The System Of Industrial Relations in Great Britain.* Oxford, Basil Blackwell.

(1959) Labour Law, in M. Ginsberg (ed.) *Law and Opinion in England in the 20th Century.* London, Stevens.

(1983) *Labour and the Law,* 3rd edn, ed. by P. Davies and M. Freedland. London, Stevens.

Kahn, P., Lewis, N., Livock, R. and Wiles, P. (1983) *Picketing: Industrial Disputes, Tactics and the Law.* London, Routledge & Kegan Paul.

Kamenka, E. and Tay, A. Erh-Soon (1975), Beyond Bourgeois Individualism: The Contemporary Crisis in Law and Legal Ideology, in E. Kamenka and R. S. Neale (eds.) *Feudalism, Capitalism and Beyond.* London, Edward Arnold.

Keegan, W. (1984) *Mrs Thatcher's Economic Experiment.* London, Allen Lane.

Kennedy, D. (1981) Cost–Benefit Analysis of Entitlement Problems: A Critique. *Stanford Law Review,* 33, 387–445.

Kennet, W. (ed.) (1982) *The Rebirth of Britain.* London, Weidenfeld & Nicolson.

Keynes, J. M. (1961) *The General Theory of Employment, Interest and Money.* London, Macmillan.

Kidner, R. (1986) Sanctions for Contempt by a Trade Union. *Legal Studies,* 6, 18–34.

King, D. S. (1987) *The New Right: Politics, Markets and Citizenship.* London, Macmillan.

King, R. (1985) Corporatism and the Local Economy, in W. Grant (ed.) *The Political Economy of Corporatism.* London, Macmillan.

Kinnock, N. (1986) *Making Our Way.* Oxford, Basil Blackwell.

Kochan, N. and Pym, H. (1987) *The Guinness Affair.* London, Christopher Helm.

Krislov, S. (1973) The OEO Lawyers Fail to Constitutionalise a Right to Welfare. *Minnesota Law Review,* 58, 211–45.

Labour Party (1986) *Statements to Conference.* London, Labour Party.

(1987) *Britain Will Win.* London, Labour Party.

Lansley, S. (1985) The Phoney War. *New Socialist,* July, 28–31.

Leach, S., Hinings, C. R., Ranson, S. and Skelcher, C. K. (1983) The Uses and Abuses of Policy Planning Systems. *Local Government Studies,* 9(1), 23–8.

Lehmbruch, G. (1979) Liberal Corporatism and Party Government, in P. Schmitter and G. Lehmbruch (eds.) *Trends Towards Corporatist Intermediation.* Beverly Hills and London, Sage.

(1982) Neo-corporatism in Comparative Perspective, in G. Lehmbruch and P. Schmitter (eds.) *Patterns of Corporatist Policy-Making*. Beverly Hills and London, Sage.

Leigh-Pemberton, R. (1984a) Changing Boundaries in Financial Services. *Bank of England Quarterly Bulletin*, 1, 40–5.

(1984b) The Future of the Securities Market. *Bank of England Quarterly Bulletin*, 2, 189–94.

(1985) Taking Stock on Issues Facing the Banking Community. *Bank of England Quarterly Bulletin*, 1, 45–6.

Leighton, P. (1986) Marginal Workers, in R. Lewis (ed.) *Labour Law in Britain*. Oxford, Basil Blackwell.

Lepage, H. (1980) *Demain le Libéralisme*. Paris, Libraire Générale Français.

Lester, A. (1984) Fundamental Rights: The United Kingdom Isolated? *Public Law*, 46–72.

Lewis, N. (1975) IBA Programme Contract Awards. *Public Law*, 317–40.

Lewis, N., Seneviratne, M. and Cracknell S. (1986) *Complaints Procedures in Local Government*. University of Sheffield.

Lewis, N. and Wiles, P. N. P. (1984) The Post-corporatist State? *Journal of Law and Society*, 11, 65–90.

Lewis, R. and Clark, J. (eds.) (1981) *Labour Law and Politics in the Weimar Republic*. Oxford, Basil Blackwell.

Lewis, R. and Simpson, R. (1981) *Striking a Balance? Employment Law after the 1980 Act*. Oxford, Martin Robertson.

Liberal Party (no date) *Nationalise—Privatise The Destructive Cycle*. Hebden Bridge, Hebden Royd.

Liberal/SDP Alliance (1983) *Towards a New Constitutional Settlement*. London, Poland Street Publications.

(1986) *People in Power*. London, SDP.

(1987) *Britain United*. London, Liberal/SDP Alliance.

Linklater, M. and Leigh, D. (1986) *Not with Honour*. Sphere, London.

Littlechild, S. (1983) *Regulation of British Telecommunications' Profitability*. London, HMSO.

(1986) *Economic Regulation of Privatised Water Authorities* London, HMSO.

Loughlin, M. (1986) The Constitutional Role for Local Government, in M. Goldsmith (ed.) *Essays on the Future of Local Government*. Wakefield, West Yorkshire County Council.

McAuslan, P. (1986) Britain's Constitutional Crisis. *Marxism Today*, August, p. 29.

McAuslan, P. and McEldowney, J. (1985) (eds.) *Law, Legitimacy and the Constitution*. London, Sweet & Maxwell.

McBride, S. (1985) Corporatism, Public Policy and the Labour Movement: A Comparative Study. *Political Studies*, 33, 439–56.

MacDonald, D. F. (1960) *The State and the Trade Unions*. London, Macmillan.

Mackintosh, M. and Wainwright, H. (eds.) (1987) *A Taste of Power: The Politics of Local Economics*. London, Verso.

Maier, C. S. (1975) *The Recasting of Bourgeois Europe*. Princeton, Princeton University Press.

Marquand, D. (1982) Social Democracy and the Collapse of the Westminster Model, in W. Kennet (ed.) *The Rebirth of Britain*. London, Weidenfeld & Nicolson.

Martin, R. M. (1980) *TUC: The Growth of a Pressure Group 1868–1976*. Oxford, Clarendon Press.

Mayer, C. and Meadowcroft, S. (1985) Selling Public Assets: Techniques and Financial Implications. *Fiscal Studies*, 6(4), 42–55.

Mellors, C. and Pollitt, D. (1984) Legislating for Privacy: Data Protection in Western Europe. *Parliamentary Affairs*, 37, 199–215.

Merkin, R. and Williams, K. (1984) *Competition Law: Antitrust Policy in the United Kingdom and the EEC.* London, Sweet & Maxwell.

Middlemas, K. (1979) *Politics in Industrial Society.* London, Andre Deutsch.

(1983) *Industry, Unions and Government.* London, Macmillan.

Miller, R. and Fine, B. (eds.) (1985) *Policing the Miners' Strike.* London, Lawrence & Wishart.

Minogue, M. and O'Grady, J. (1985) Contracting out Local Authority Services in Britain. *Local Government Studies*, 11(3), 35–50.

Mitchell, A. (1987) New Rights Diary. *New Statesman,* 13 February, p. 4.

Moore, J. (1986a) The Success of Privatisation, in J. Kay, C. Mayer and D. Thompson (eds.) *Privatisation and Regulation: The UK Experience.* Oxford, Clarendon Press.

(1986b) Why Privatise? in J. Kay, C. Mayer and D. Thompson (eds.) *Privatisation and Regulation: The UK Experience.* Oxford, Clarendon Press.

Moran, M. (1984) *The Politics of Banking.* London, Macmillan.

Mosley, P. (1984) *The Making of Economic Policy.* Brighton, Wheatsheaf.

Moss, R. (1975) *The Collapse of Democracy.* London, Temple Smith.

Mullard, M. (1987) *The Politics of Public Expenditure.* London, Croom Helm.

Murphy, W. T. and Roberts, S. (1987) Introduction. *Modern Law Review*, 50, 677–87.

Nash, R. and Cibinic, J. (1977) *Federal Procurement Law*, 3rd edn. Washington, DC, George Washington University.

National Audit Office (1987) *Competitive Tendering for Support Services in the NHS.* HC 318, 1986–7. London, HMSO.

National Economic Development Office (1976) *A Study of UK Nationalised Industries.* London, HMSO.

Newton, N. and Karran, T. (1985) *The Politics of Local Expenditure.* London, Macmillan.

Nitsch, N. (1981) Les Principes généraux du droit à L'epréuve du droit public économique. *Revue Du Droit Public*, 97, 1549–79.

Noreng, O. (1980) *The Oil Industry and Government Strategy in the North Sea.* London, Croom Helm.

Nove, A. (1983) *The Economics of Feasible Socialism.* London, Allen & Unwin.

Nozick, R. (1974) *Anarchy, State and Utopia.* Oxford, Basil Blackwell.

Nuti, D. (1986) Economic Planning in Market Economies: Scope, Instruments, Institutions. *The Socialist Register 1985–6*, 373–82.

O'Brien, D. P. (1982) Competition Policy in Britain: The Silent Revolution. *The Antitrust Bulletin*, 27, 217–39.

O'Connor, J. (1973) *The Fiscal Crisis of the State.* New York, St Martins Press.

Offe, C. (1975) The Theory of the Capitalist State and the Problem of Policy Formation, in L. Lindberg, R. Alford, C. Crouch and C. Offe (eds.) *Stress and Contradiction in Modern Capitalism.* Lexington Mass., Lexington Books.

Office of Fair Trading (1977, 1979, 1980, 1983, 1984) *Annual Report.* London, HMSO.

OFTEL (1987) *British Telecom's Quality of Service 1987.* London, OFTEL.

O'Hagan, T. (1984) *The End of Law?* Oxford, Basil Blackwell

O'Leary, B. (1987) Why Was the GLC Abolished? *International Journal of Urban and Regional Research*, 11, 193–217.

Olson, M. (1965) *The Logic of Collective Action*. Cambridge, Mass., Harvard University Press.

(1982) *The Rise and Decline of Nations*. London, Yale University Press.

Owen, D. (1981) *Face the Future*. London, Jonathan Cape.

(1982) The Enabling Society, in W. Kennet (ed.) *The Rebirth of Britain*. London, Weidenfeld & Nicolson.

(1987) *Social Market and Social Justice*. London, Tawney Society.

PA Management Consultants (1985) *The Proposed Abolition of the Metropolitan County Councils: A Study of Non-Financial Aspects*. London, PA Management Consultants.

Panitch, L. (1980) Recent Theorizations of Corporatism: Reflections on a Growth Industry. *British Journal of Sociology*, 31, 159–87.

Parkinson, M. and Wilks, S. (1986) The Politics of Inner City Partnerships, in M. Goldsmith (ed.) *New Research in Central–Local Relations*, Aldershot, Gower.

Pelling, H. (1976) *A History of British Trade Unionism*. London, Penguin.

Pirie, M. (1985) *Privatisation*. London, Adam Smith Institute.

Poggi, G. (1978) *The Development of the Modern State*. London, Hutchinson.

Pratten, C. (1987) Mrs Thatcher's Economic Legacy, in K. Minogue and M. Biddiss (eds.) *Thatcherism: Personalities and Politics*. London, Macmillan.

Prosser, T. (1982) Towards a Critical Public Law. *Journal of Law and Society*, 9, 1–19.

(1983) *Test Cases for the Poor*. London, Child Poverty Action Group.

(1986) *Nationalised Industries and Public Control*. Oxford, Basil Blackwell.

Radical Statistics Health Group (1987) *Facing the Figures: What Really is Happening to the NHS?* London, British Society for Social Responsibility in Science.

Review Board for Government Contracts (1984) *Report on the Fourth General Review of the Profit Formula for Non-Competitive Government Contracts*. London, HMSO.

Rhodes, R. (1986) *The National World of Local Government*. London, Allen & Unwin.

(1988) *Beyond Westminster and Whitehall: The Sub-central Government of Britain*. London, Allen & Unwin.

Richardson, J. J. and Jordan, A. G. (1979) *Governing under Pressure: The Policy Process in a Post-parliamentary Democracy*. Oxford, Basil Blackwell.

Riddell, P. (1983) *The Thatcher Government*. Oxford, Basil Blackwell.

Rodgers, W. (1982) Towards an Industrial Partnership, in W. Kennet (ed.) *The Rebirth of Britain*, London, Weidenfeld & Nicolson.

Rustin, M. (1986) Restructuring the State. *New Left Review*, 158, 43–58.

Sargent, J. A. (1983a) *The Organisation of Business Interests in the UK Pharmaceutical Industry*. Berlin, International Institute of Management.

(1983b) *The Pharmaceutical Price Regulation Scheme*. Berlin, International Institute of Management.

Scargill, A. (1986) Proportional Representation: A Socialist Concept. *New Left Review*, 158, 76–80.

Scarman, Lord (1981) *Report*. Command Paper 8427. London, HMSO.

Schmitter, P. (1979) Still the Century of Corporatism? in P. Schmitter and G. Lehmbruch (eds.) *Trends Towards Corporatist Intermediation*, London, Sage.

Schumpeter, J. A. (1974) *Capitalism and Social Democracy*. London, Allen & Unwin.

Sharpe, T. (1979) Unfair Competition by Public Support of Private Enterprises. *Law Quarterly Review*, 95, 205–43.

Shonfield, A. (1965) *Modern Capitalism: The Changing Balance of Public and Private*

Power. London, Oxford University Press.

Simpson, R. (1980) NWL Ltd v. Woods. *Modern Law Review*, 43, 327–36.

Smith, B. (1971) Accountability and Independence in the Modern State, in B. Smith and D. Hague (eds.) *The Dilemma of Accountability in Modern Government.* London, Macmillan.

Smith, D. (1987) *The Rise and Fall of Monetarism.* London, Penguin.

Social Democratic Party (1983) *Controlling the State: Towards Fairer Administration.* London, SDP.

(no date [a]) *Citizens Rights.* London, SDP.

(no date [b]) *Industrial Strategy.* London, SDP.

(no date [c]) *Decentralising Government.* London, SDP.

Sparer, E. (1970) The Right to Welfare, in W. Dorsen (ed.) *The Rights of Americans.* New York, Pantheon.

Steadman, J. M. (1976) Banned in Boston—and Birmingham and Boise and ... : Due Process in the Debarment and Suspension of Government Contractors. *Hastings Law Journal*, 27, 793–823.

Steel, D. (1984) Government and the New Hybrids, in D. Steel and D. Heald (eds.) *Privatizing Public Enterprises.* London, Royal Institute of Public Administration.

Stock Exchange (1979, 1980, 1984) *Annual Report and Accounts.* London, Stock Exchange.

(1986) *Dealings in the Shares of Westland PLC.* London, Stock Exchange.

Stock Exchange Council (1984) The Choice of a New Dealing System for Equities. *Stock Exchange Quarterly*, September, 10–28.

Stoker, G. (1988) *The Politics of Local Government.* London, Macmillan.

Streek, W. and Schmitter P. (1985) *Private Interest Government.* Beverly Hills and London, Sage.

Sunkin, M. (1987) What is Happening to Applications for Judicial Review? *Modern Law Review*, 50, 432–67.

Teubner, G. (1983) Substantive and Reflexive Elements in Modern Law. *Law and Society Review*, 17, 239–85.

Thain, C. (1984) The Education of the Treasury: The Medium-Term Financial Strategy 1980–84. *Public Administration*, 62, 261–85.

Thatcher, M. (1986) Two More Terms to Eliminate Socialism. Interview in *Financial Times*, 19 November.

Thompson, A. W. J. and Engleman, S. R. (1975) *The Industrial Relations Act: A Review and Analysis.* London, Martin Robertson.

Trades Union Congress (1974) *Annual Report of the TUC.* London, TUC.

(1984) *Contractors' Failures: The Privatisation Experience.* London, TUC.

Travers, T. (1986) *The Politics of Local Government Finance.* London, Allen & Unwin.

Treasury (1984) *Nationalised Industries Consultation Proposals.* London, HM Treasury.

Truchet, D. (1980) Réfléxions sur le droit économique public en droit français. *Revue du Droit Public*, 96, 1009–42.

Tulloch, G. (1976) *The Vote Motive.* London, Institute of Economic Affairs.

Turpin, C. (1972) *Government Contracts.* Harmondsworth, Penguin.

Veljanovski, C. (1987) *Selling the State.* London, Weidenfeld and Nicolson.

Vickers, J. and Yarrow, G. (1985) *Privatisation and the Natural Monopolies.* London, Public Policy Centre.

Vickerstaff, S. (1985) Industrial Training in Britain: The Dilemmas of a Neo-corporatist Policy, in A. Cawson (ed.) *Organized Interests and the State.* Beverly Hills and London, Sage.

Wallington, P. (ed.) (1984) *Civil Liberties 1984.* Oxford, Martin Robertson.

(1985) Policing the Miners' Strike. *Industrial Law Journal,* 14, 145–59.

Watts, T. (1981) Planning the Next Decade, in R. Leach and E. Stamp (eds.) *British Accounting Standards: The First 10 Years.* Cambridge, Woodhead-Faulkner.

(1983) *The Role of the Accounting Standards Committee.* University College, Cardiff.

Webb, S. and Webb, B. (1919) *The History of Trade Unionism, 1666–1920.* London, Special Edition.

Weber, M. (1969) *Economy and Society.* New York, Bedminster Press.

Wedderburn, Lord (1978) The New Structure of Labour Law in Britain. *Israel Law Review,* 13, 435–58.

(1980) Industrial Relations and the Courts. *Industrial Law Journal,* 9, 65–94.

(1986) *The Worker and the Law,* 3rd edn. London, Penguin.

Weekes, B., Mellish, M., Dickens, L. and Lloyd, J. (1975) *Industrial Relations and the Law.* Oxford, Basil Blackwell.

Weir, S. (1982) The Citizen and the Town Hall. *New Society,* 9 March, 345–6.

Wheen, F. (1985) *The Battle for London.* London, Pluto Press.

Whitley, J. H. (1917) *Interim Report on Joint Standing Industrial Councils by the Sub-Committee on Relations between Employers and Employed of the Committee of Reconstruction.* Command Paper 8606, London, HMSO.

Widdicombe, D. (1986) *The Conduct of Local Authority Business.* Command Paper 9797. London, HMSO.

Wilks, S. (1987) Administrative Culture and Policy-Making in the Department of the Environment. *Public Policy and Administration,* 2, 25–41.

Williams, S. (1982) On Modernizing Britain, in W. Kennet (ed.) *The Rebirth of Britain,* London, Weidenfeld & Nicolson.

Williams, T. (1983) *Fighting Privatisation: The Victory in Gloucester.* London, Institute for Workers' Control.

Willetts, D. (1987) The Role of the Prime Minister's Policy Unit. *Public Administration,* 65, 443–54.

Wilson, G. (1987) English Legal Scholarship. *Modern Law Review,* 50, 818–54.

Wilson, Sir H. (1980) Committee to Review the Functioning of Financial Institutions, *Report.* Command Paper 7937, London, HMSO.

Winkler, J. T. (1975) Law, State and Economy: The Industry Act 1975 in Context. *British Journal of Law and Society,* 2, 103–28.

Winter, D. (1986) Socialism, Markets and Market Socialism, in I. Forbes (ed.) *Market Socialism: Whose Choice?* Fabian Tract 116. London, Fabian Society.

Wood, B. (1976) *The Process of Local Government Reform.* London, Allen & Unwin.

Young, H. and Sloman, A. (1986) *The Thatcher Phenomenon.* London, BBC Publications.

Young, K. (1984) Metropolitan Government: The Development of the Concept and the Reality, in S. Leach (ed.) *The Future of Metropolitan Government.* Birmingham, INLOGOV.

(1986) Widdicombe from the Researcher's Angle. *Local Government Studies,* 12(6), 27–32.

Young, S. (1985) The Use of Subsidies as Part of the Conservative Government's Privatisation Strategy in Britain 1979–85. Paper to European Consortium for

Political Research, Barcelona, March.

(1986) The Nature of Privatisation in Britain 1979–85. *West European Politics*, 9, 235–52.

Young, S. with Lowe, A. V. (1974) *Intervention in the Mixed Economy: The Evolution of British Industrial Policy*. London, Croom Helm.

Zysman, J. (1983) *Governments, Markets and Growth*. Ithaca, NY, Cornell University Press.

Index